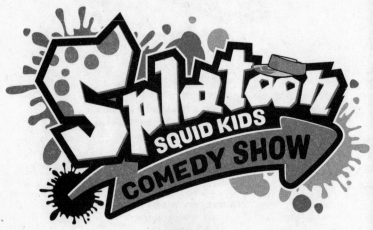

SQUID KIDS

COMEDY SHOW

STORY AND ART BY
HIDEKI GOTO

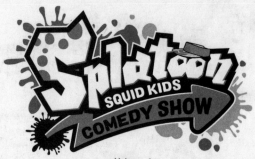

Volume 4
VIZ Media Edition

Story and Art by
Hideki Goto

Translation **Tetsuichiro Miyaki**
English Adaptation **Bryant Turnage**
Lettering **John Hunt**
Design **Kam Li**
Editor **Joel Enos**

SPLATOON IKASU KIDS 4KOMA FES Vol. 4 by Hideki GOTO
© 2018 Hideki GOTO
All rights reserved.
Original Japanese edition published by SHOGAKUKAN.
English translation rights in the United States of America, Canada, the United
Kingdom, Ireland, Australia and New Zealand arranged with SHOGAKUKAN.

Original Design vol.ONE

Printed in the U.S.A.

Published by VIZ Media, LLC
P.O. Box 77010
San Francisco, CA 94107

10 9 8 7 6 5 4 3 2 1
First Printing, July 2021

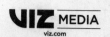

viz.com

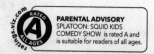

Splatoon
SQUID KIDS COMEDY SHOW
4

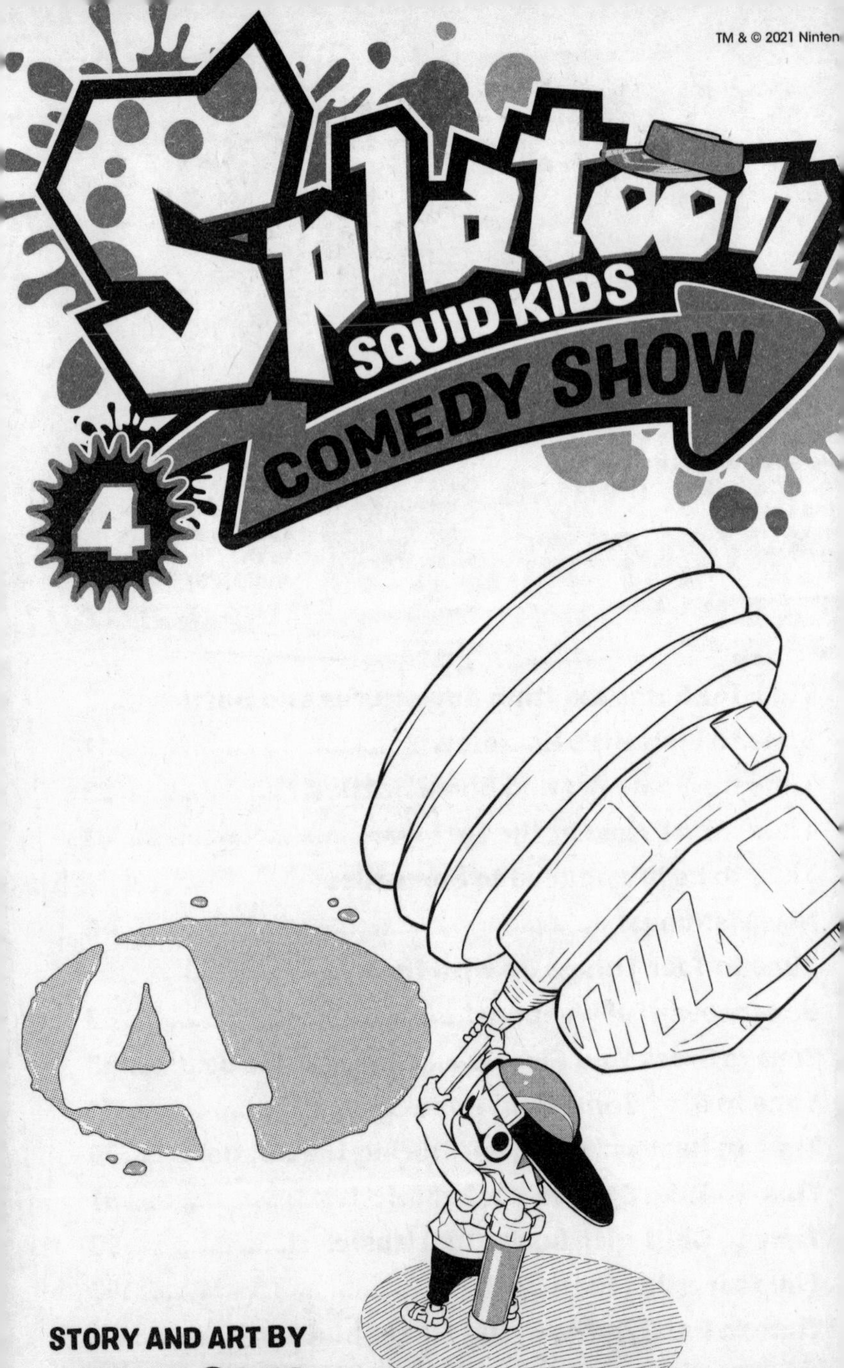

STORY AND ART BY
HIDEKI GOTO

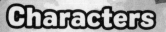

Characters

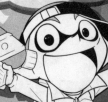

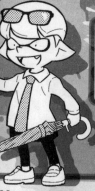

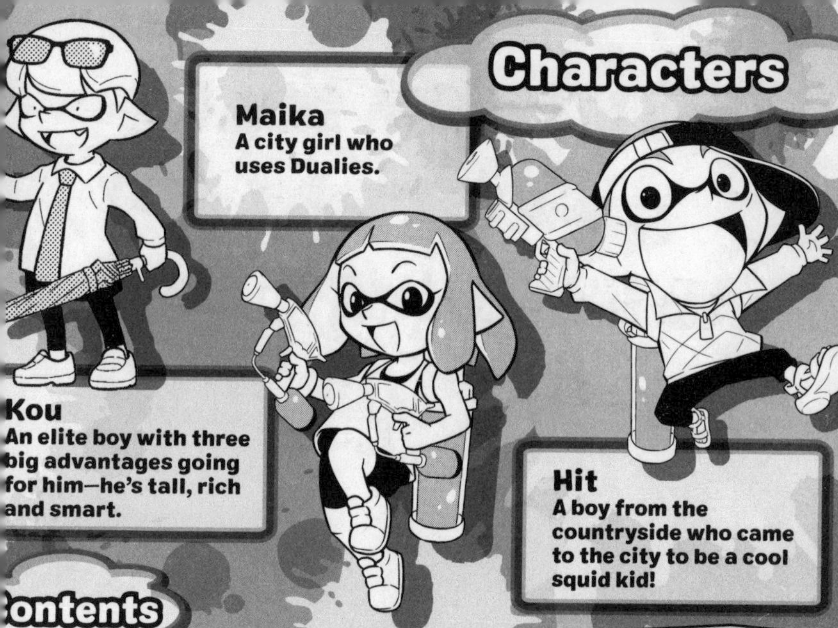

Maika
A city girl who uses Dualies.

Kou
An elite boy with three big advantages going for him—he's tall, rich and smart.

Hit
A boy from the countryside who came to the city to be a cool squid kid!

Contents

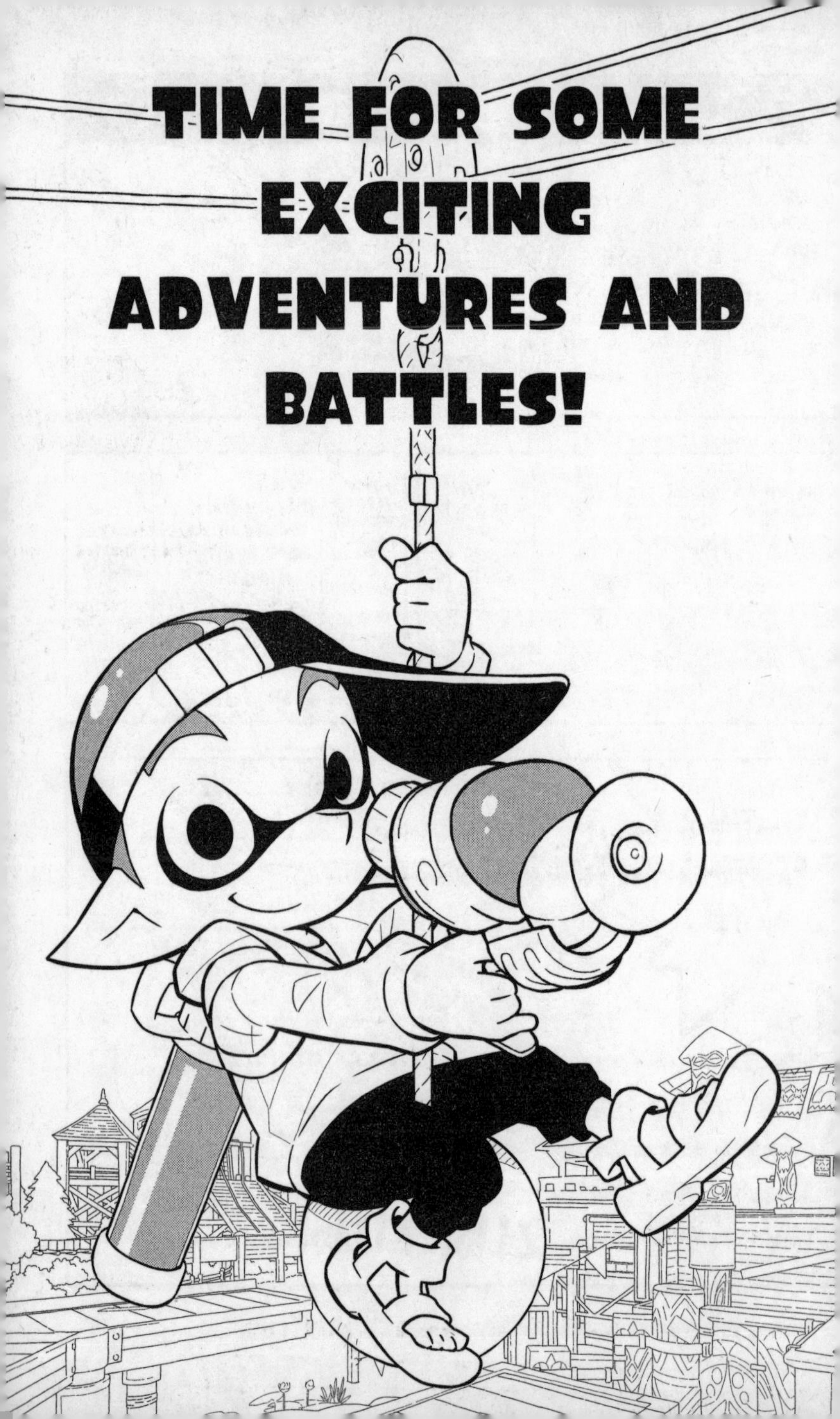
TIME FOR SOME
EXCITING
ADVENTURES AND
BATTLES!

NET CLIMBING

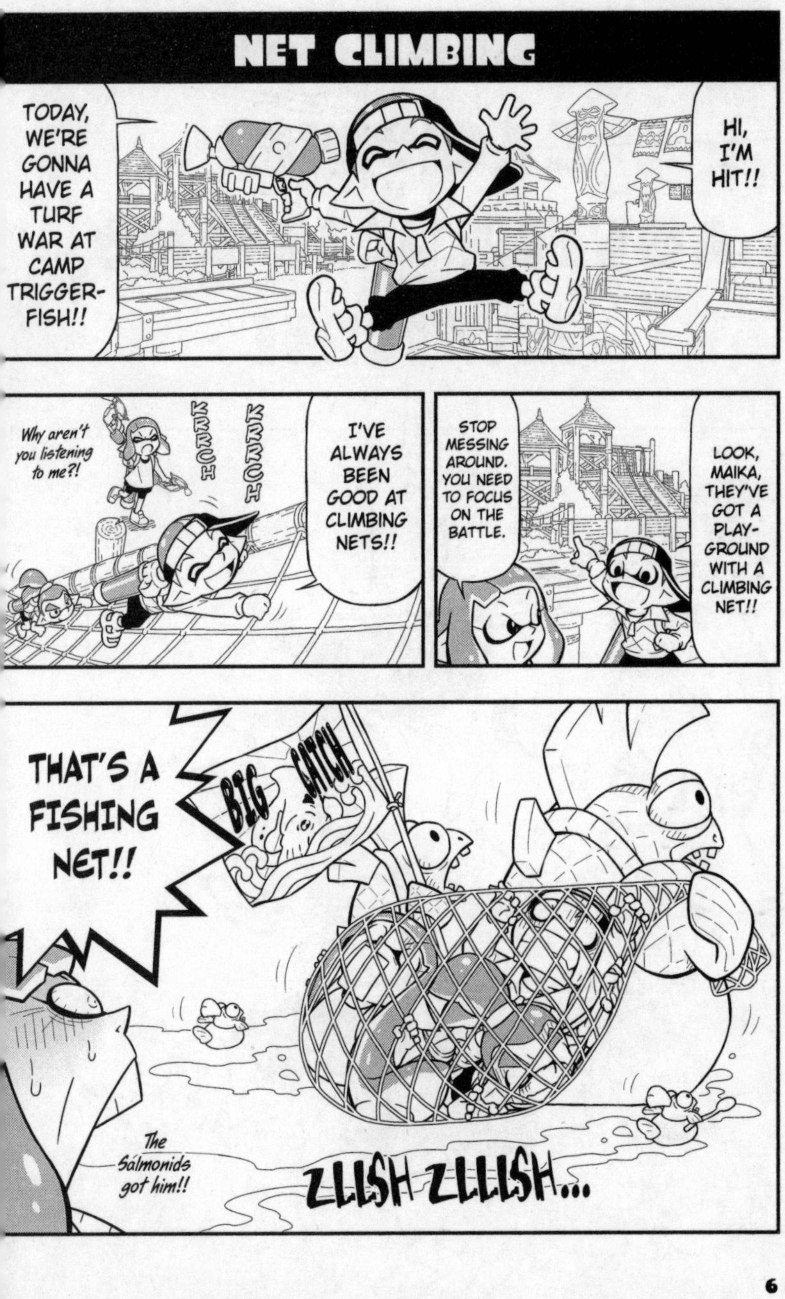

HI, I'M HIT!!
TODAY, WE'RE GONNA HAVE A TURF WAR AT CAMP TRIGGER-FISH!!
LOOK, MAIKA, THEY'VE GOT A PLAY-GROUND WITH A CLIMBING NET!!
STOP MESSING AROUND. YOU NEED TO FOCUS ON THE BATTLE.
I'VE ALWAYS BEEN GOOD AT CLIMBING NETS!!
KRRCH
KRRCH
Why aren't you listening to me?!
BIG CATCH
THAT'S A FISHING NET!!
The Salmonids got him!!
ZLISH ZLLISH...

TURF-TIED

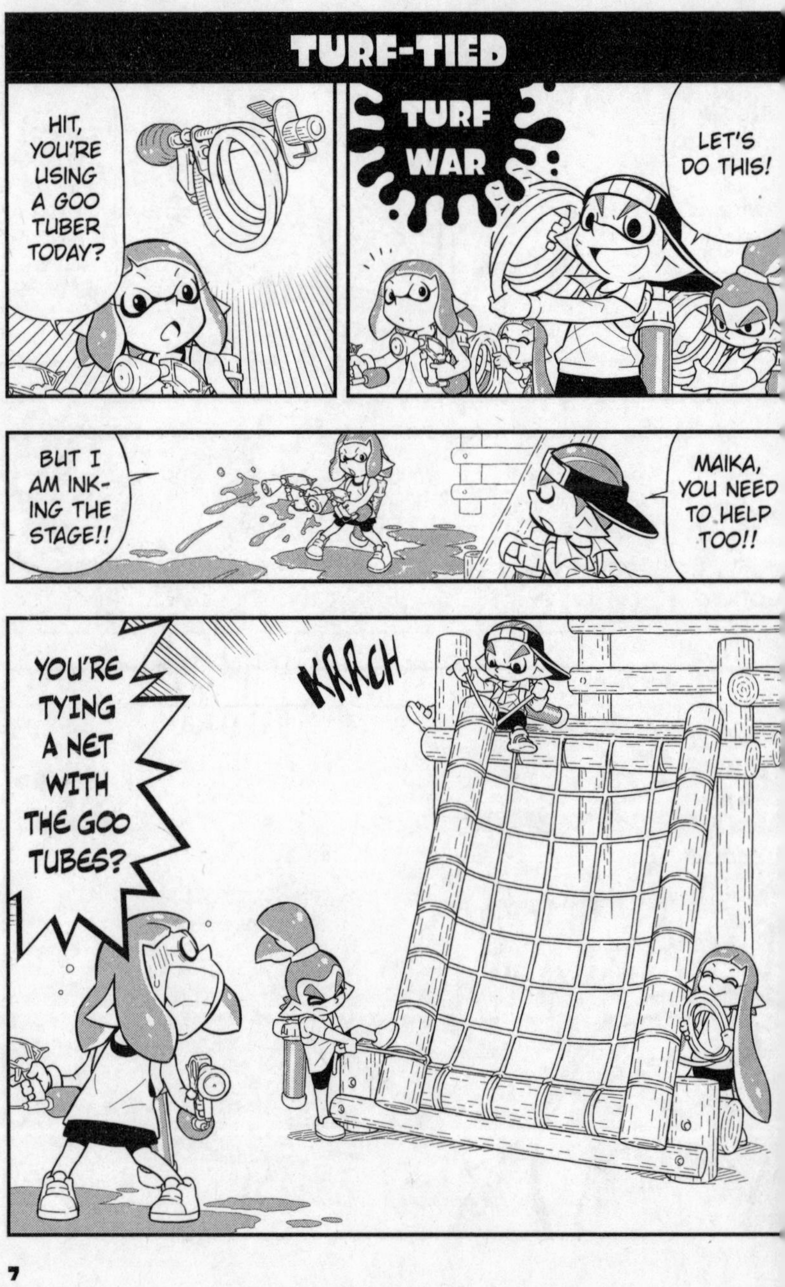
TURF WAR
LET'S DO THIS!
HIT, YOU'RE USING A GOO TUBER TODAY?
MAIKA, YOU NEED TO HELP TOO!!
BUT I AM INKING THE STAGE!!
KRRCH
YOU'RE TYING A NET WITH THE GOO TUBES?

ULTRA STAMP SPAMMING

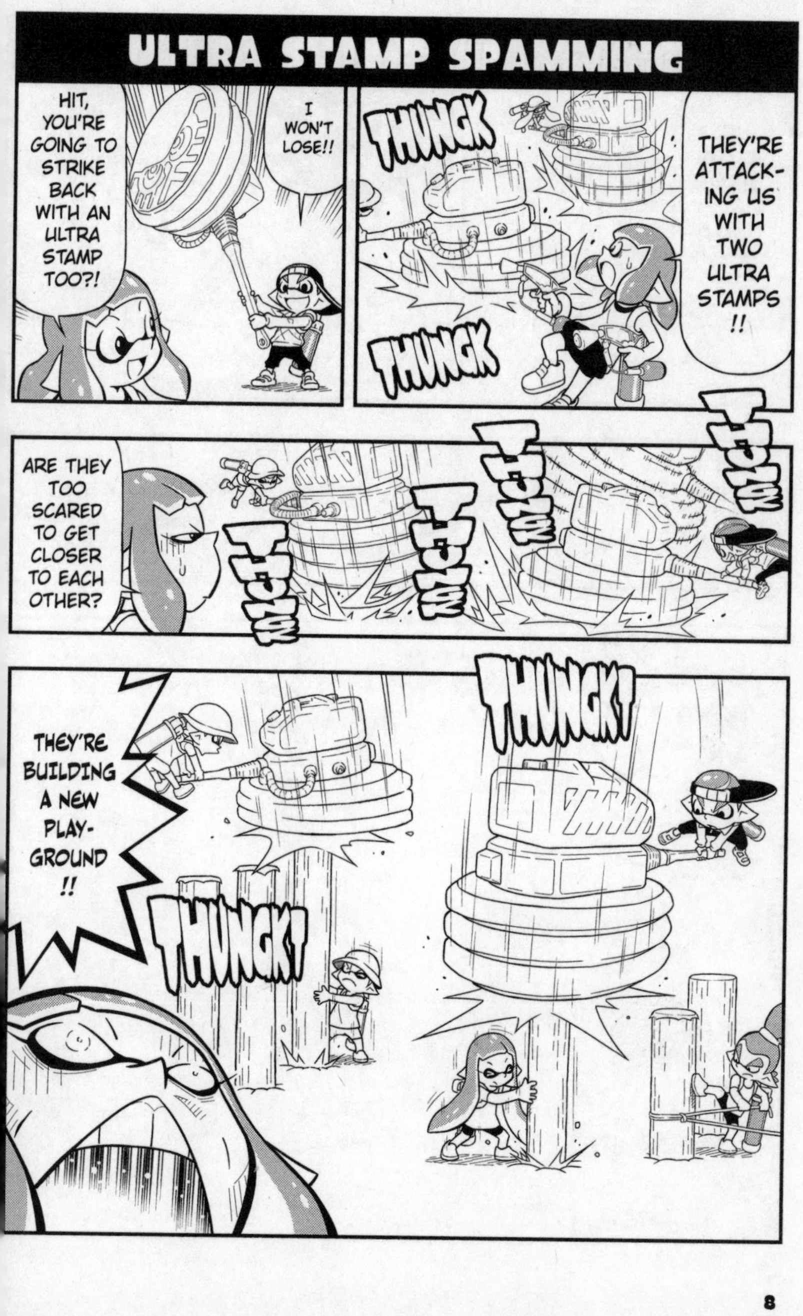
THEY'RE ATTACKING US WITH TWO ULTRA STAMPS!!
THUNGK
THUNGK
I WON'T LOSE!!
HIT, YOU'RE GOING TO STRIKE BACK WITH AN ULTRA STAMP TOO?!
THUNK
THUNK
THUNK
THUNK
ARE THEY TOO SCARED TO GET CLOSER TO EACH OTHER?
THUNGK!
THUNGK!
THEY'RE BUILDING A NEW PLAYGROUND!!

DEFENSIVE INK

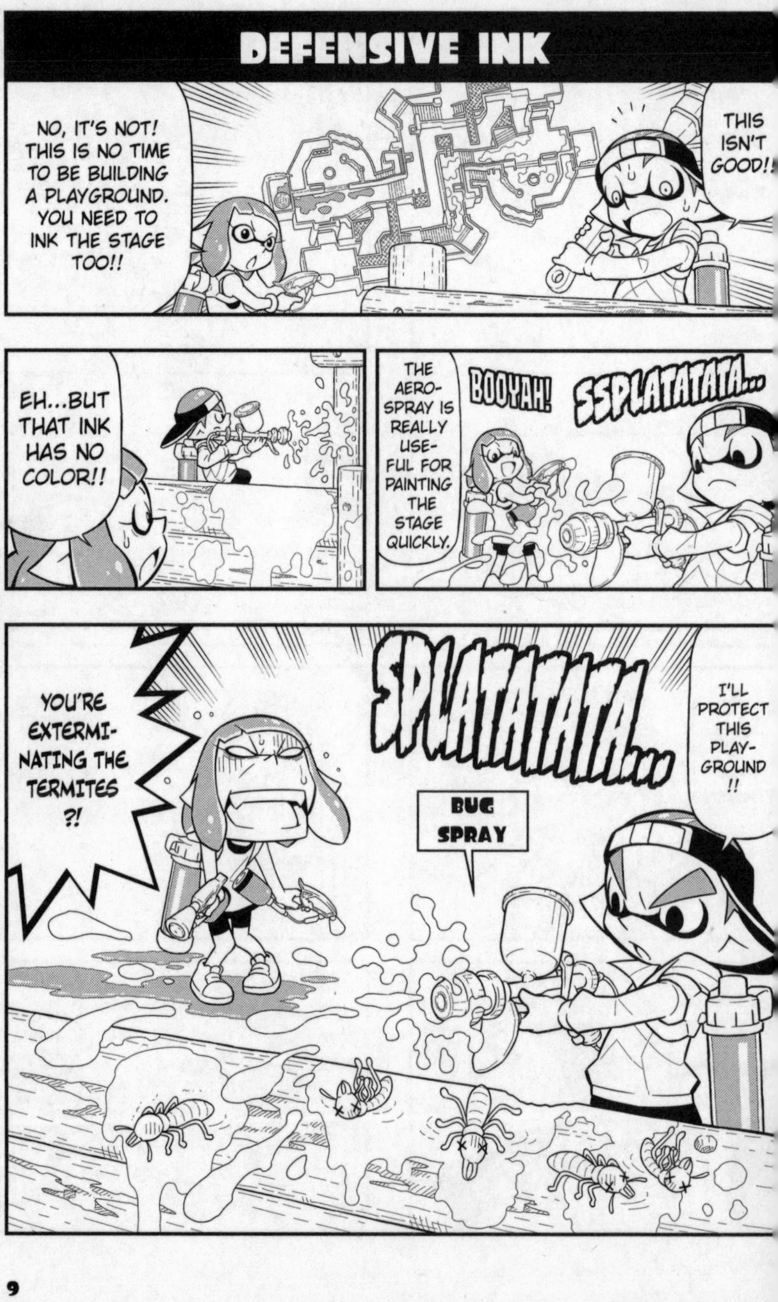
THIS ISN'T GOOD!!
NO, IT'S NOT! THIS IS NO TIME TO BE BUILDING A PLAYGROUND. YOU NEED TO INK THE STAGE TOO!!
SSPLATATATA...
BOOYAH!
THE AERO-SPRAY IS REALLY USE-FUL FOR PAINTING THE STAGE QUICKLY.
EH...BUT THAT INK HAS NO COLOR!!
I'LL PROTECT THIS PLAY-GROUND!!
SPLATATATA...
BUG SPRAY
YOU'RE EXTERMI-NATING THE TERMITES?!

HIDDEN ENEMY SPOTTED

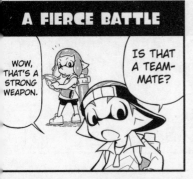

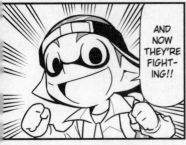

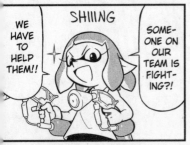

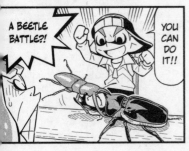

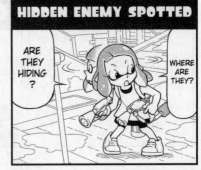

WHERE ARE THEY?
ARE THEY HIDING?
I FOUND THEM!!
WHAT?! WHERE?!
LOOK AT THIS HUGE STAG BEETLE!!
GO HOME, BUG!!

A FIERCE BATTLE

IS THAT A TEAMMATE?
WOW, THAT'S A STRONG WEAPON.
AND NOW THEY'RE FIGHTING!!
SOMEONE ON OUR TEAM IS FIGHTING?!
SHIIING
WE HAVE TO HELP THEM!!
YOU CAN DO IT!!
A BEETLE BATTLE?!

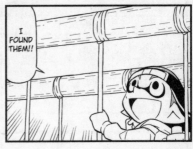

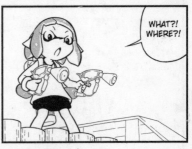

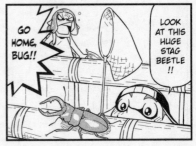

MAXIMUM DANGER!!

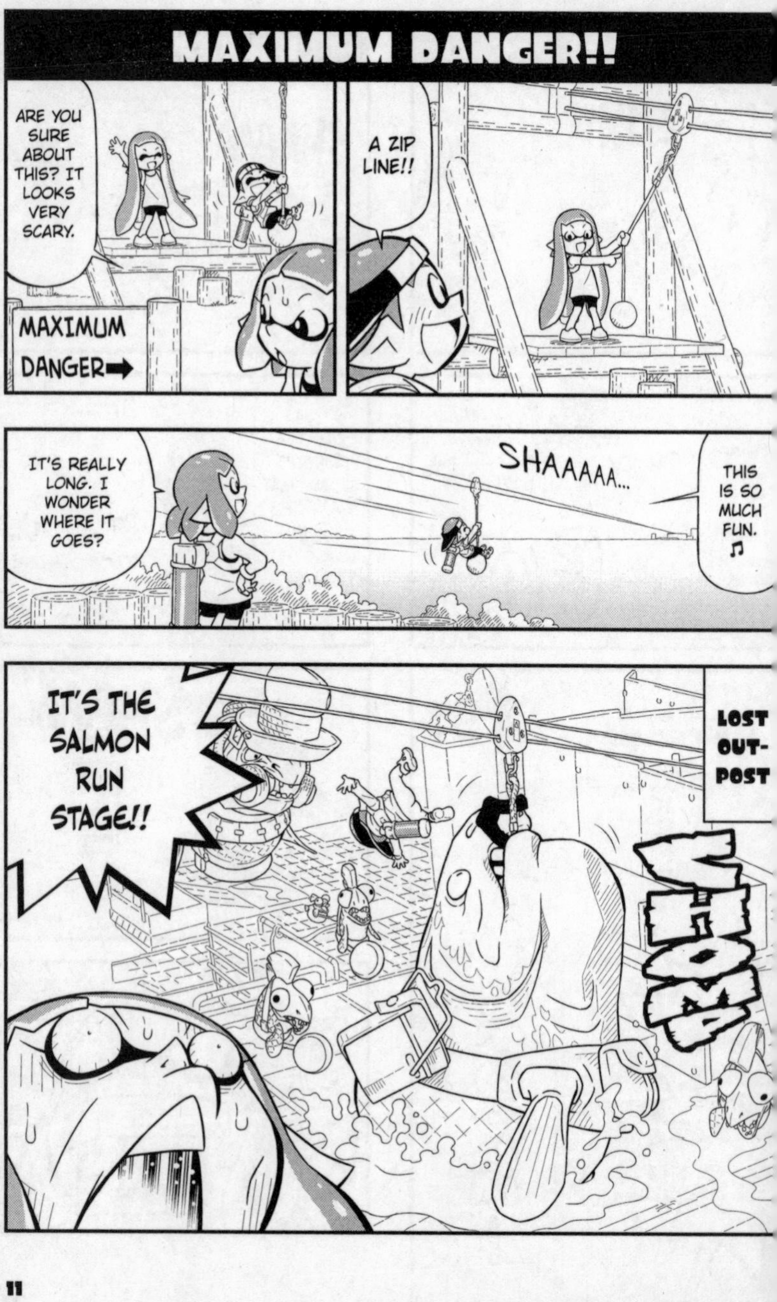
A ZIP LINE!!
ARE YOU SURE ABOUT THIS? IT LOOKS VERY SCARY.
MAXIMUM DANGER➡
THIS IS SO MUCH FUN. ♫
SHAAAAA...
IT'S REALLY LONG. I WONDER WHERE IT GOES?
LOST OUT-POST
WHOA
IT'S THE SALMON RUN STAGE!!

BENEATH YOU

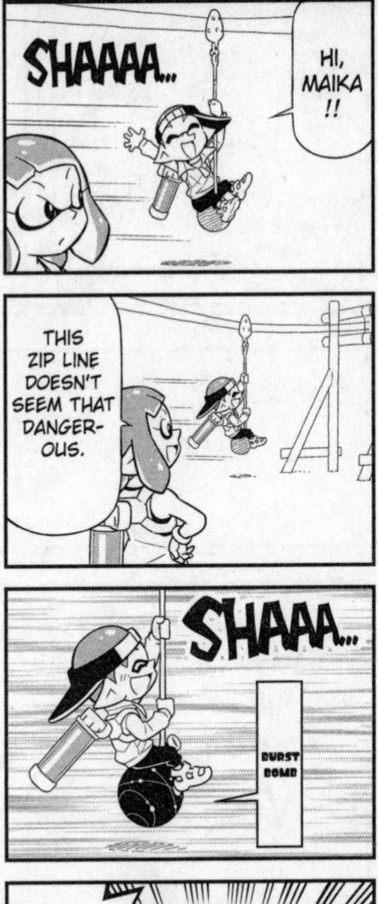
HI, MAIKA!!
SHAAAA...
THIS ZIP LINE DOESN'T SEEM THAT DANGER-OUS.
SHAAA...
BURST BOMB
UNDER-NEATH YOU!!
ACK!

RESCUING WITH A WEAPON

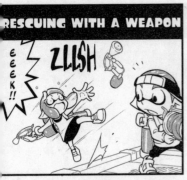

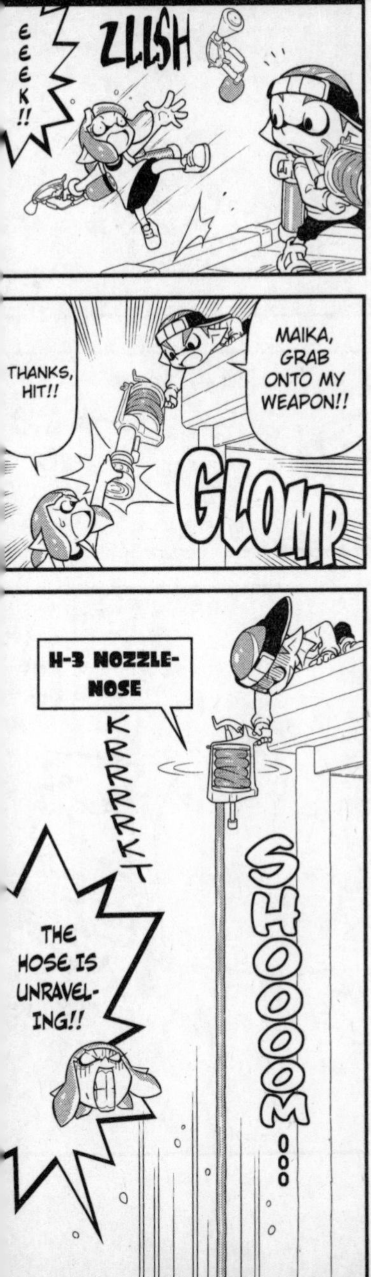
ZLLSH
EEEK!!
MAIKA, GRAB ONTO MY WEAPON!!
GLOMP
THANKS, HIT!!
H-3 NOZZLE-NOSE
KRRRRRKT
SHOOOOOMooo
THE HOSE IS UNRAVEL-ING!!

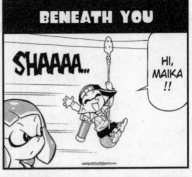

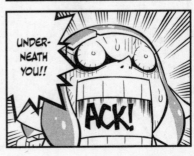

LOG HOPPING

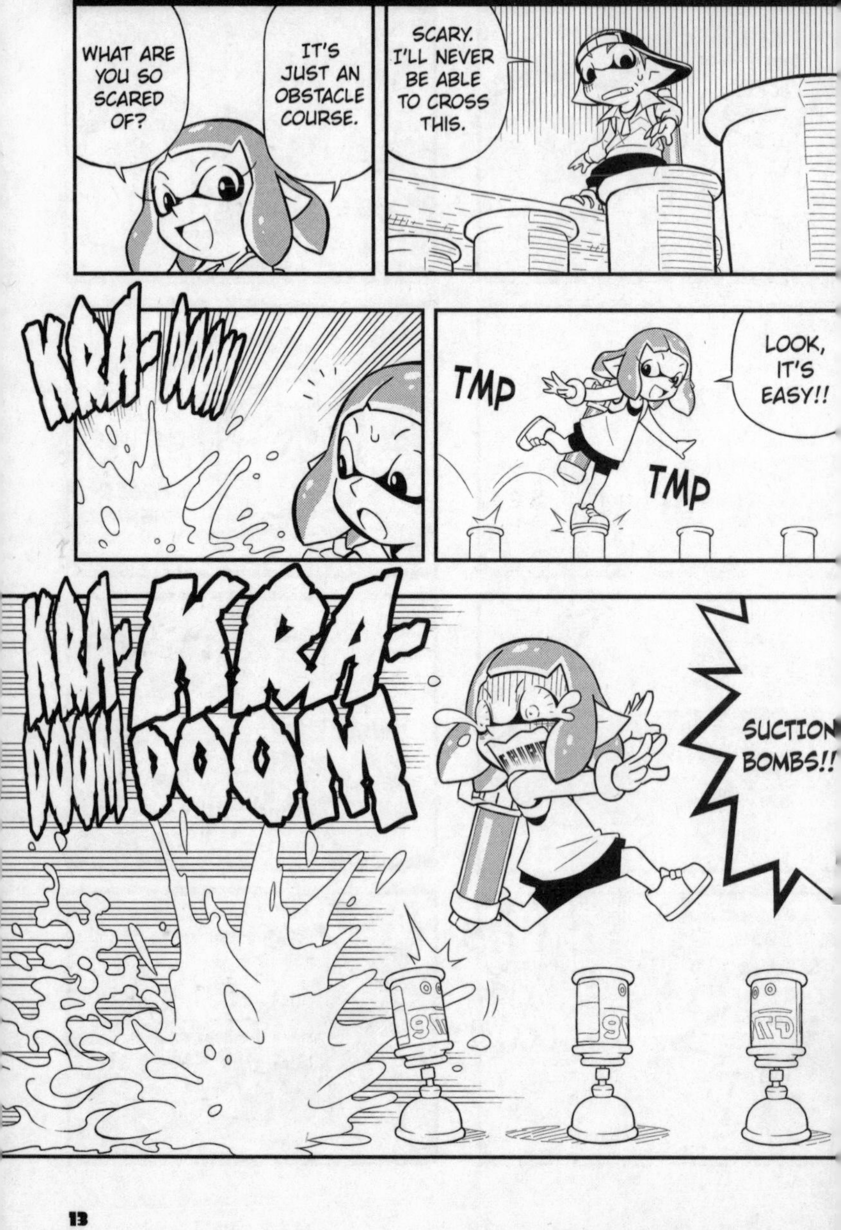
SCARY. I'LL NEVER BE ABLE TO CROSS THIS.
WHAT ARE YOU SO SCARED OF?
IT'S JUST AN OBSTACLE COURSE.
LOOK, IT'S EASY!!
TMP
TMP
KRA-DOOM
KRA-DOOM
KRA-DOOM
SUCTION BOMBS!!

CAMOUFLAGE

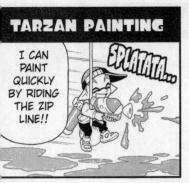

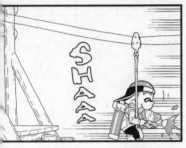

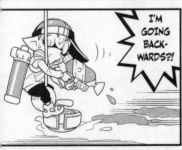

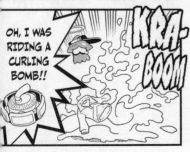

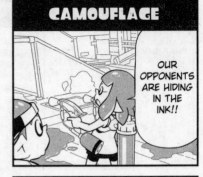

OUR OPPONENTS ARE HIDING IN THE INK!!
THEN WE'LL USE THE PERFECT DISGUISE FOR CAMP TRIGGER-FISH!!
YOU'RE GOING TO USE THE TENTA CAMO BRELLA, RIGHT?
The camouflaged design weapon!!
A DUCK DECOY? CANARD CAMO?

TARZAN PAINTING

SPLATATA...
I CAN PAINT QUICKLY BY RIDING THE ZIP LINE!!
SHAAAA
I'M GOING BACK-WARDS?!
KRA-BOOM
OH, I WAS RIDING A CURLING BOMB!!

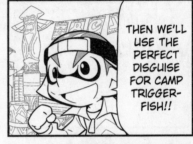

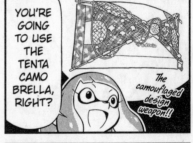

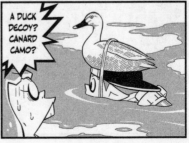

NET TUNNEL

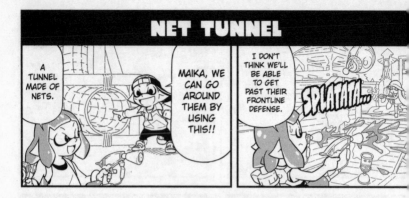

I DON'T THINK WE'LL BE ABLE TO GET PAST THEIR FRONTLINE DEFENSE.
SPLATATA...
MAIKA, WE CAN GO AROUND THEM BY USING THIS!!
A TUNNEL MADE OF NETS.
BE CAREFUL, HIT. YOUR WEAPON COULD GET STUCK IN THE NET!!
SSH
THE SPLAT-TERSHOT IS ROUND, SO IT DIDN'T GET STUCK.
BUT YOUR PANTS DID!
PLIP
And your underwear too!!

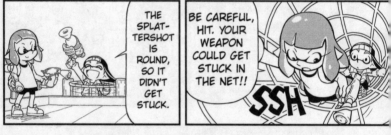

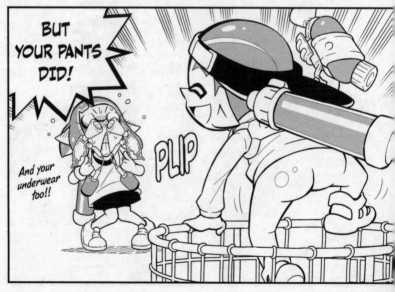

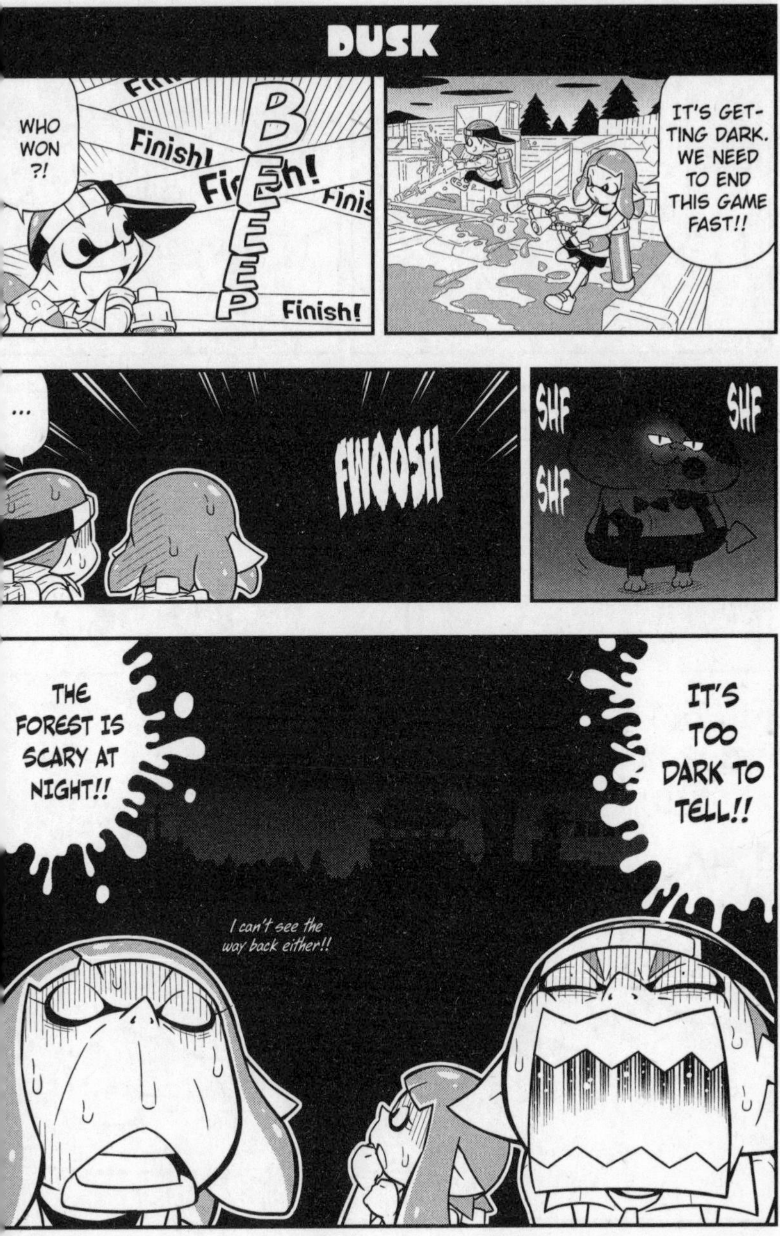
DUSK
IT'S GET-TING DARK. WE NEED TO END THIS GAME FAST!!
WHO WON ?!
Finish!
Finish!
Finish!
Finish!
BEEEEP
Finish!
SHF
SHF
SHF
FWOOSH
...
IT'S TOO DARK TO TELL!!
THE FOREST IS SCARY AT NIGHT!!
I can't see the way back either!!

TIME TO VISIT HIT'S HOMETOWN!

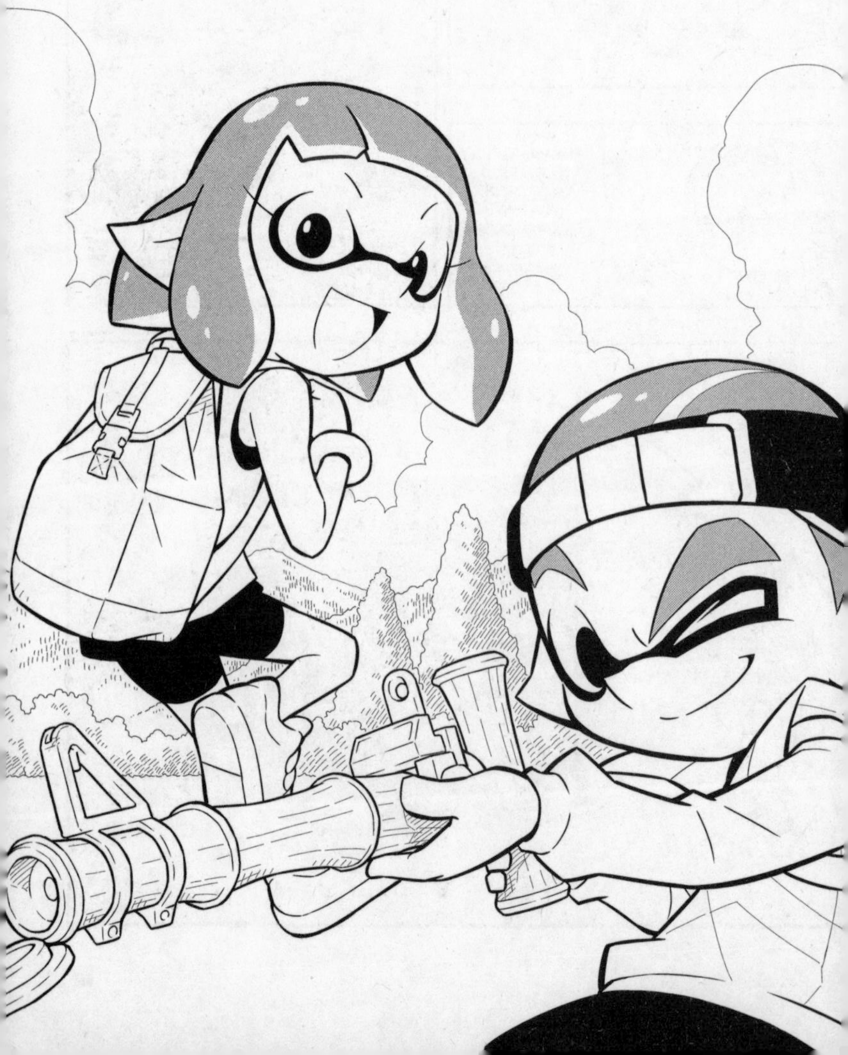

LIFE IN THE COUNTRY

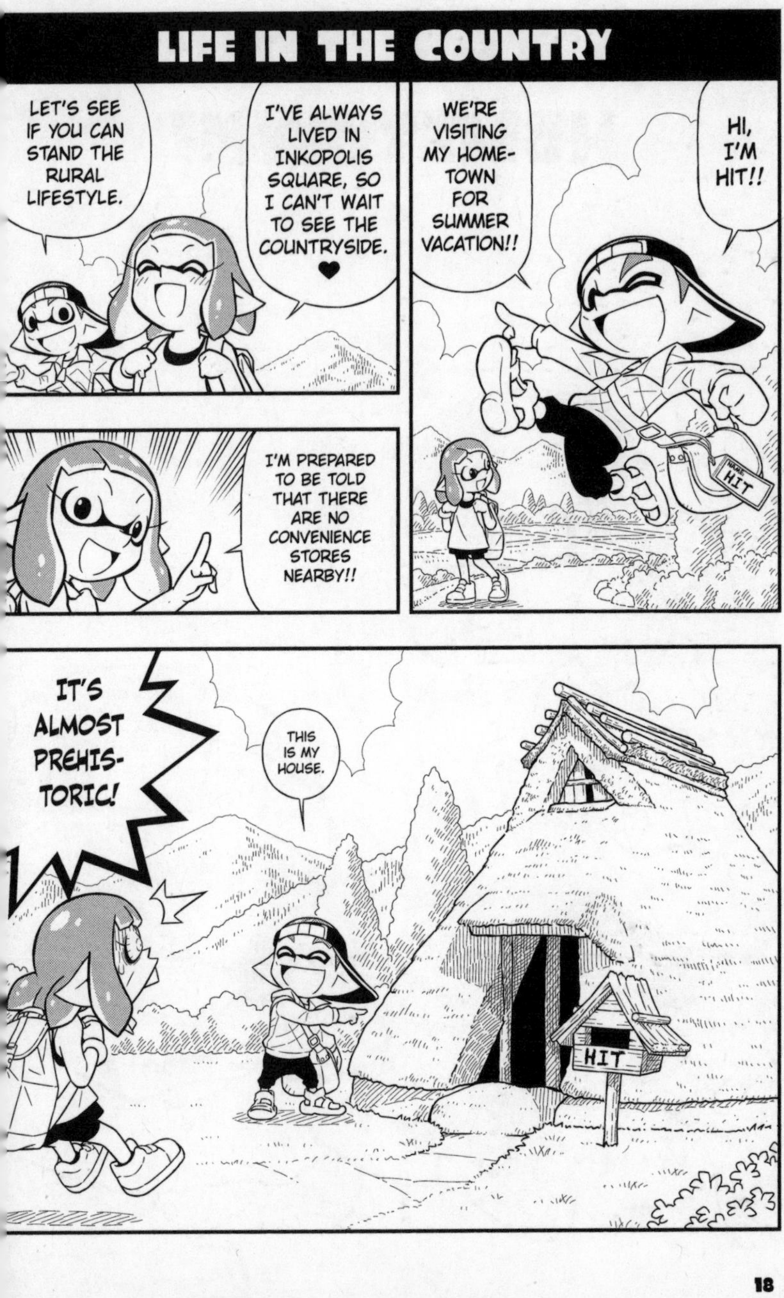
HI, I'M HIT!!
WE'RE VISITING MY HOME-TOWN FOR SUMMER VACATION!!
NAME HIT
I'VE ALWAYS LIVED IN INKOPOLIS SQUARE, SO I CAN'T WAIT TO SEE THE COUNTRYSIDE. ♥
LET'S SEE IF YOU CAN STAND THE RURAL LIFESTYLE.
I'M PREPARED TO BE TOLD THAT THERE ARE NO CONVENIENCE STORES NEARBY!!
THIS IS MY HOUSE.
HIT
IT'S ALMOST PREHIS-TORIC!

DOING IT OLD-SCHOOL... REAL OLD-SCHOOL

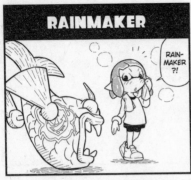

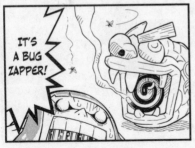

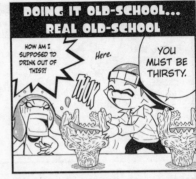

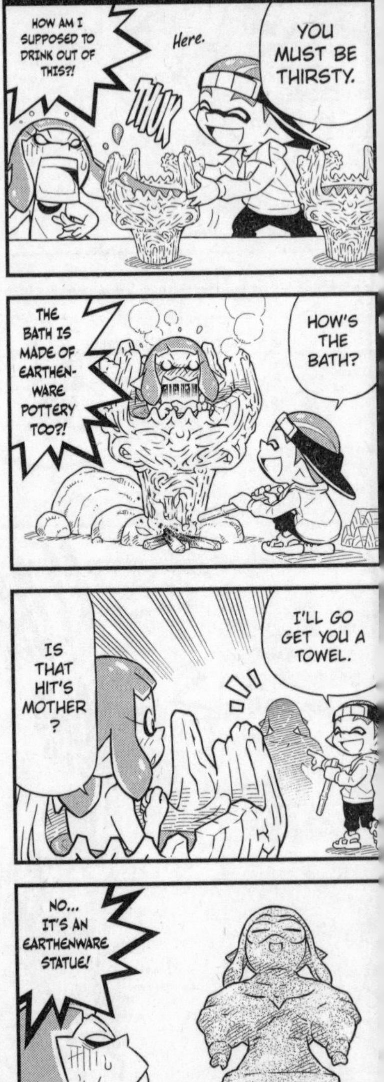
YOU MUST BE THIRSTY.
Here.
THUK
HOW AM I SUPPOSED TO DRINK OUT OF THIS?!
HOW'S THE BATH?
THE BATH IS MADE OF EARTHEN-WARE POTTERY TOO?!
I'LL GO GET YOU A TOWEL.
IS THAT HIT'S MOTHER ?
NO... IT'S AN EARTHENWARE STATUE!

RAINMAKER

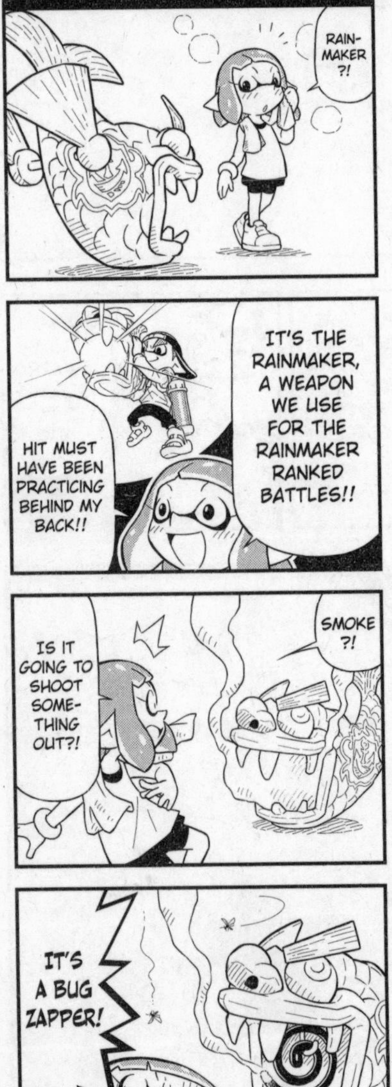
RAIN-MAKER ?!
IT'S THE RAINMAKER, A WEAPON WE USE FOR THE RAINMAKER RANKED BATTLES!!
HIT MUST HAVE BEEN PRACTICING BEHIND MY BACK!!
SMOKE ?!
IS IT GOING TO SHOOT SOME-THING OUT?!
IT'S A BUG ZAPPER!

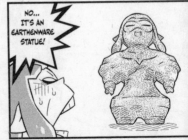

SWIMMING UPSTREAM

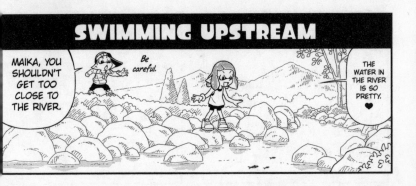

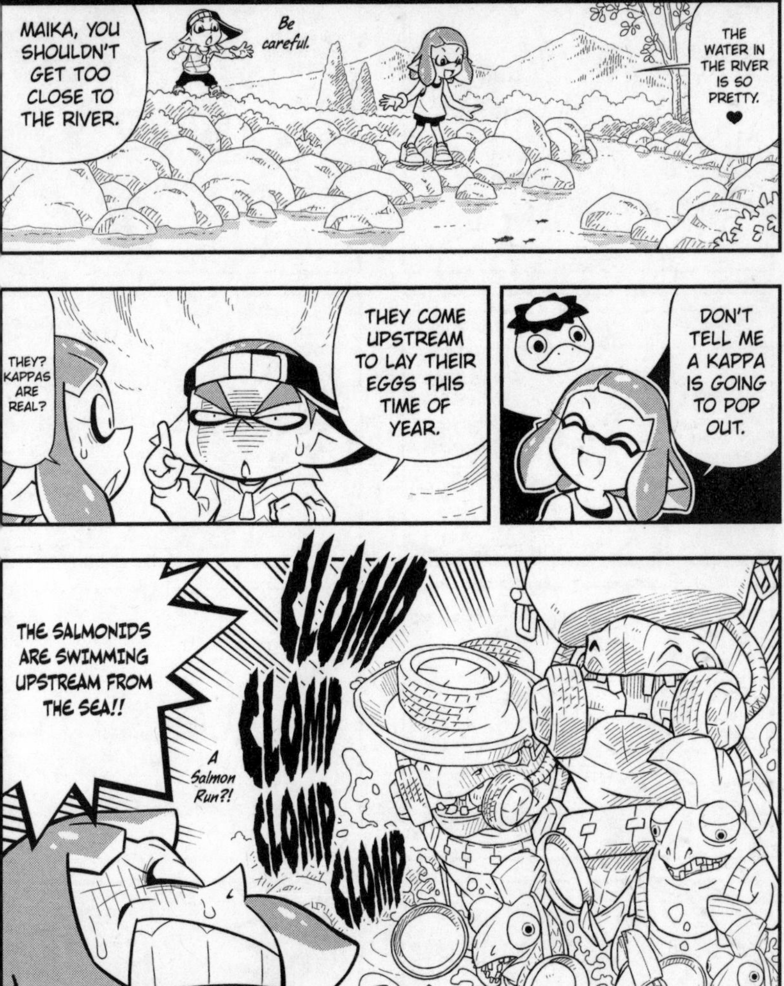
THE WATER IN THE RIVER IS SO PRETTY. ❤
MAIKA, YOU SHOULDN'T GET TOO CLOSE TO THE RIVER.
Be careful.
DON'T TELL ME A KAPPA IS GOING TO POP OUT.
THEY COME UPSTREAM TO LAY THEIR EGGS THIS TIME OF YEAR.
THEY? KAPPAS ARE REAL?
CLOMP
CLOMP
CLOMP
CLOMP
THE SALMONIDS ARE SWIMMING UPSTREAM FROM THE SEA!!
A Salmon Run?!

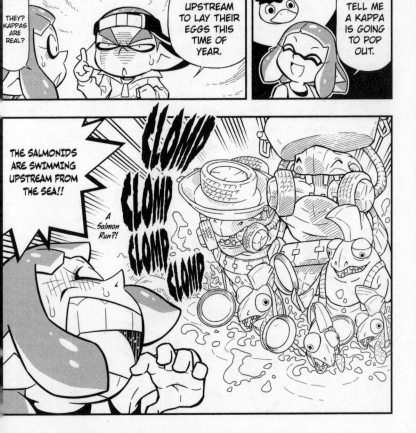

COUNTRY WEAPONS

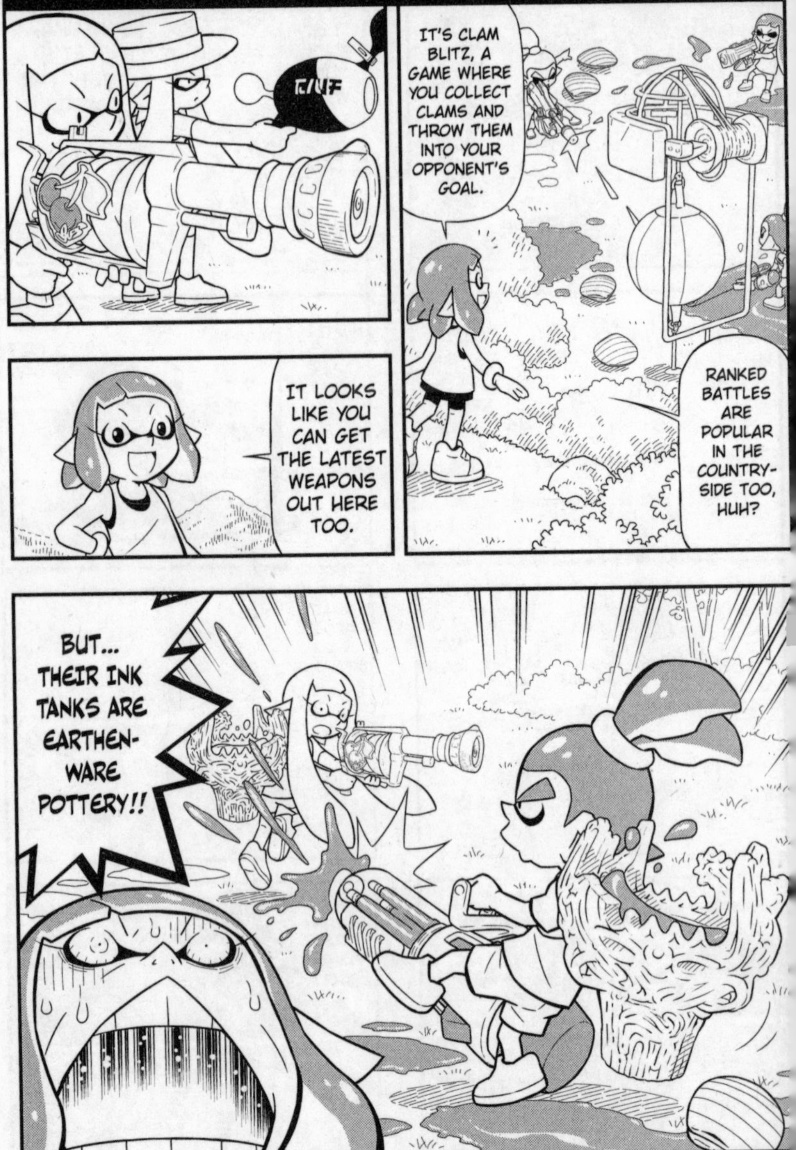
IT'S CLAM BLITZ, A GAME WHERE YOU COLLECT CLAMS AND THROW THEM INTO YOUR OPPONENT'S GOAL.
RANKED BATTLES ARE POPULAR IN THE COUNTRY-SIDE TOO, HUH?
IT LOOKS LIKE YOU CAN GET THE LATEST WEAPONS OUT HERE TOO.
BUT... THEIR INK TANKS ARE EARTHEN-WARE POTTERY!!

BAMBOO STYLE

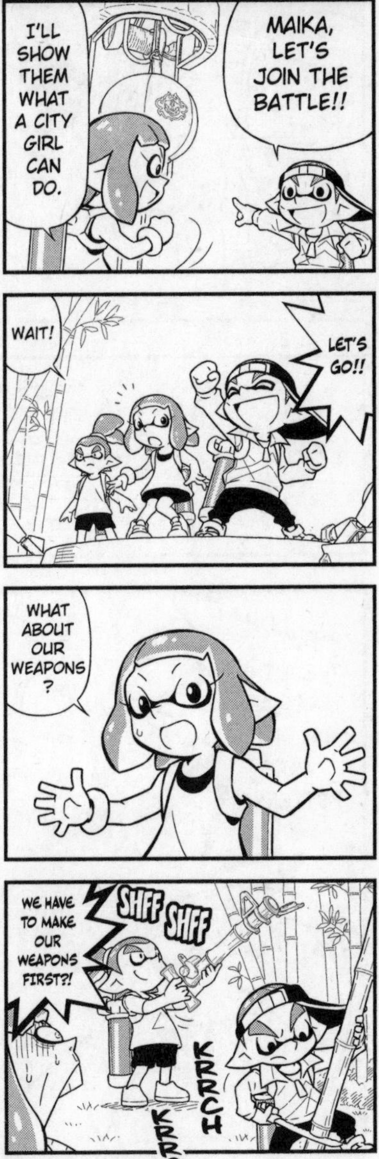
MAIKA, LET'S JOIN THE BATTLE!!
I'LL SHOW THEM WHAT A CITY GIRL CAN DO.
LET'S GO!!
WAIT!
WHAT ABOUT OUR WEAPONS?
SHFF SHFF
KRRCH
WE HAVE TO MAKE OUR WEAPONS FIRST?!
KRRCH

COUNTRYSIDE STAGE

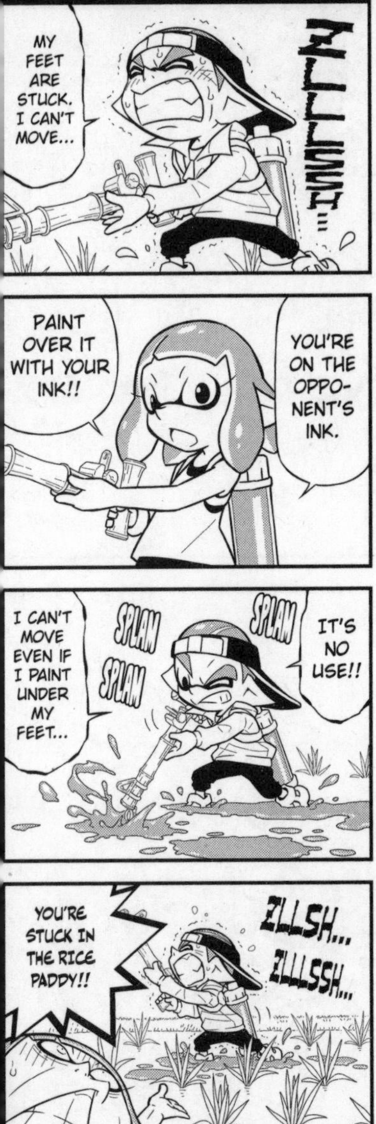
ZLLLSSH...
MY FEET ARE STUCK. I CAN'T MOVE...
YOU'RE ON THE OPPONENT'S INK.
PAINT OVER IT WITH YOUR INK!!
IT'S NO USE!!
SPLAM
SPLAM
SPLAM
I CAN'T MOVE EVEN IF I PAINT UNDER MY FEET...
ZLLSH...
ZLLLSSH...
YOU'RE STUCK IN THE RICE PADDY!!

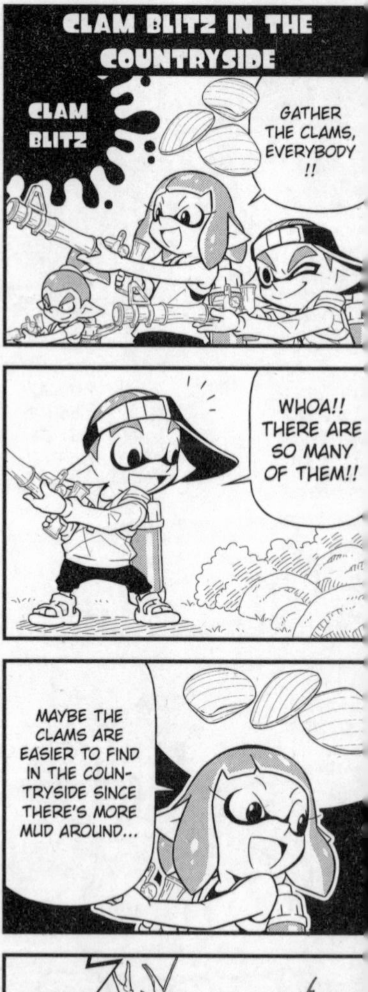
CLAM BLITZ IN THE COUNTRYSIDE
GATHER THE CLAMS, EVERYBODY!!
CLAM BLITZ
WHOA!! THERE ARE SO MANY OF THEM!!
MAYBE THE CLAMS ARE EASIER TO FIND IN THE COUNTRYSIDE SINCE THERE'S MORE MUD AROUND...
WE DON'T NEED ANY CRAWFISH!!

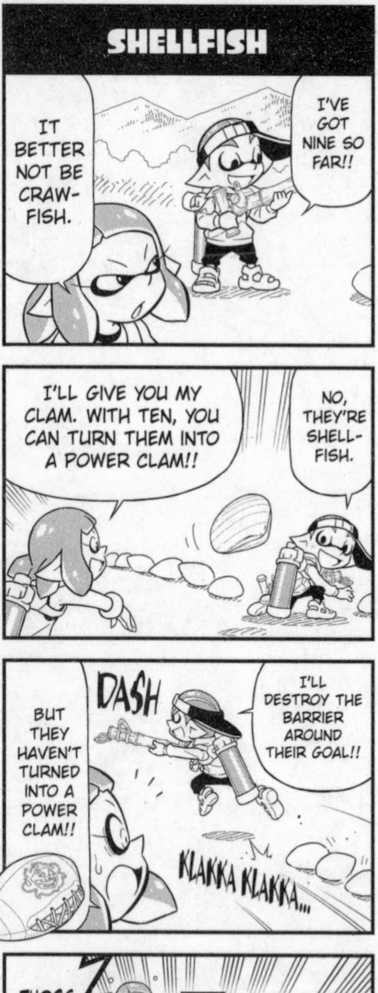
SHELLFISH
I'VE GOT NINE SO FAR!!
IT BETTER NOT BE CRAWFISH.
NO, THEY'RE SHELLFISH.
I'LL GIVE YOU MY CLAM. WITH TEN, YOU CAN TURN THEM INTO A POWER CLAM!!
I'LL DESTROY THE BARRIER AROUND THEIR GOAL!!
DASH
BUT THEY HAVEN'T TURNED INTO A POWER CLAM!!
KLAKKA KLAKKA...
RIVER SNAIL
THOSE AREN'T CLAMS!!

*Gather ten clams to get a Power Clam.

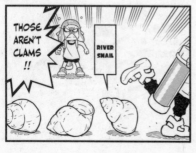

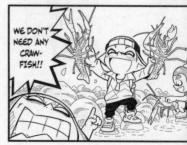

HIDING IN THE BUSH

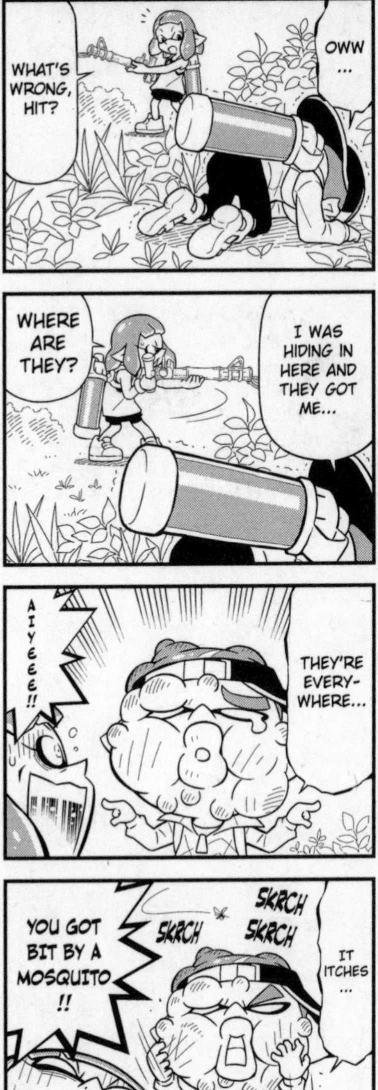
OWW ...
WHAT'S WRONG, HIT?
I WAS HIDING IN HERE AND THEY GOT ME...
WHERE ARE THEY?
THEY'RE EVERY-WHERE...
AIYEEEE!!
SKRCH SKRCH
IT ITCHES ...
SKRCH
YOU GOT BIT BY A MOSQUITO!!

SPLASHDOWN NULLIFIED

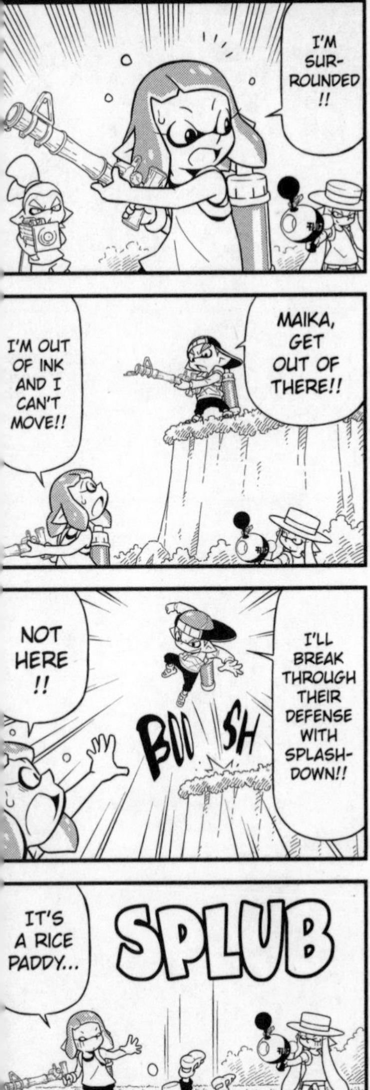
I'M SUR-ROUNDED!!
MAIKA, GET OUT OF THERE!!
I'M OUT OF INK AND I CAN'T MOVE!!
I'LL BREAK THROUGH THEIR DEFENSE WITH SPLASH-DOWN!!
BOOSH
NOT HERE!!
SPLUB
IT'S A RICE PADDY...

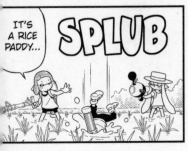

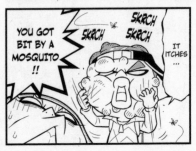

FULL NET

AND WE'VE WON!!
BOOSH
BEEEEP
Finish!
Finish!
BOOYAH!
WE GO A LOT POINTS
I PUT 30 OF THEM INSIDE.
WHAT ?!
THEM ...?
RUSTLE RUSTLE
RUSTLE RUSTLE
IT'S NOT AN INSECT CAGE!!
EEEEK!!
RUSTLE RUSTLE

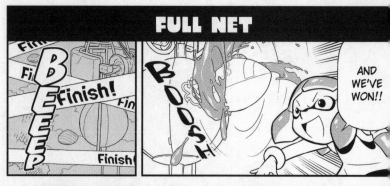

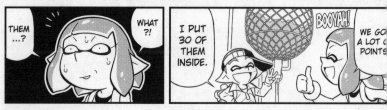

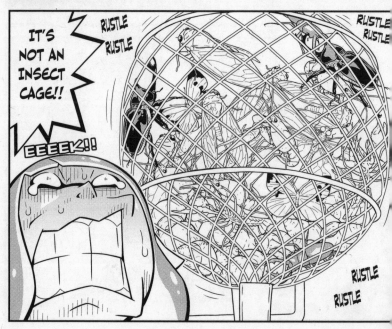

FIREFLIES

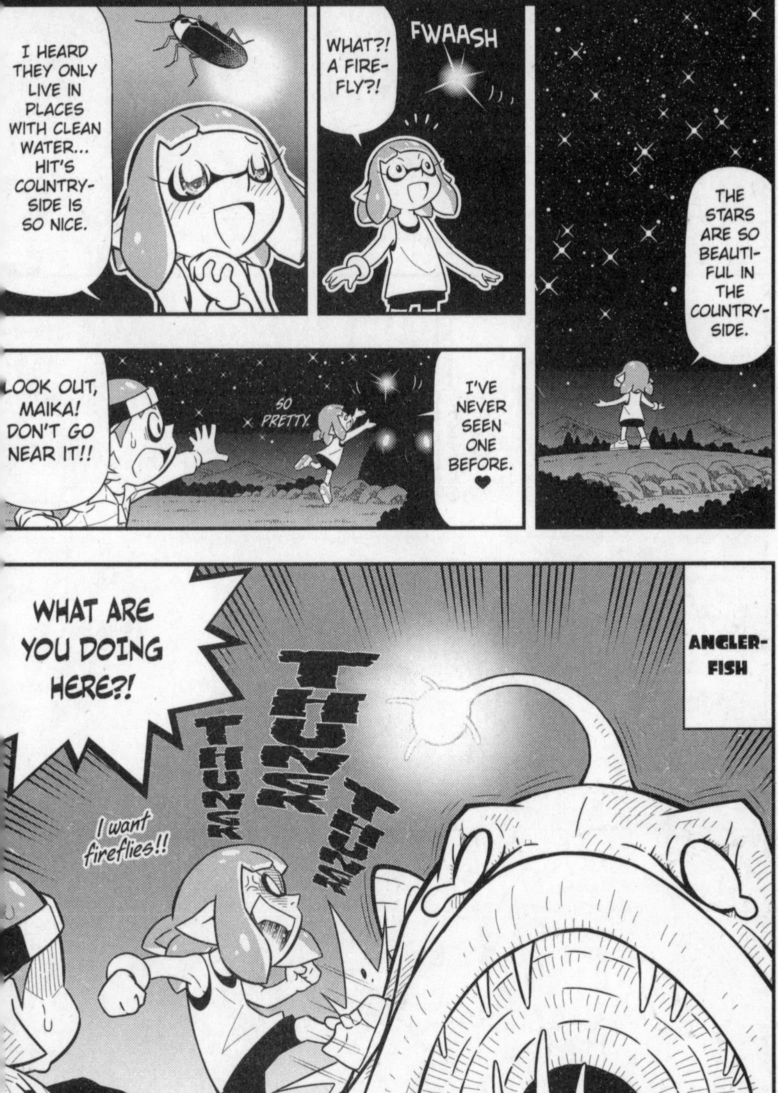
THE STARS ARE SO BEAUTIFUL IN THE COUNTRYSIDE.
WHAT?! A FIREFLY?!
FWAASH
I HEARD THEY ONLY LIVE IN PLACES WITH CLEAN WATER... HIT'S COUNTRYSIDE IS SO NICE.
I'VE NEVER SEEN ONE BEFORE. ♥
SO PRETTY.
LOOK OUT, MAIKA! DON'T GO NEAR IT!!
ANGLERFISH
THUNK
THUNK
WHAT ARE YOU DOING HERE?!
I want fireflies!!

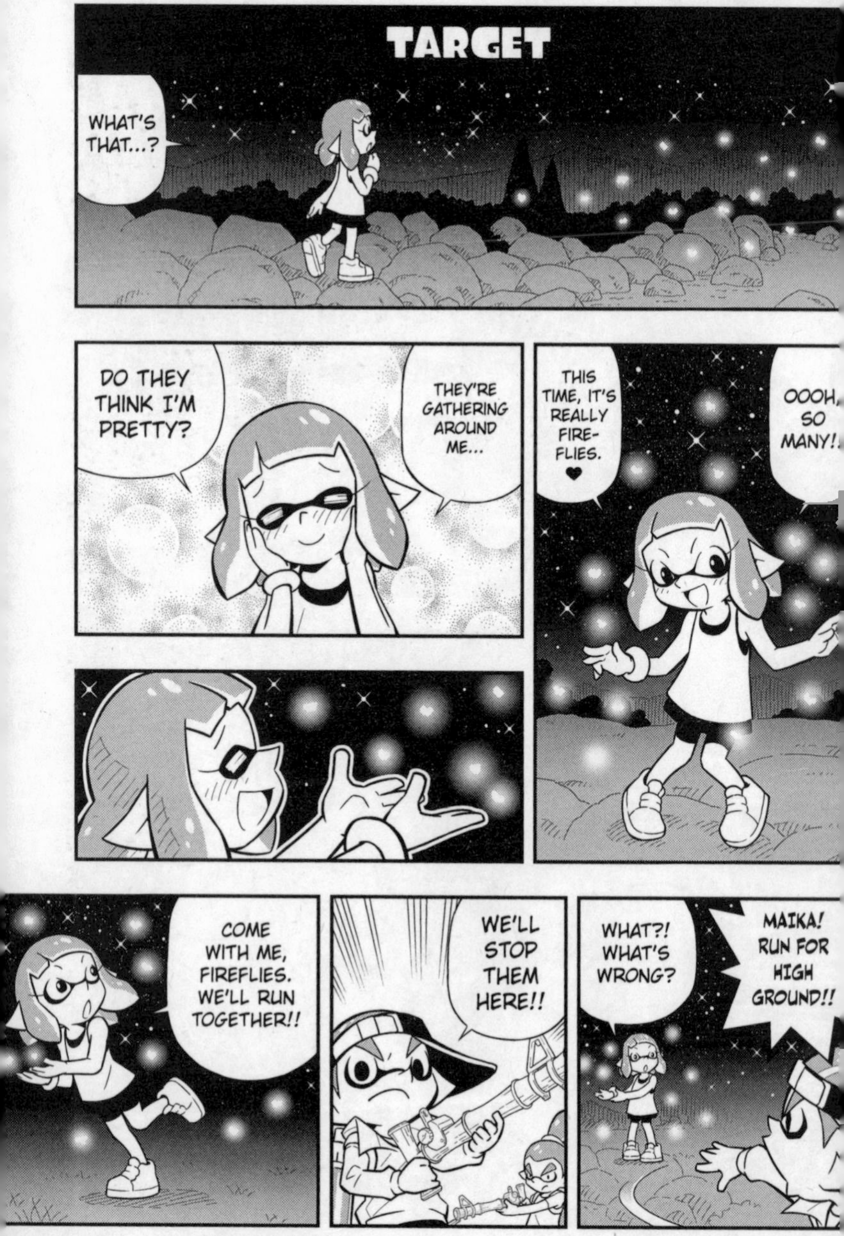
TARGET
WHAT'S THAT...?
OOOH, SO MANY!!
THIS TIME, IT'S REALLY FIRE-FLIES. ♥
THEY'RE GATHERING AROUND ME...
DO THEY THINK I'M PRETTY?
MAIKA! RUN FOR HIGH GROUND!!
WHAT?! WHAT'S WRONG?
WE'LL STOP THEM HERE!!
COME WITH ME, FIREFLIES. WE'LL RUN TOGETHER!!

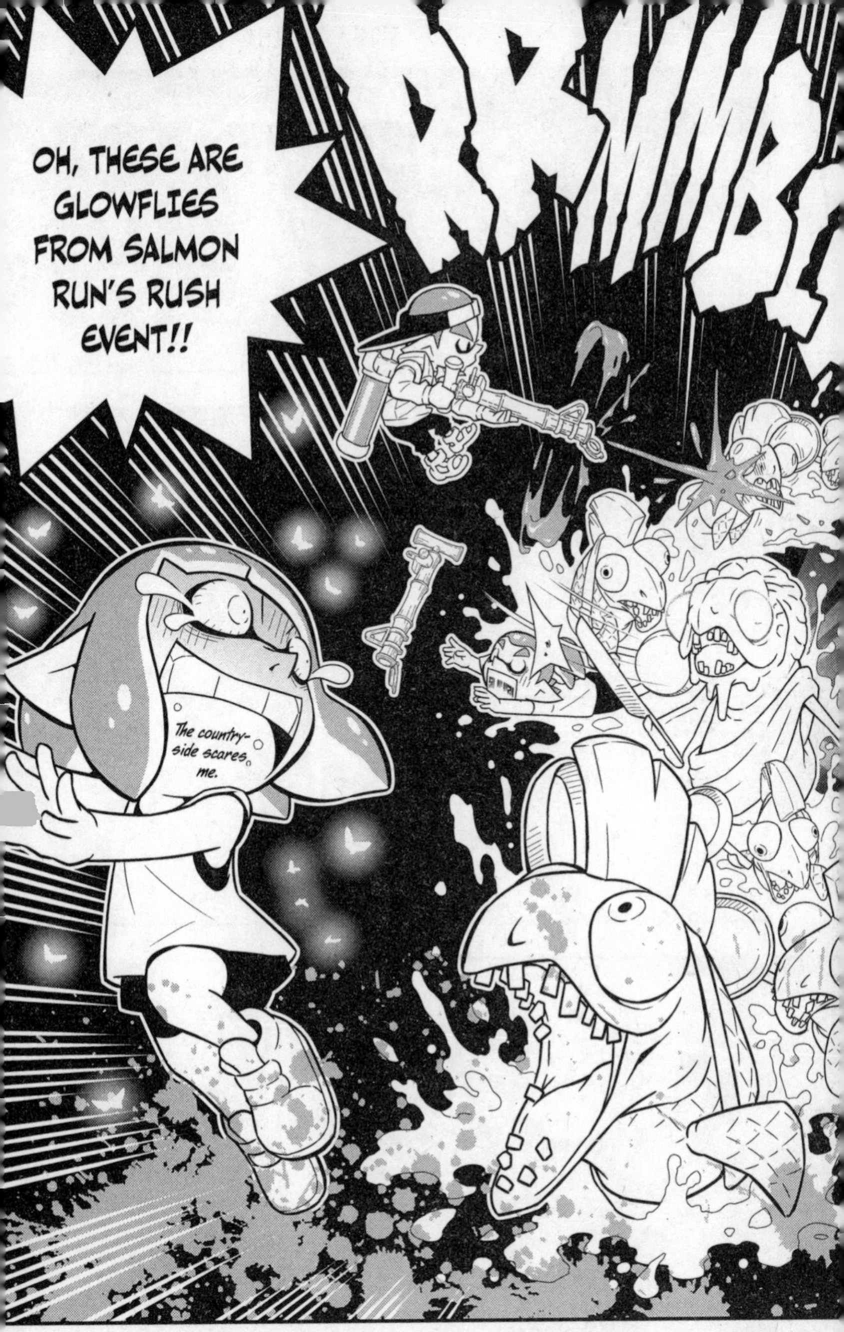
OH, THESE ARE GLOWFLIES FROM SALMON RUN'S RUSH EVENT!!
The country-side scares me.

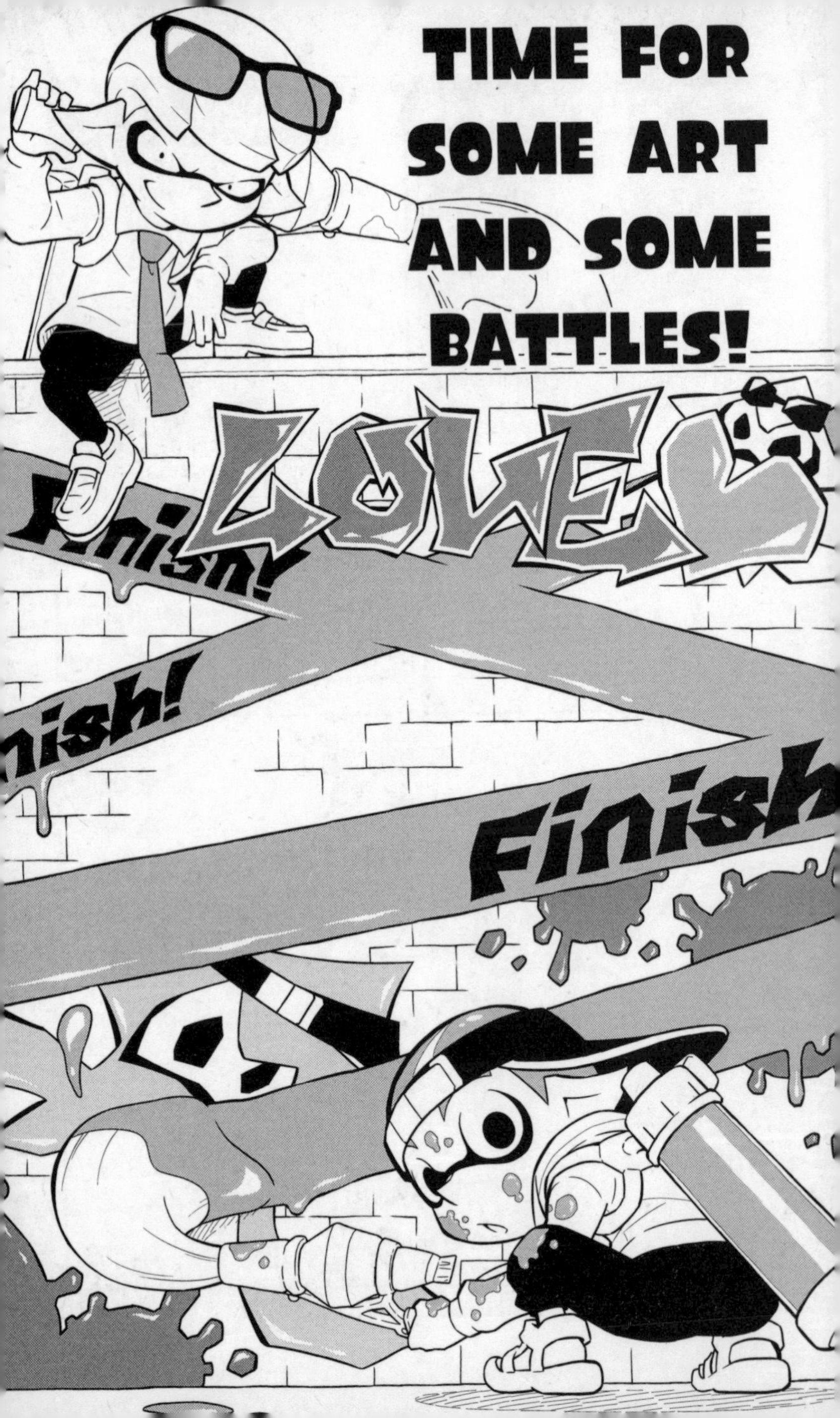

TIME FOR SOME ART AND SOME BATTLES!
LOVE
Finish!
Finish!
Finish

AUTUMN IS FOR ART

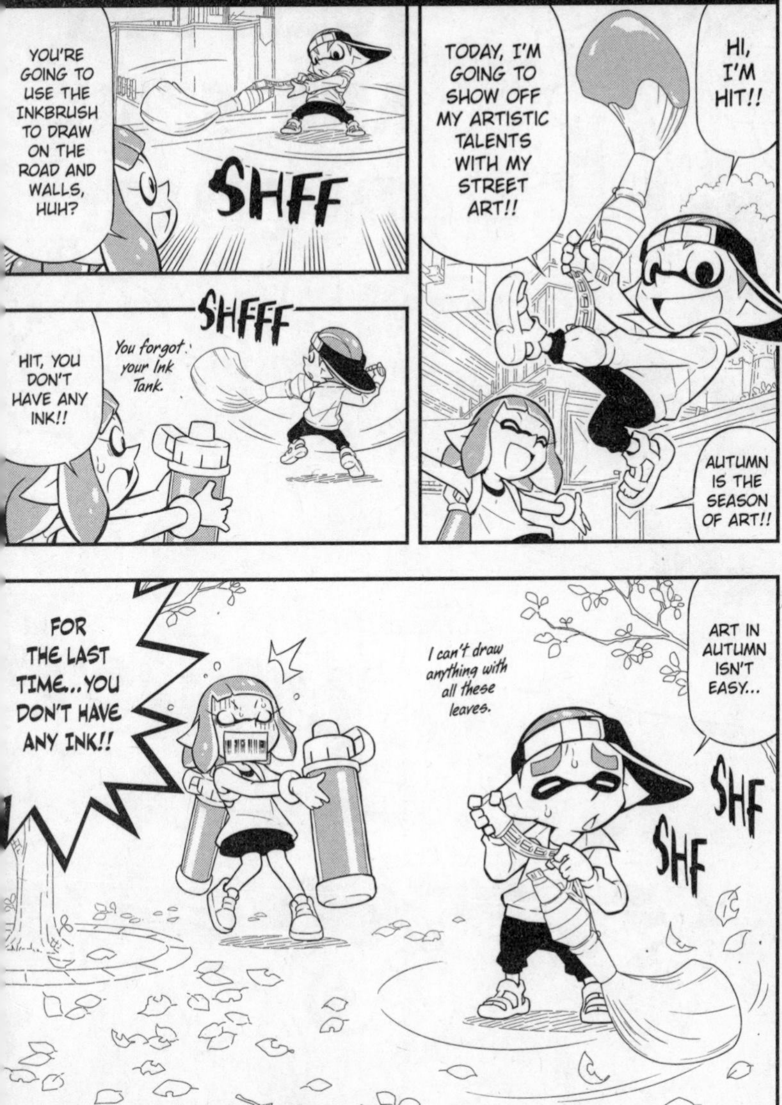

HI, I'M HIT!!
TODAY, I'M GOING TO SHOW OFF MY ARTISTIC TALENTS WITH MY STREET ART!!
AUTUMN IS THE SEASON OF ART!!
YOU'RE GOING TO USE THE INKBRUSH TO DRAW ON THE ROAD AND WALLS, HUH?
SHFF
SHFFF
You forgot your Ink Tank.
HIT, YOU DON'T HAVE ANY INK!!
ART IN AUTUMN ISN'T EASY...
SHF
SHF
I can't draw anything with all these leaves.
FOR THE LAST TIME...YOU DON'T HAVE ANY INK!!

PAINTING WITH THE INKBRUSH

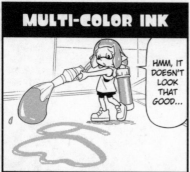

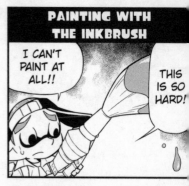

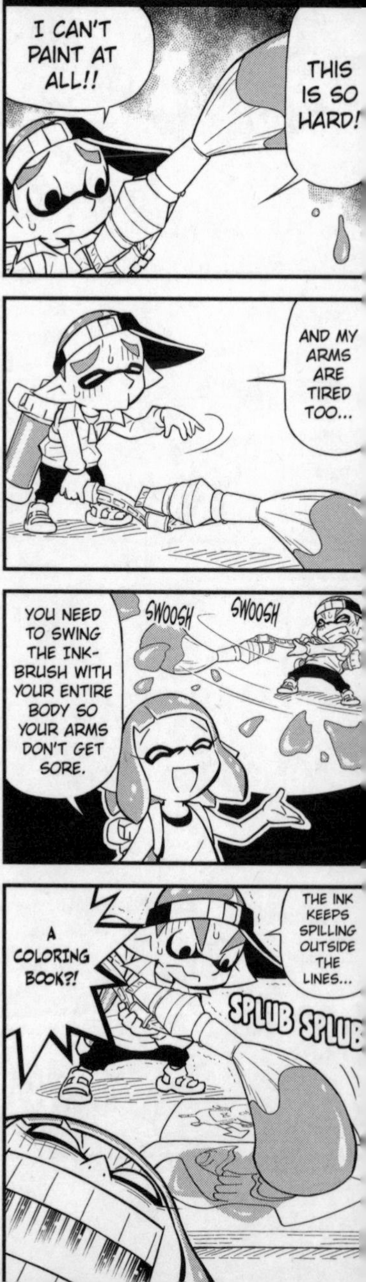
THIS IS SO HARD!
I CAN'T PAINT AT ALL!!
AND MY ARMS ARE TIRED TOO...
SWOOSH
SWOOSH
YOU NEED TO SWING THE INK-BRUSH WITH YOUR ENTIRE BODY SO YOUR ARMS DON'T GET SORE.
THE INK KEEPS SPILLING OUTSIDE THE LINES...
SPLUB SPLUB
A COLORING BOOK?!

MULTI-COLOR INK

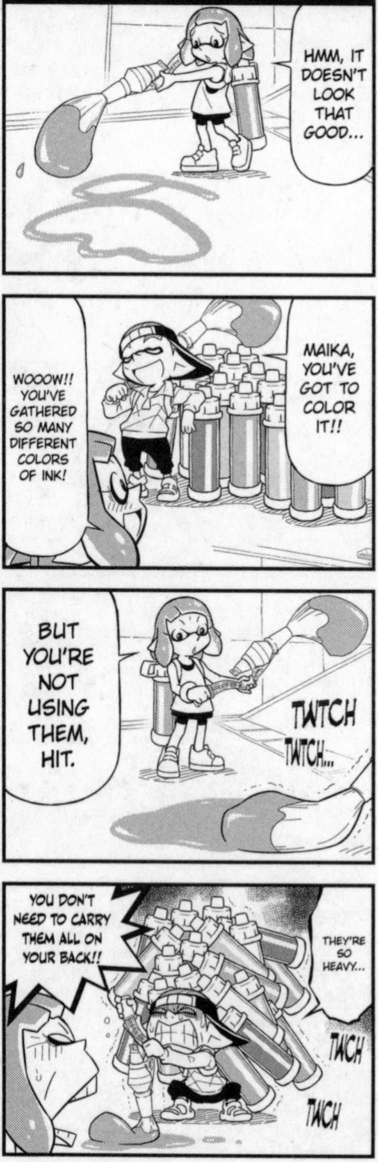
HMM, IT DOESN'T LOOK THAT GOOD...
MAIKA, YOU'VE GOT TO COLOR IT!!
WOOOW!! YOU'VE GATHERED SO MANY DIFFERENT COLORS OF INK!
TWTCH TWTCH...
BUT YOU'RE NOT USING THEM, HIT.
THEY'RE SO HEAVY...
TWCH
TWCH
YOU DON'T NEED TO CARRY THEM ALL ON YOUR BACK!!

FLINGZA ROLLER

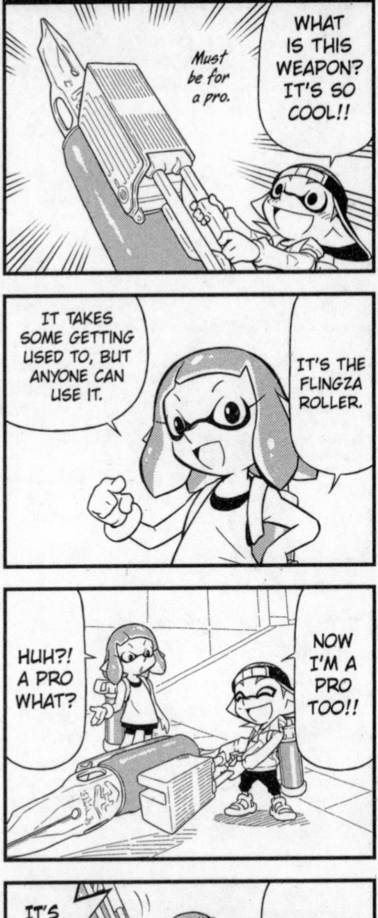
WHAT IS THIS WEAPON? IT'S SO COOL!!
Must be for a pro.
IT'S THE FLINGZA ROLLER.
IT TAKES SOME GETTING USED TO, BUT ANYONE CAN USE IT.
NOW I'M A PRO TOO!!
HUH?! A PRO WHAT?
HOW DO THE MANGA ARTISTS EVEN DRAW WITH THIS?
SKRT
SKRT
IT'S NOT A DIP PEN!!

WATER SOLUBLE

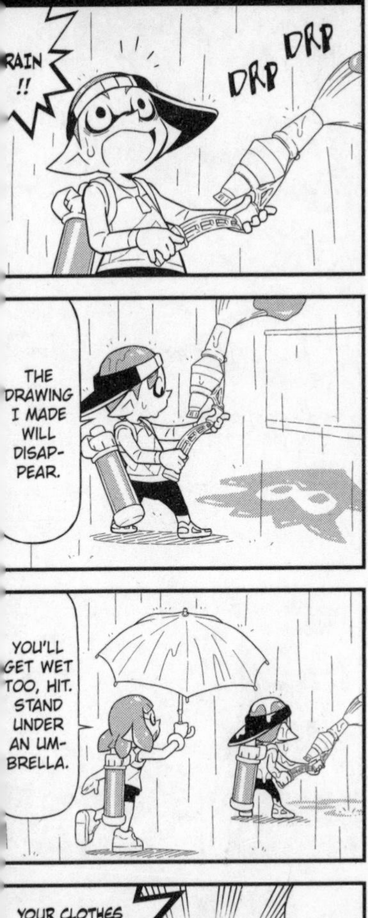
DRP DRP
RAIN!!
THE DRAWING I MADE WILL DISAPPEAR.
YOU'LL GET WET TOO, HIT. STAND UNDER AN UMBRELLA.
THANKS, MAIKA.
YOUR CLOTHES WERE INK TOO, WEREN'T THEY?
NAAAKED

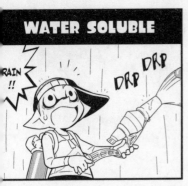

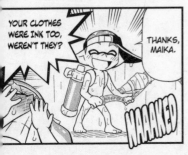

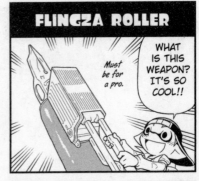

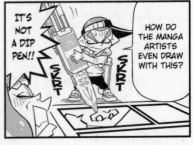

CLASH BLASTER

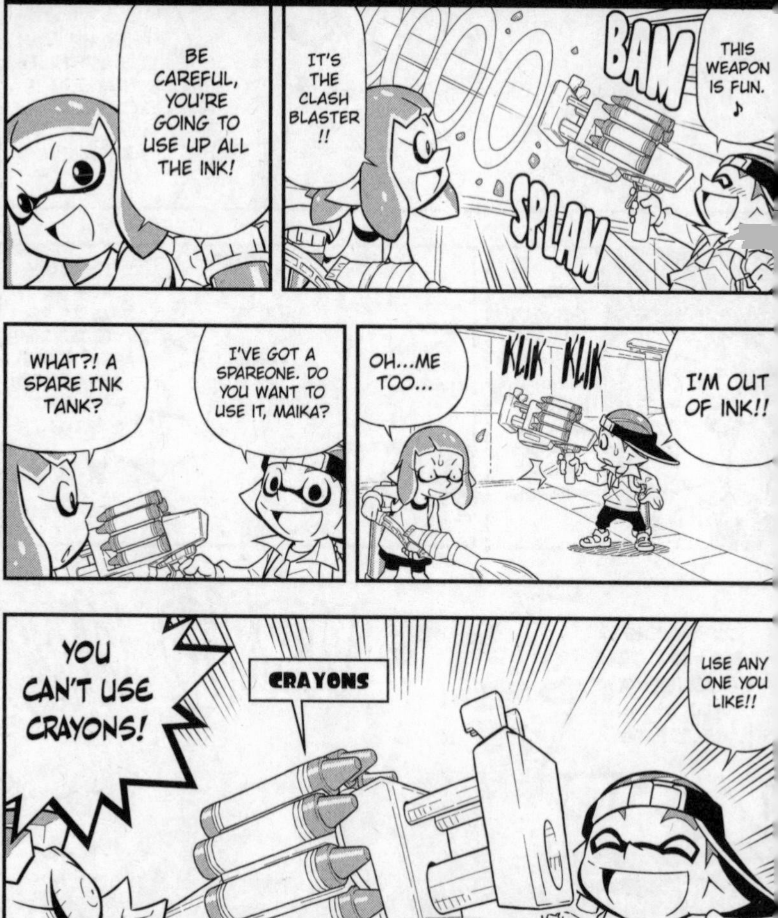
THIS WEAPON IS FUN. ♪
BAM
SPLAW
IT'S THE CLASH BLASTER!!
BE CAREFUL, YOU'RE GOING TO USE UP ALL THE INK!
I'M OUT OF INK!!
KLIK KLIK
OH...ME TOO...
I'VE GOT A SPAREONE. DO YOU WANT TO USE IT, MAIKA?
WHAT?! A SPARE INK TANK?
USE ANY ONE YOU LIKE!!
CRAYONS
YOU CAN'T USE CRAYONS!

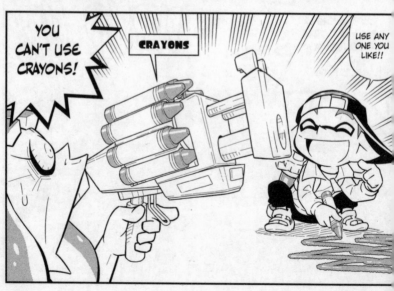

BATH BATTLE

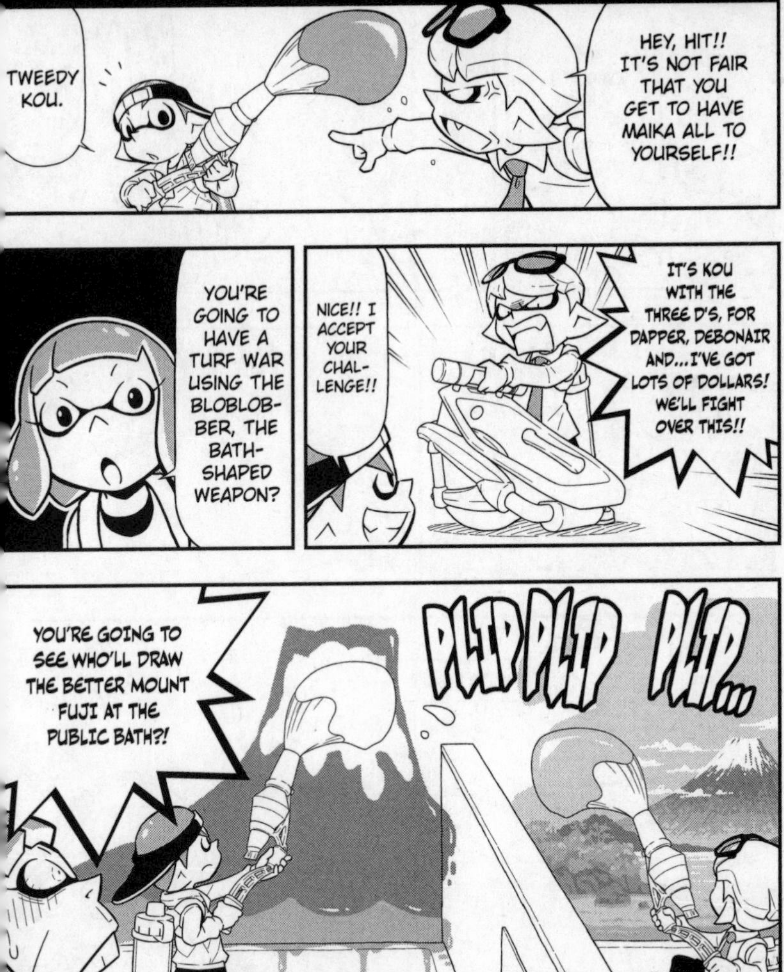
HEY, HIT!! IT'S NOT FAIR THAT YOU GET TO HAVE MAIKA ALL TO YOURSELF!!
TWEEDY KOU.
IT'S KOU WITH THE THREE D'S, FOR DAPPER, DEBONAIR AND...I'VE GOT LOTS OF DOLLARS! WE'LL FIGHT OVER THIS!!
NICE!! I ACCEPT YOUR CHAL-LENGE!!
YOU'RE GOING TO HAVE A TURF WAR USING THE BLOBLOB-BER, THE BATH-SHAPED WEAPON?
PLIP PLIP PLIP...
YOU'RE GOING TO SEE WHO'LL DRAW THE BETTER MOUNT FUJI AT THE PUBLIC BATH?!

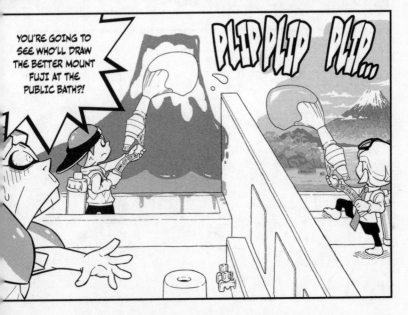

PAINTING AREA

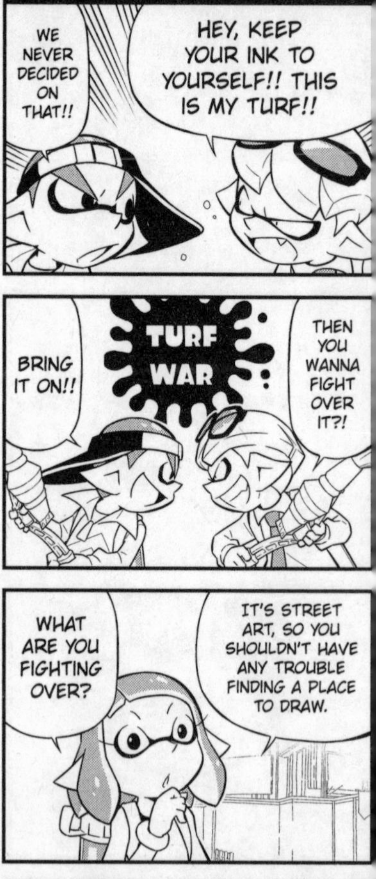
HEY, KEEP YOUR INK TO YOURSELF!! THIS IS MY TURF!!
WE NEVER DECIDED ON THAT!!
THEN YOU WANNA FIGHT OVER IT?!
TURF WAR
BRING IT ON!!
IT'S STREET ART, SO YOU SHOULDN'T HAVE ANY TROUBLE FINDING A PLACE TO DRAW.
WHAT ARE YOU FIGHTING OVER?
A COLORING BOOK?!
COLORING BOOK FOR CHILDREN

SMALL WEAPON

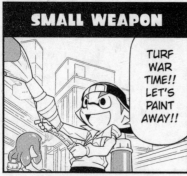

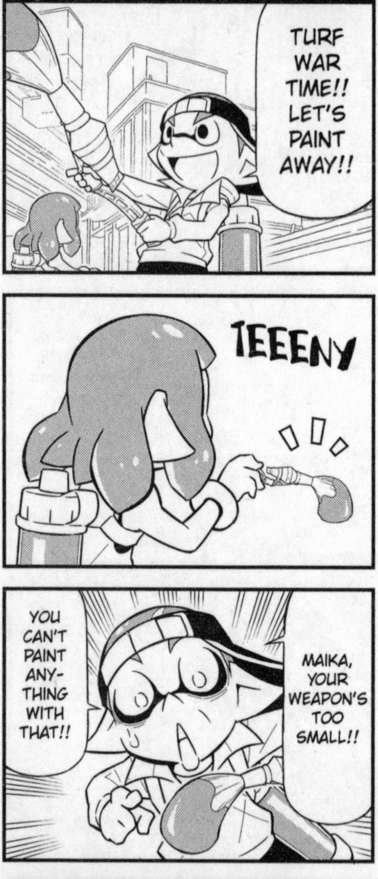
TURF WAR TIME!! LET'S PAINT AWAY!!
TEEENY
MAIKA, YOUR WEAPON'S TOO SMALL!!
YOU CAN'T PAINT ANYTHING WITH THAT!!
IT'S THE PERFECT SIZE.
IT'S FOR MAKEUP ?!
Um... lookin'...um... good...yeah... good.

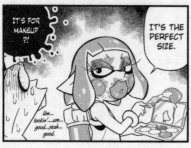

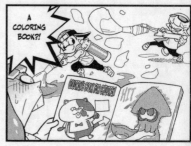

SNEAKY WITH CAMOUFLAGE

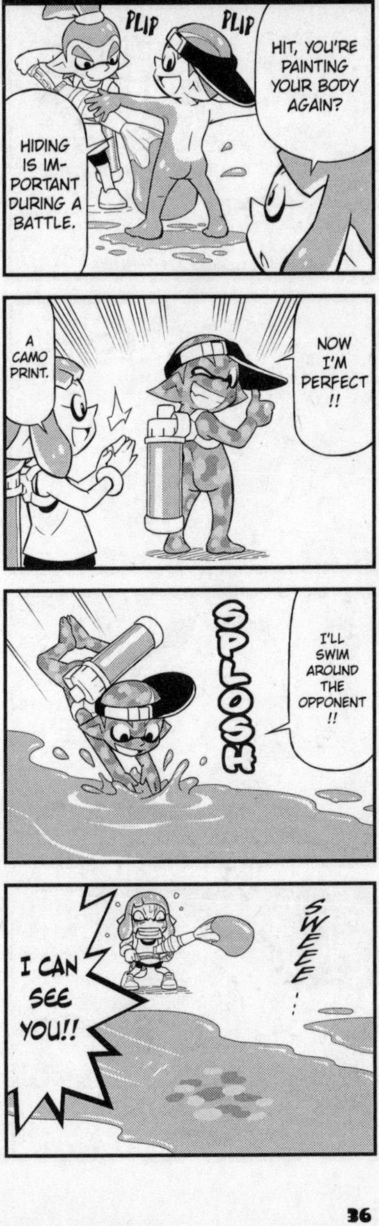
PLIP
PLIP
HIT, YOU'RE PAINTING YOUR BODY AGAIN?
HIDING IS IMPORTANT DURING A BATTLE.
NOW I'M PERFECT!!
A CAMO PRINT.
SPLOSH
I'LL SWIM AROUND THE OPPONENT!!
SWEEE...
I CAN SEE YOU!!

MAIKA SHADOW CLONE

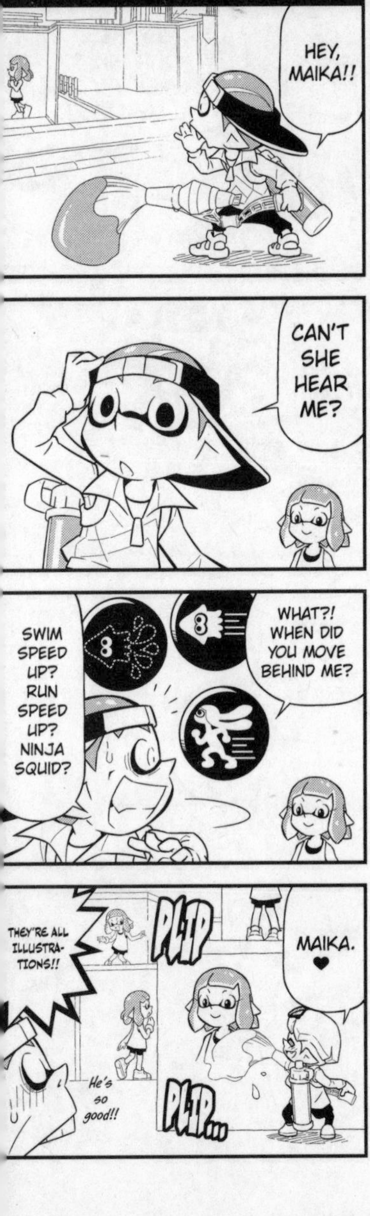
HEY, MAIKA!!
CAN'T SHE HEAR ME?
WHAT?! WHEN DID YOU MOVE BEHIND ME?
SWIM SPEED UP? RUN SPEED UP? NINJA SQUID?
MAIKA. ♥
PLIP
PLIP...
THEY'RE ALL ILLUSTRATIONS!!
He's so good!!

STREET ART BATTLE

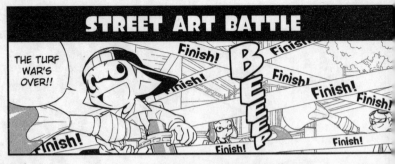

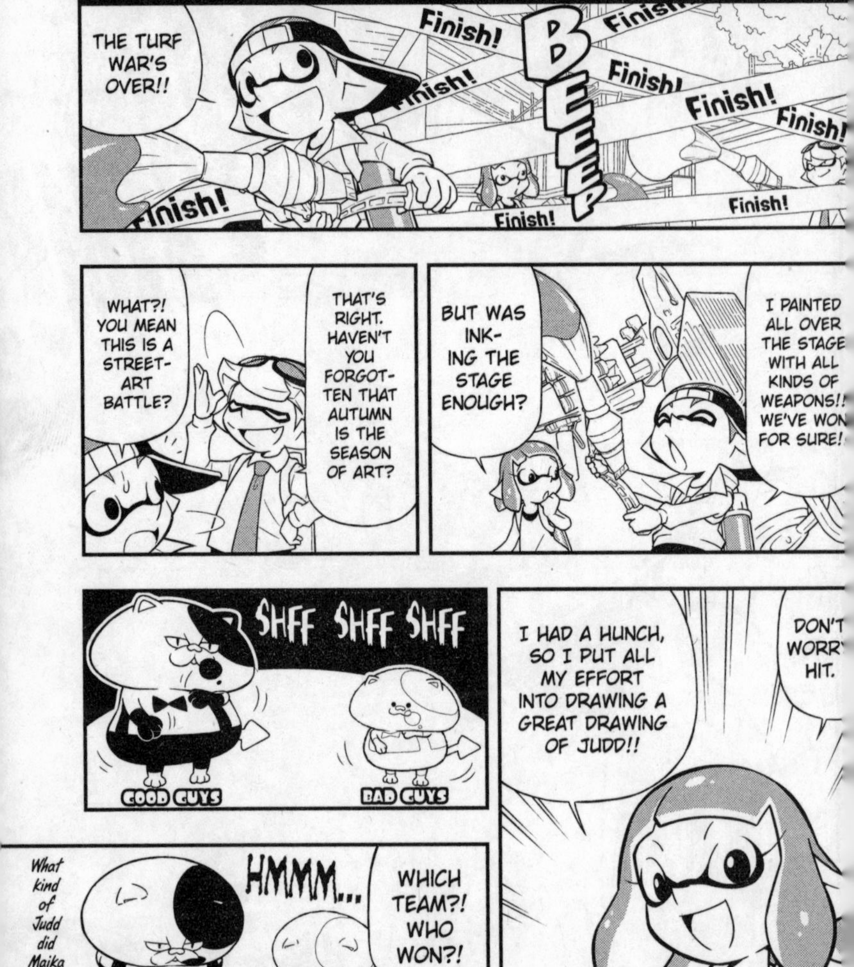
Finish!
Finish!
Finish!
Finish!
BEEEEP
Finish!
Finish!
Finish!
Finish!
THE TURF WAR'S OVER!!
I PAINTED ALL OVER THE STAGE WITH ALL KINDS OF WEAPONS!! WE'VE WON FOR SURE!
BUT WAS INKING THE STAGE ENOUGH?
THAT'S RIGHT. HAVEN'T YOU FORGOTTEN THAT AUTUMN IS THE SEASON OF ART?
WHAT?! YOU MEAN THIS IS A STREET-ART BATTLE?
DON'T WORR HIT.
I HAD A HUNCH, SO I PUT ALL MY EFFORT INTO DRAWING A GREAT DRAWING OF JUDD!!
SHFF SHFF SHFF
GOOD GUYS
BAD GUYS
WHICH TEAM?! WHO WON?!
HMMM...
What kind of Judd did Maika draw?
GOOD GUYS
BAD GUYS

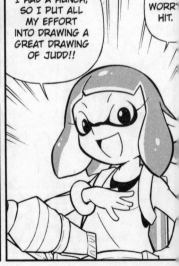

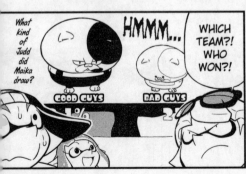

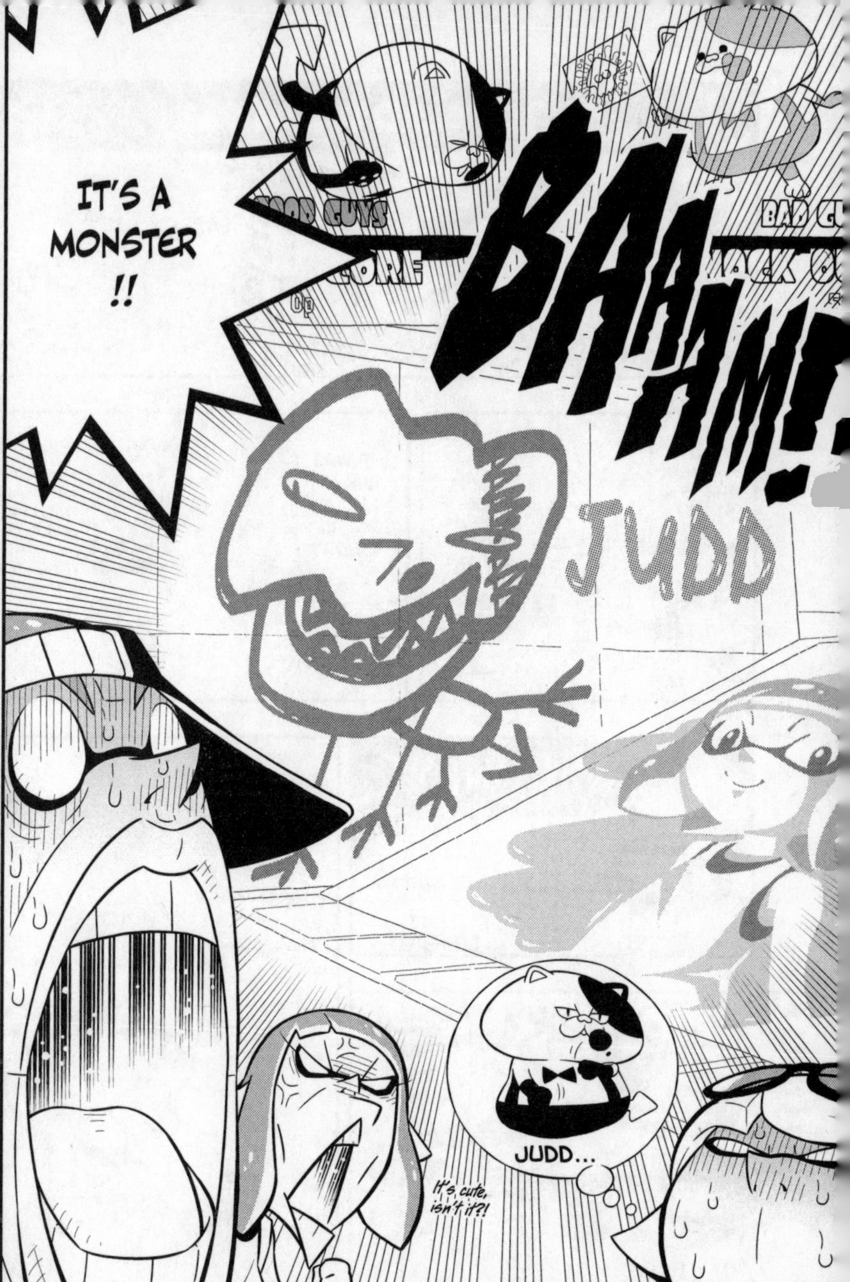
BAAAM!
IT'S A MONSTER !!
JUDD
JUDD...
It's cute, isn't it?!

Splatoon SQUID KIDS COMEDY SHOW

THIS is Judd.
It's a snowman!!

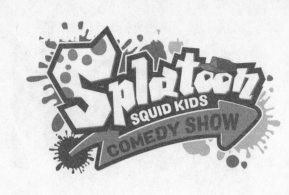

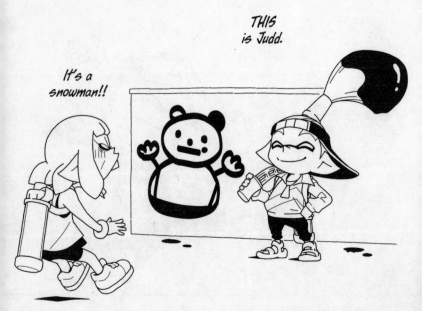

Splatoon
SQUID KIDS COMEDY SHOW

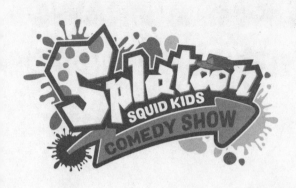

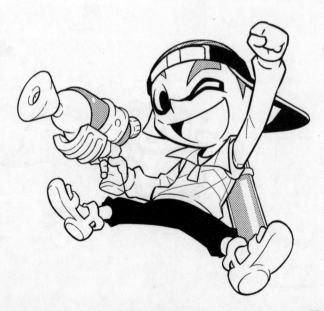

TIME FOR A BRAWL AT THE TURF WAR!

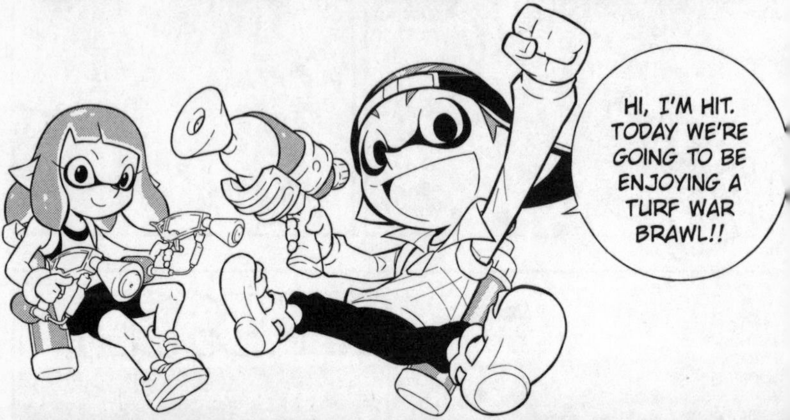
HI, I'M HIT. TODAY WE'RE GOING TO BE ENJOYING A TURF WAR BRAWL!!

STAMP

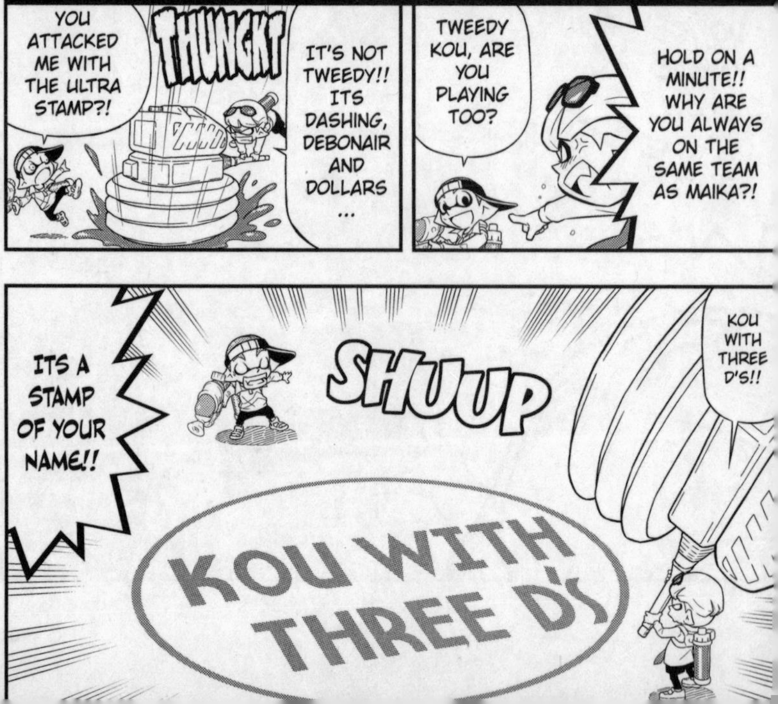
TWEEDY KOU, ARE YOU PLAYING TOO?
HOLD ON A MINUTE!! WHY ARE YOU ALWAYS ON THE SAME TEAM AS MAIKA?!
THUNGKT
YOU ATTACKED ME WITH THE ULTRA STAMP?!
IT'S NOT TWEEDY!! ITS DASHING, DEBONAIR AND DOLLARS ...
KOU WITH THREE D'S!!
SHUUP
ITS A STAMP OF YOUR NAME!!
KOU WITH THREE D'S

CALLING TO ATTENTION

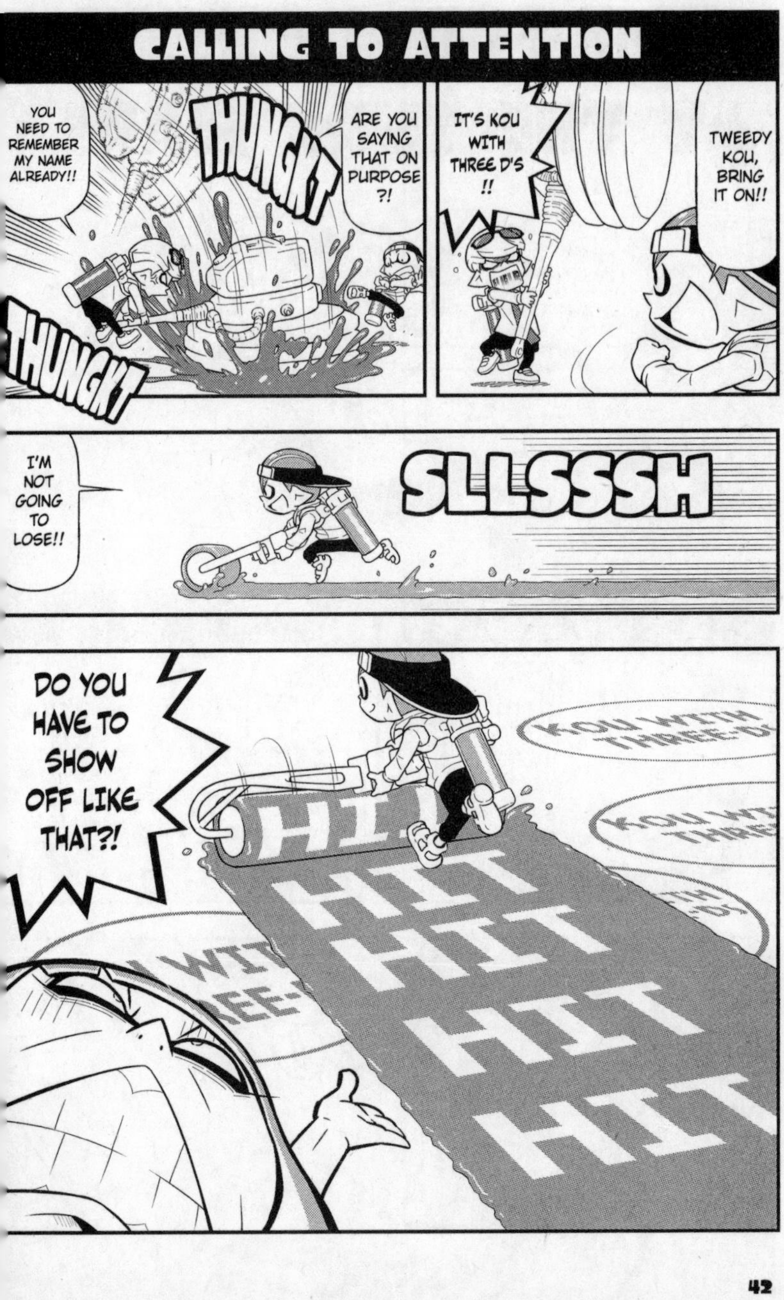
TWEEDY KOU, BRING IT ON!!
IT'S KOU WITH THREE D'S!!
ARE YOU SAYING THAT ON PURPOSE?!
THUNGKT
YOU NEED TO REMEMBER MY NAME ALREADY!!
THUNGKT
SLLSSSH
I'M NOT GOING TO LOSE!!
KOU WITH THREE-D
HIT
HIT
HIT
HIT
DO YOU HAVE TO SHOW OFF LIKE THAT?!

SMASH AND STRETC

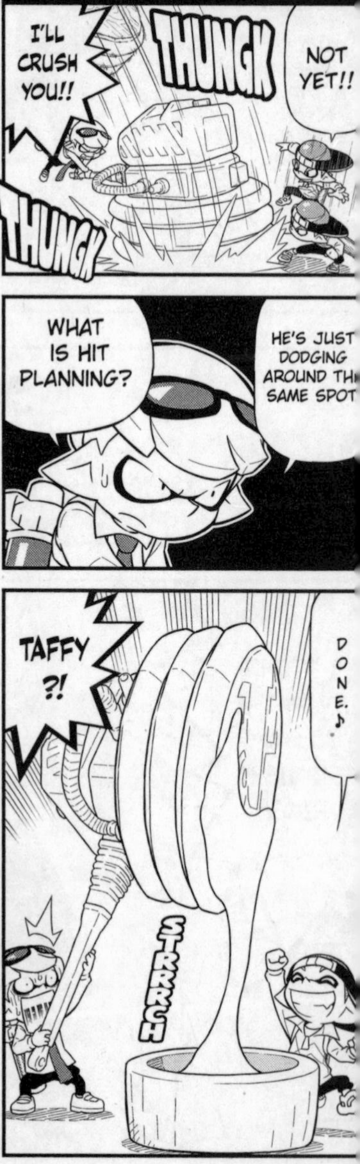
NOT YET!!
THUNGK
I'LL CRUSH YOU!!
THUNGK
HE'S JUST DODGING AROUND TH SAME SPOT
WHAT IS HIT PLANNING?
DONE.♪
TAFFY ?!
STRRRCH

DEFEND YOURSELF WITH A BOMB

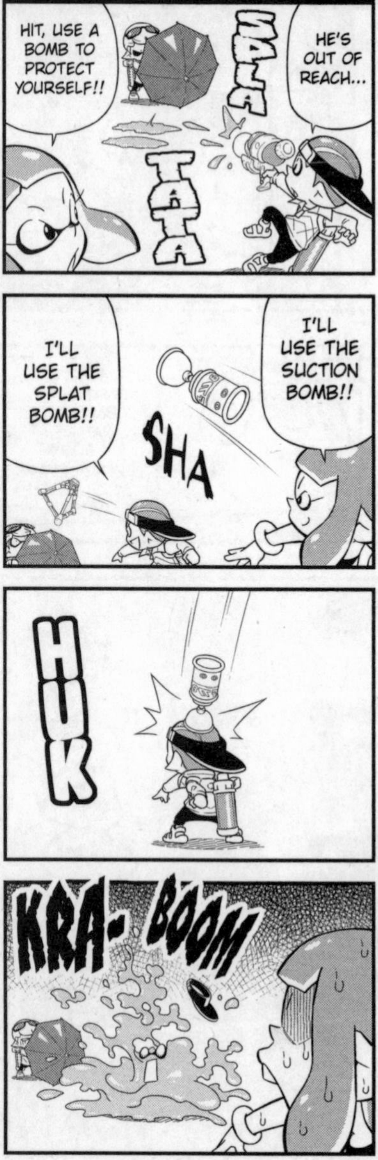
HE'S OUT OF REACH...
SPLA
HIT, USE A BOMB TO PROTECT YOURSELF!!
I'LL USE THE SUCTION BOMB!!
SHA
I'LL USE THE SPLAT BOMB!!
HUK
KRA-BOOM

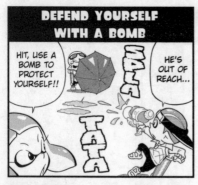

HUGE BALL

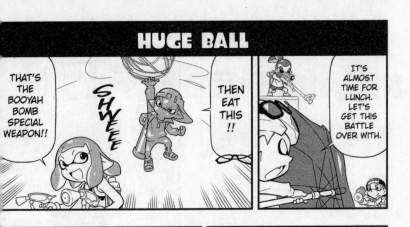

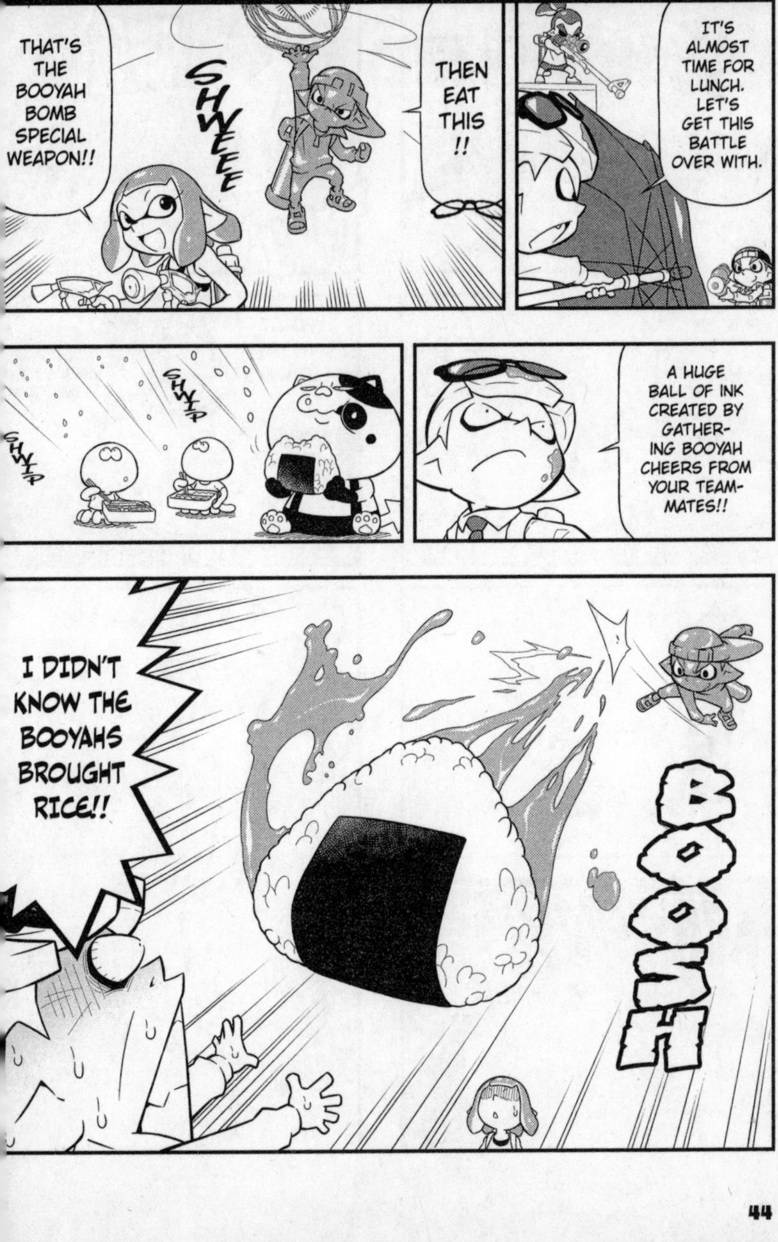
IT'S ALMOST TIME FOR LUNCH. LET'S GET THIS BATTLE OVER WITH.
THEN EAT THIS!!
SHWEEE
THAT'S THE BOOYAH BOMB SPECIAL WEAPON!!
A HUGE BALL OF INK CREATED BY GATHER-ING BOOYAH CHEERS FROM YOUR TEAM-MATES!!
SHWIP
SHWIP
BOOSH
I DIDN'T KNOW THE BOOYAHS BROUGHT RICE!!

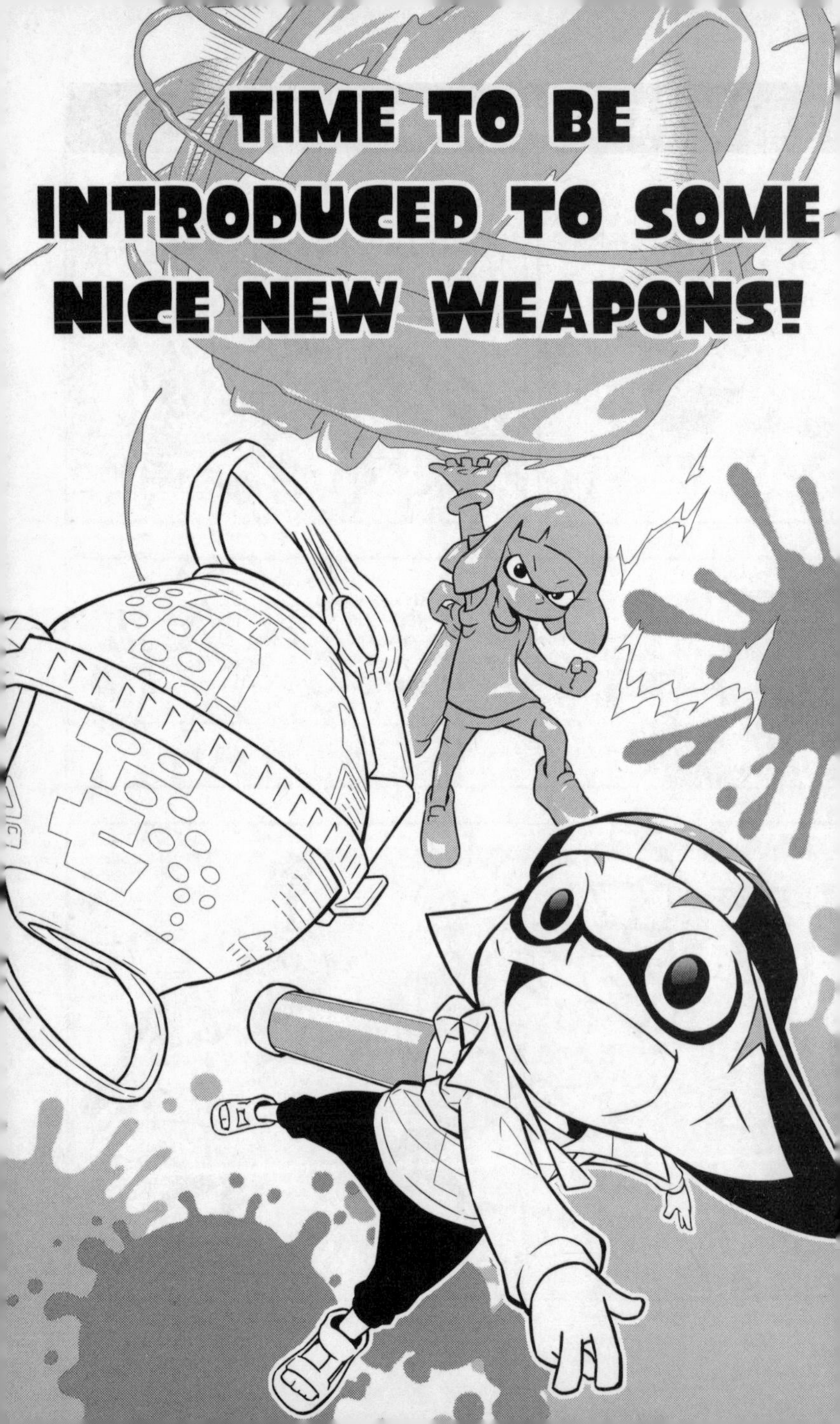
TIME TO BE INTRODUCED TO SOME NICE NEW WEAPONS!

KENSA COLLECTION

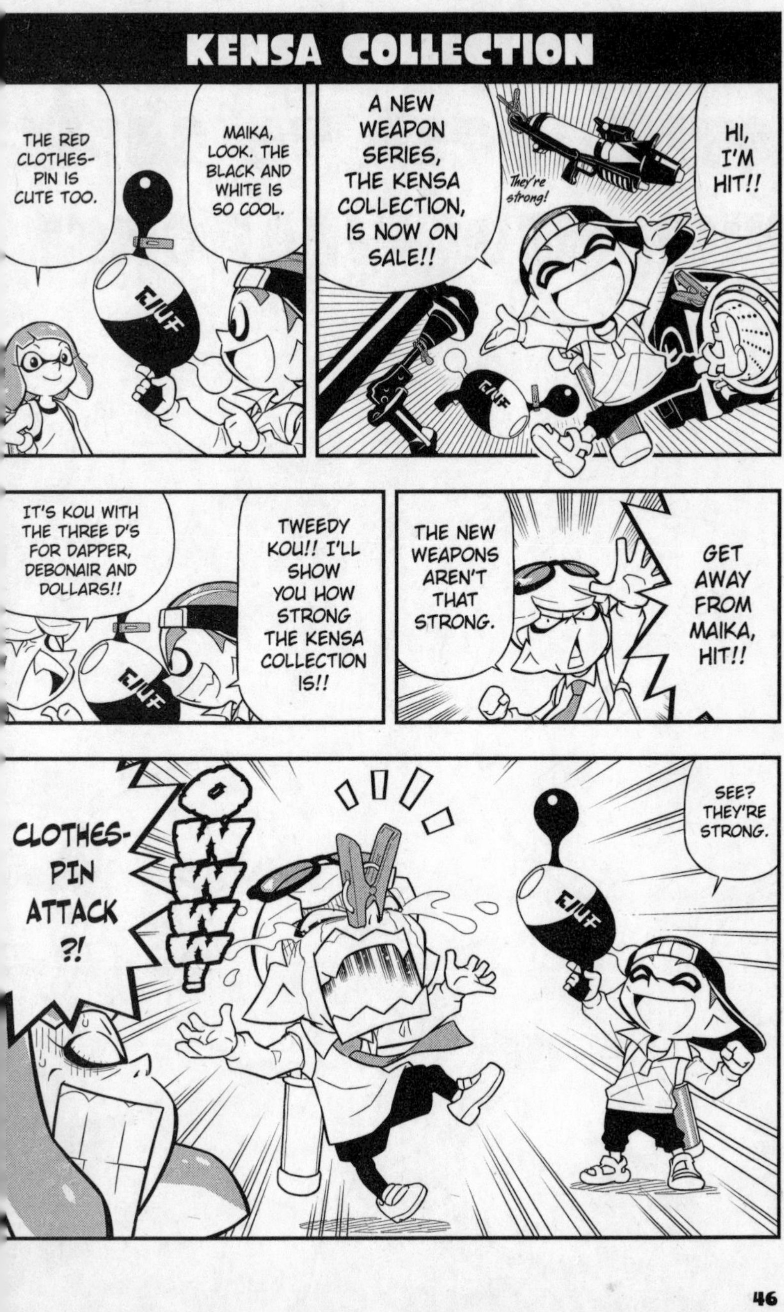
HI, I'M HIT!!
They're strong!
A NEW WEAPON SERIES, THE KENSA COLLECTION, IS NOW ON SALE!!
MAIKA, LOOK. THE BLACK AND WHITE IS SO COOL.
THE RED CLOTHES-PIN IS CUTE TOO.
GET AWAY FROM MAIKA, HIT!!
THE NEW WEAPONS AREN'T THAT STRONG.
TWEEDY KOU!! I'LL SHOW YOU HOW STRONG THE KENSA COLLECTION IS!!
IT'S KOU WITH THE THREE D'S FOR DAPPER, DEBONAIR AND DOLLARS!!
SEE? THEY'RE STRONG.
OWWWW!
CLOTHES-PIN ATTACK ?!

FIZZY BOMB

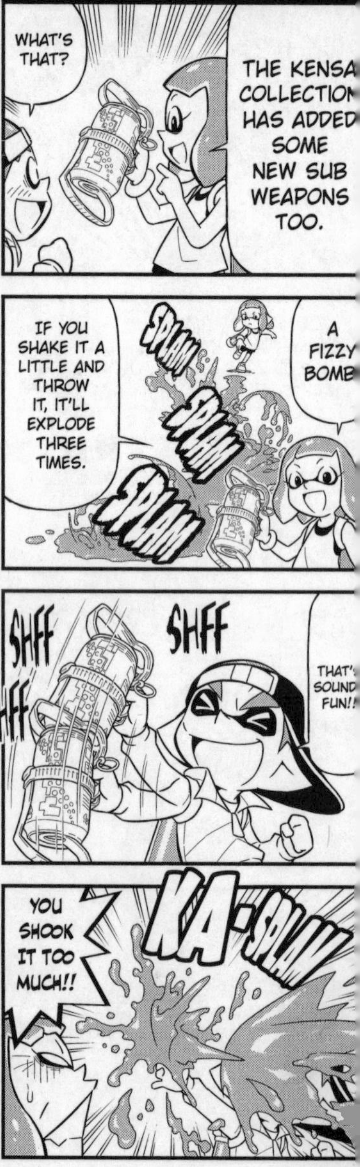
THE KENSA COLLECTION HAS ADDED SOME NEW SUB WEAPONS TOO.
WHAT'S THAT?
A FIZZY BOMB
SPLAM
SPLAM
SPLAM
IF YOU SHAKE IT A LITTLE AND THROW IT, IT'LL EXPLODE THREE TIMES.
THAT'S SOUND FUN!!
SHFF
SHFF
SHFF
KA-SPLAM
YOU SHOOK IT TOO MUCH!!

FIZZY

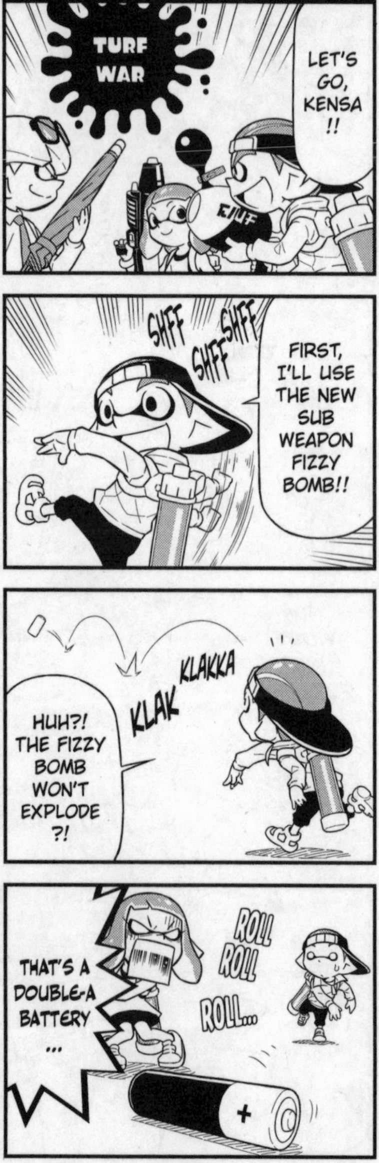
LET'S GO, KENSA!!
TURF WAR
SHFF
SHFF
SHFF
FIRST, I'LL USE THE NEW SUB WEAPON FIZZY BOMB!!
KLAKKA
KLAK
HUH?! THE FIZZY BOMB WON'T EXPLODE?!
ROLL
ROLL
ROLL...
THAT'S A DOUBLE-A BATTERY...

NON-FIZZY BOMB

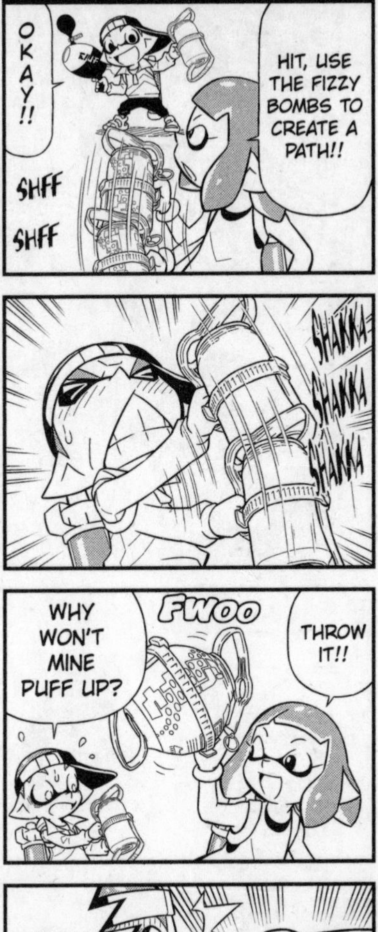
HIT, USE THE FIZZY BOMBS TO CREATE A PATH!!
OKAY!!
SHFF
SHFF
SHAKKA
SHAKKA
SHAKKA
THROW IT!!
FWOO
WHY WON'T MINE PUFF UP?
WRONG BOTTLE... NO CARBON-ATION.
APPLE JUICE
100%

SHAKE WELL

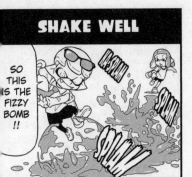

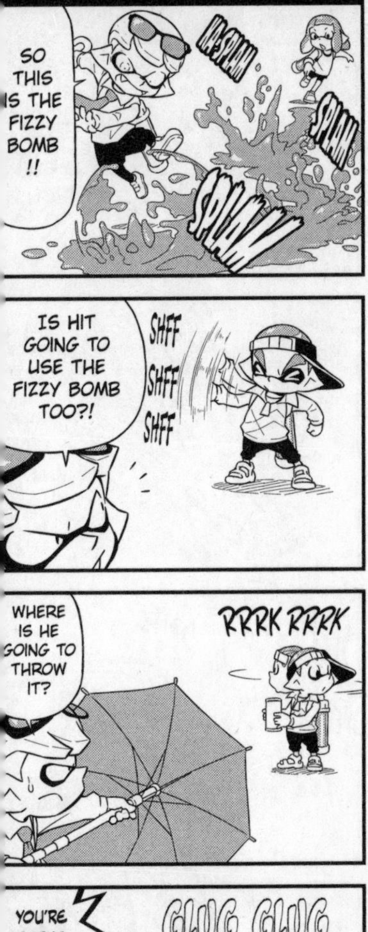
SO THIS IS THE FIZZY BOMB!!
SHFF
SHFF
SHFF
IS HIT GOING TO USE THE FIZZY BOMB TOO?!
RRRK RRRK
WHERE IS HE GOING TO THROW IT?
GLUG GLUG
YOU'RE GOING TO DRINK IT?!

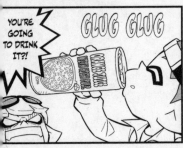

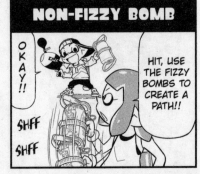

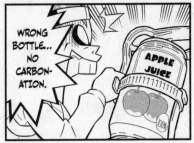

FULL STOMACH

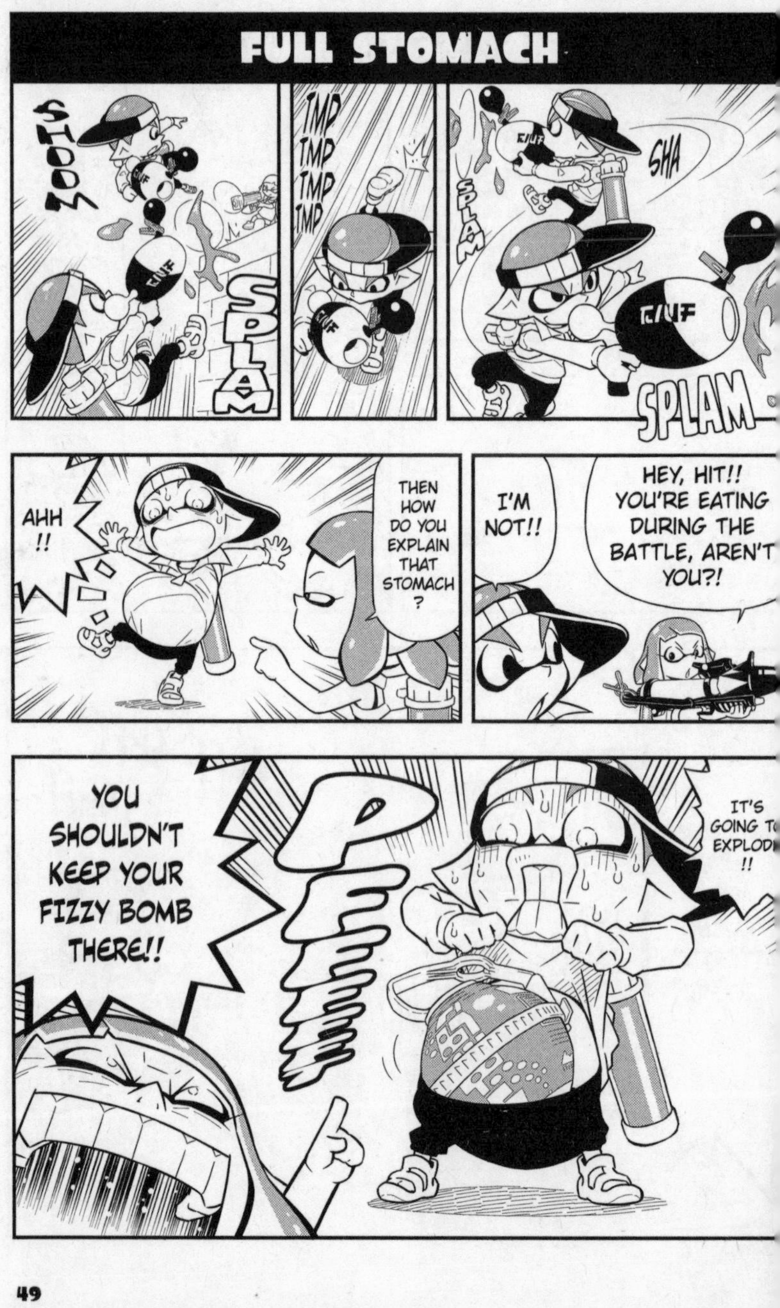
SHA
SPLAM
SPLAM
TMP
TMP
TMP
TMP
SPLAM
HEY, HIT!! YOU'RE EATING DURING THE BATTLE, AREN'T YOU?!
I'M NOT!!
THEN HOW DO YOU EXPLAIN THAT STOMACH?
AHH!!
IT'S GOING T EXPLOD !!
YOU SHOULDN'T KEEP YOUR FIZZY BOMB THERE!!

BOOYAH BOMB

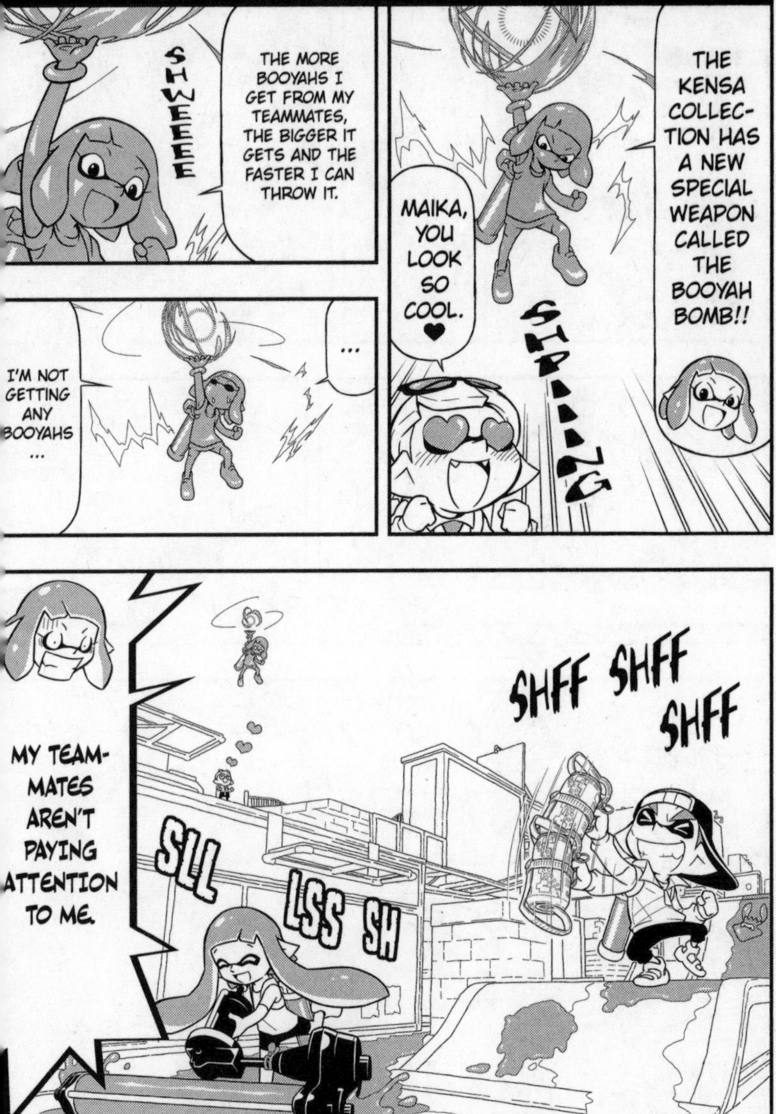
THE KENSA COLLECTION HAS A NEW SPECIAL WEAPON CALLED THE BOOYAH BOMB!!
MAIKA, YOU LOOK SO COOL. ♥
SHWEEEE
THE MORE BOOYAHS I GET FROM MY TEAMMATES, THE BIGGER IT GETS AND THE FASTER I CAN THROW IT.
...
I'M NOT GETTING ANY BOOYAHS ...
SHFF SHFF SHFF
MY TEAM-MATES AREN'T PAYING ATTENTION TO ME.
SLL
LSS SH

GIVE ME YOUR NICE SCREAMS

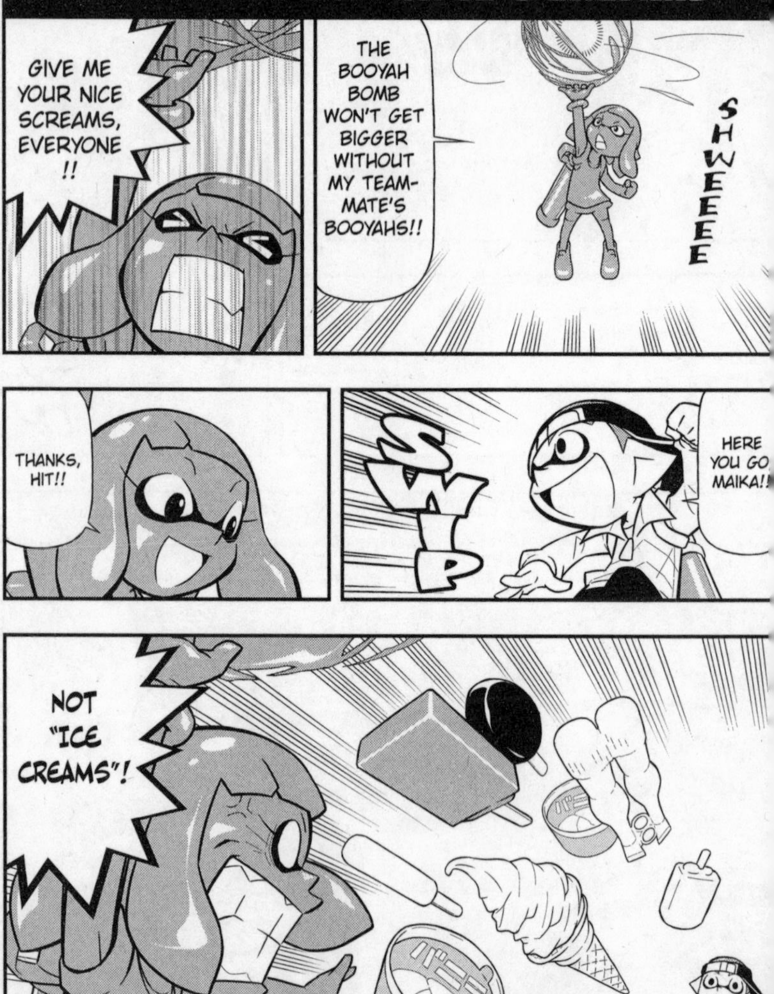

THE BOOYAH BOMB WON'T GET BIGGER WITHOUT MY TEAM-MATE'S BOOYAHS!!
SHWEEEE
GIVE ME YOUR NICE SCREAMS, EVERYONE!!
HERE YOU GO MAIKA!!
SWIP
THANKS, HIT!!
NOT "ICE CREAMS"!

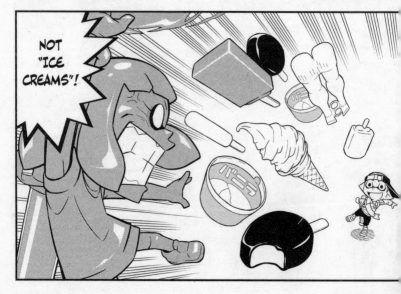

LOTS OF BOOYAH

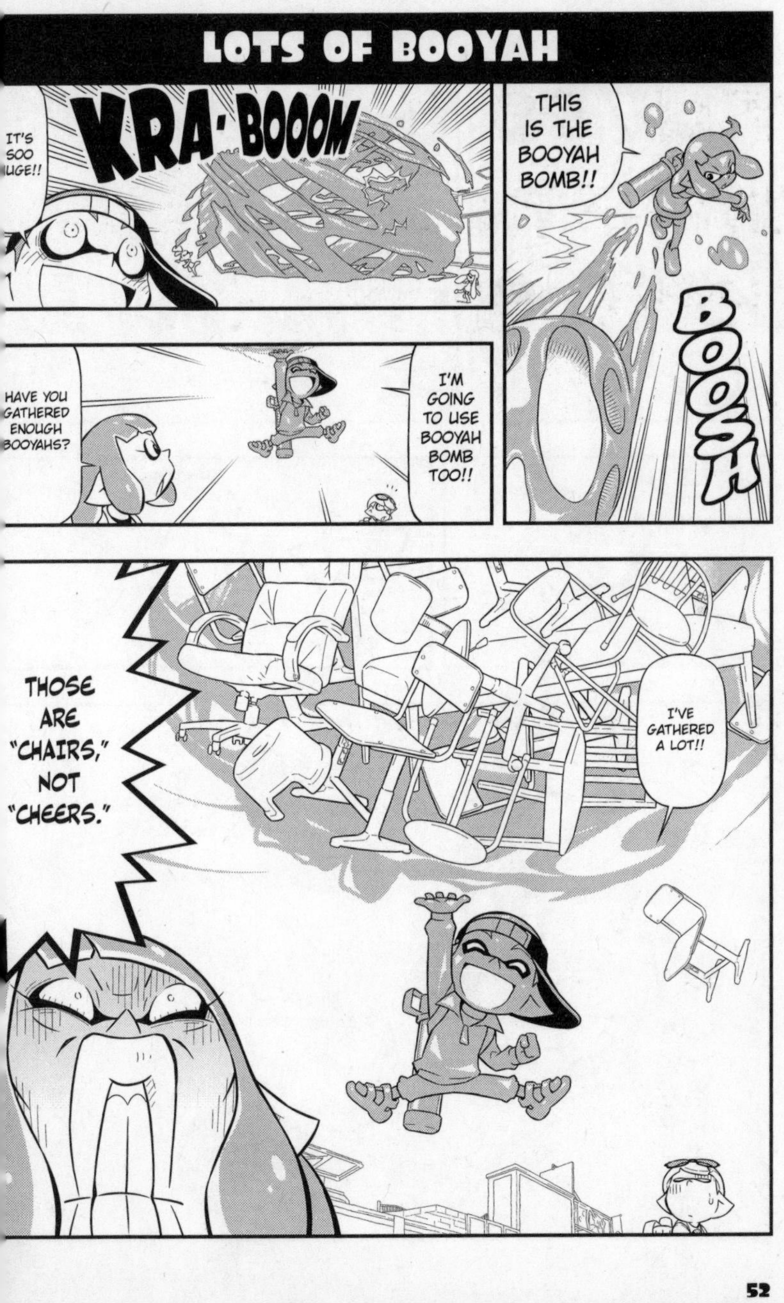

THIS IS THE BOOYAH BOMB!!
BOOSH
KRA-BOOOM
IT'S SOO
UGE!!
I'M GOING TO USE BOOYAH BOMB TOO!!
HAVE YOU GATHERED ENOUGH BOOYAHS?
I'VE GATHERED A LOT!!
THOSE ARE "CHAIRS," NOT "CHEERS."

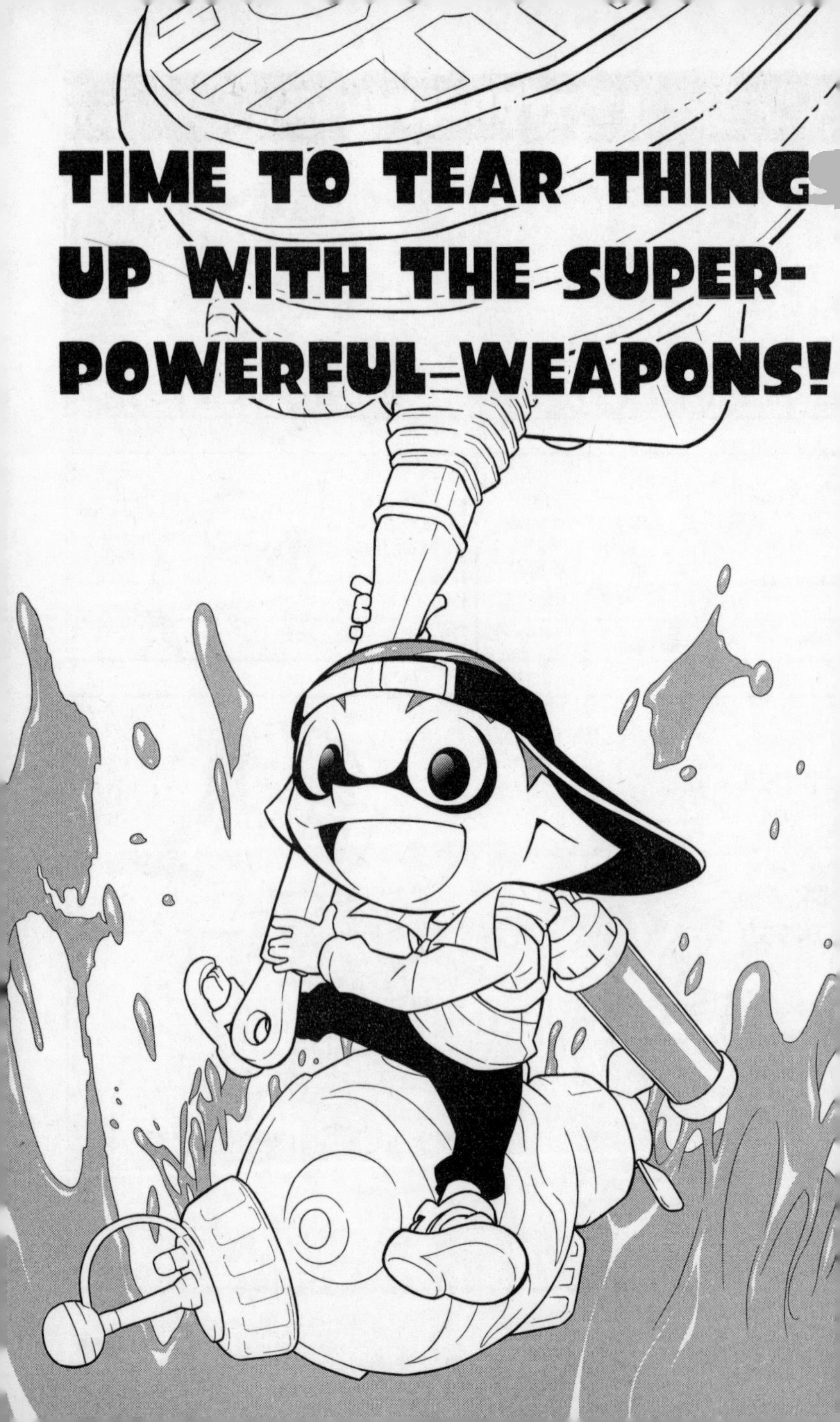
TIME TO TEAR THINGS
UP WITH THE SUPER-
POWERFUL WEAPONS!

TORPEDO

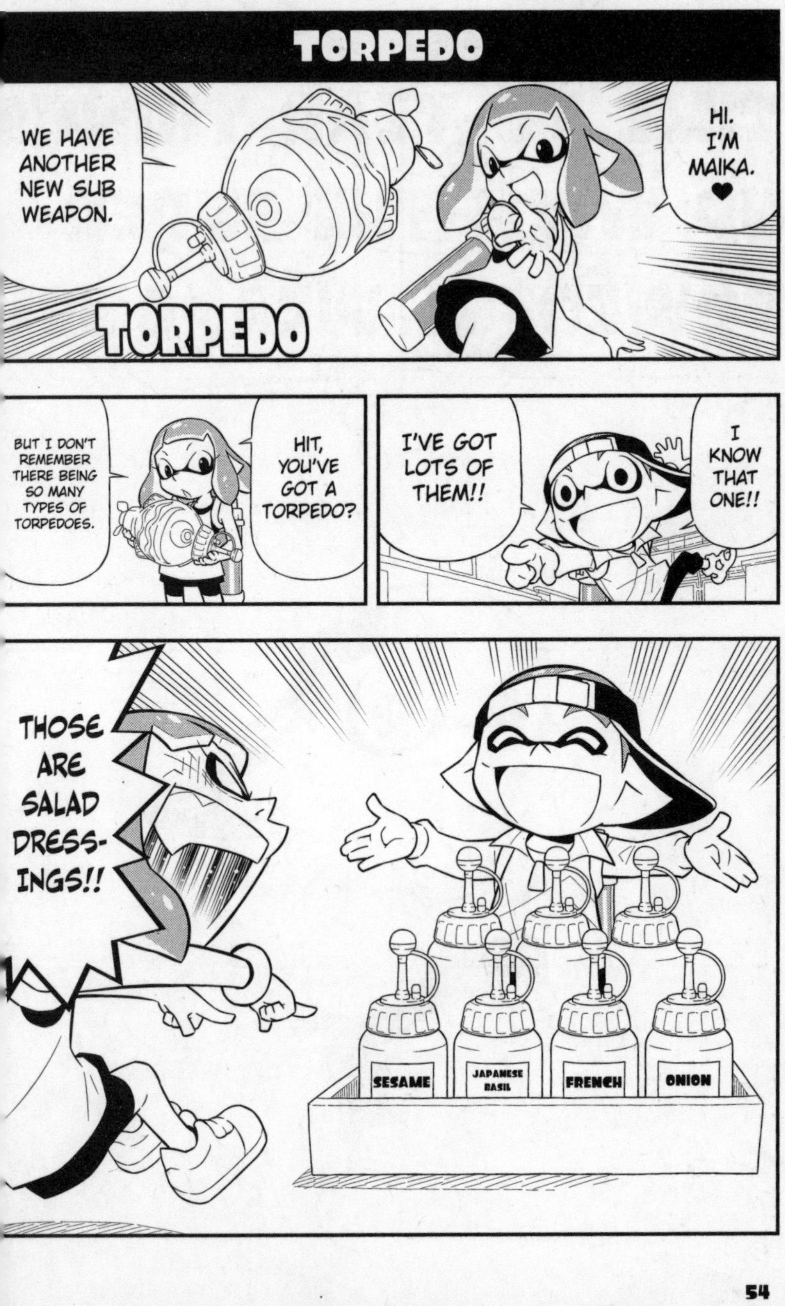
HI. I'M MAIKA. ♥
WE HAVE ANOTHER NEW SUB WEAPON.
TORPEDO
I KNOW THAT ONE!!
I'VE GOT LOTS OF THEM!!
HIT, YOU'VE GOT A TORPEDO?
BUT I DON'T REMEMBER THERE BEING SO MANY TYPES OF TORPEDOES.
THOSE ARE SALAD DRESS-INGS!!
ONION
FRENCH
JAPANESE BASIL
SESAME

FOLLOW

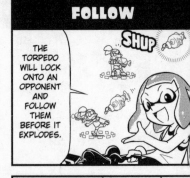

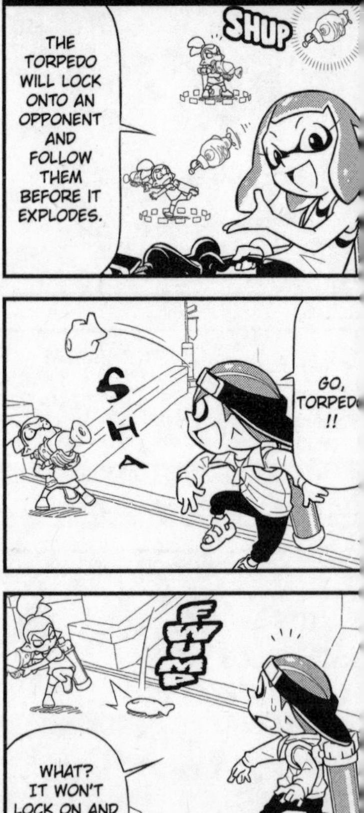
SHUP
THE TORPEDO WILL LOCK ONTO AN OPPONENT AND FOLLOW THEM BEFORE IT EXPLODES.
GO, TORPED !!
SHA
FWUMP
WHAT? IT WON'T LOCK ON AND FOLLOW...
IT'S A TAIYAKI PASTRY!!

LOCK ON

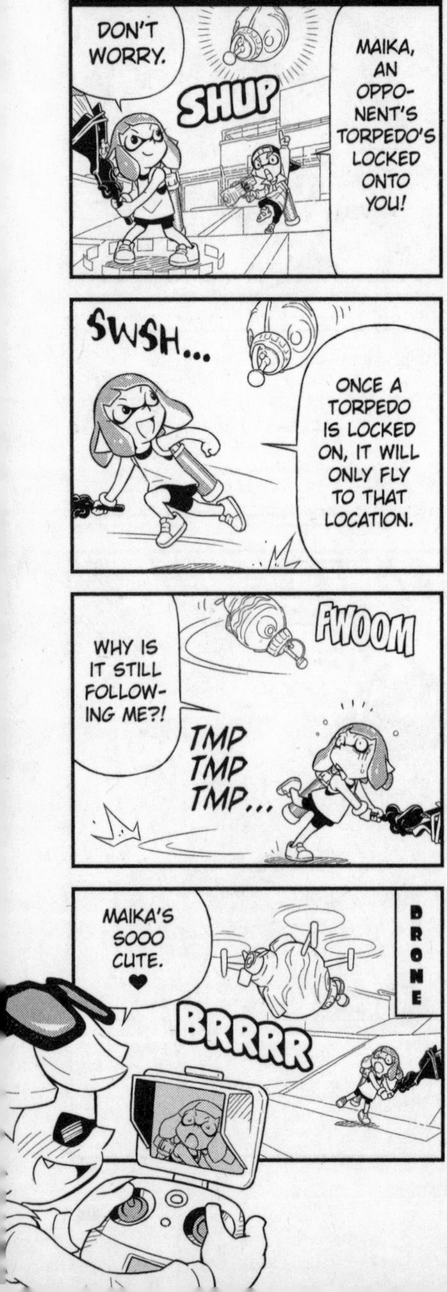
MAIKA, AN OPPO-NENT'S TORPEDO'S LOCKED ONTO YOU!
SHUP
DON'T WORRY.
ONCE A TORPEDO IS LOCKED ON, IT WILL ONLY FLY TO THAT LOCATION.
SWSH...
FWOOM
WHY IS IT STILL FOLLOW-ING ME?!
TMP TMP TMP...
DRONE
MAIKA'S SOOO CUTE. ♥
BRRRR

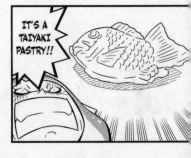

TORPEDO IN A BOX

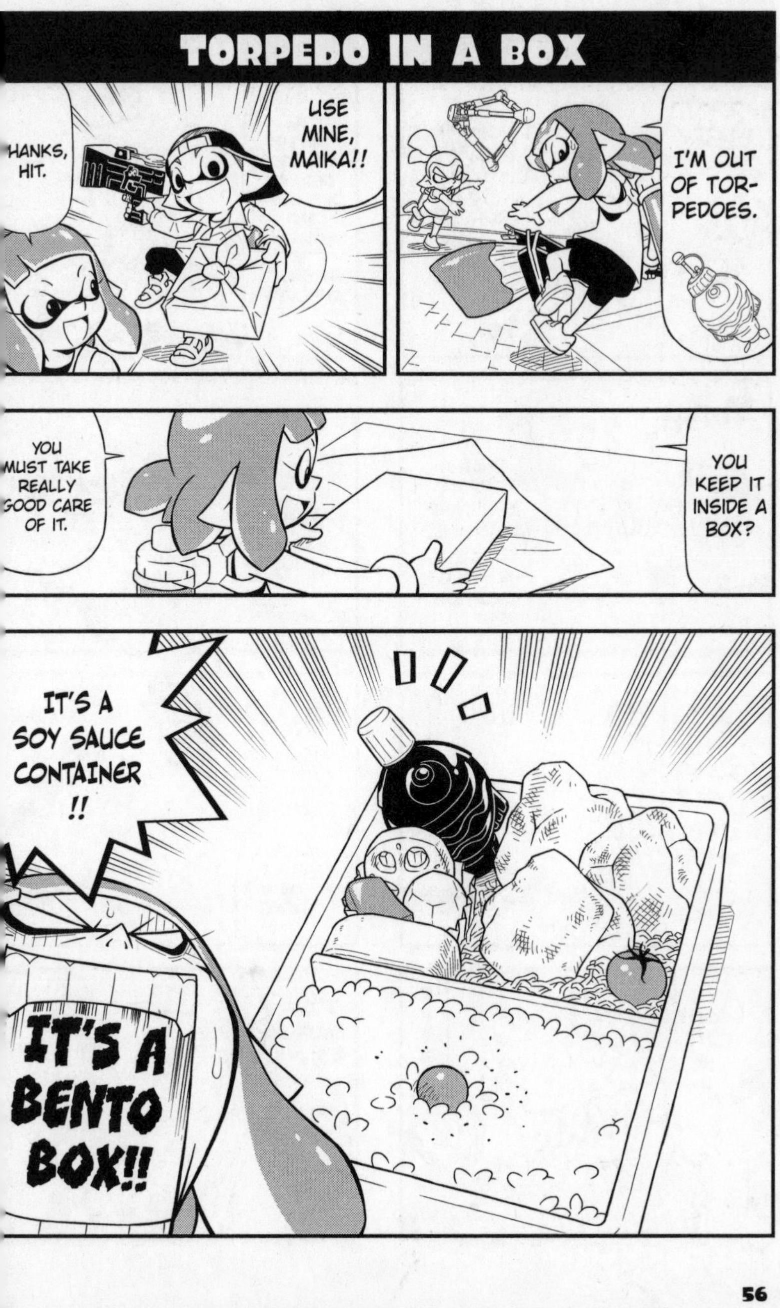
I'M OUT OF TOR-PEDOES.
USE MINE, MAIKA!!
HANKS, HIT.
YOU KEEP IT INSIDE A BOX?
YOU MUST TAKE REALLY GOOD CARE OF IT.
IT'S A SOY SAUCE CONTAINER !!
IT'S A BENTO BOX!!

PROPELLER

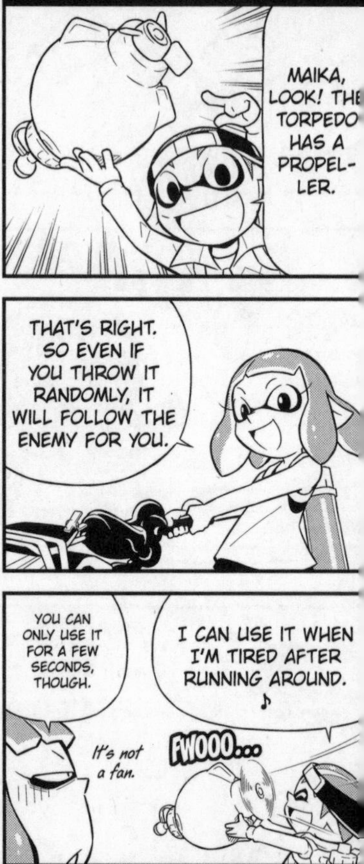
MAIKA, LOOK! THE TORPEDO HAS A PROPEL-LER.
THAT'S RIGHT. SO EVEN IF YOU THROW IT RANDOMLY, IT WILL FOLLOW THE ENEMY FOR YOU.
I CAN USE IT WHEN I'M TIRED AFTER RUNNING AROUND. ♪
YOU CAN ONLY USE IT FOR A FEW SECONDS, THOUGH.
FWOOO...
It's not a fan.
NO?
KRA-SPLAM
IT'S A BOMB.

ULTRA STAMP

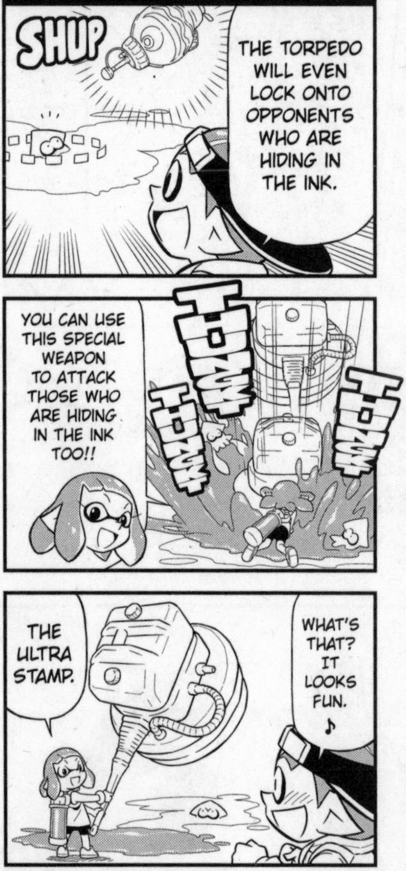
THE TORPEDO WILL EVEN LOCK ONTO OPPONENTS WHO ARE HIDING IN THE INK.
SHUP
THUNK
THUNK
THUNK
YOU CAN USE THIS SPECIAL WEAPON TO ATTACK THOSE WHO ARE HIDING IN THE INK TOO!!
WHAT'S THAT? IT LOOKS FUN. ♪
THE ULTRA STAMP.
I WANT TO PLAY WHACK-A-MOLE TOO!!
THIS IS TURF WAR!!

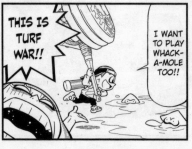

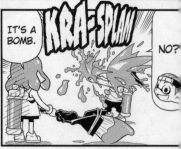

GIANT WEAPON

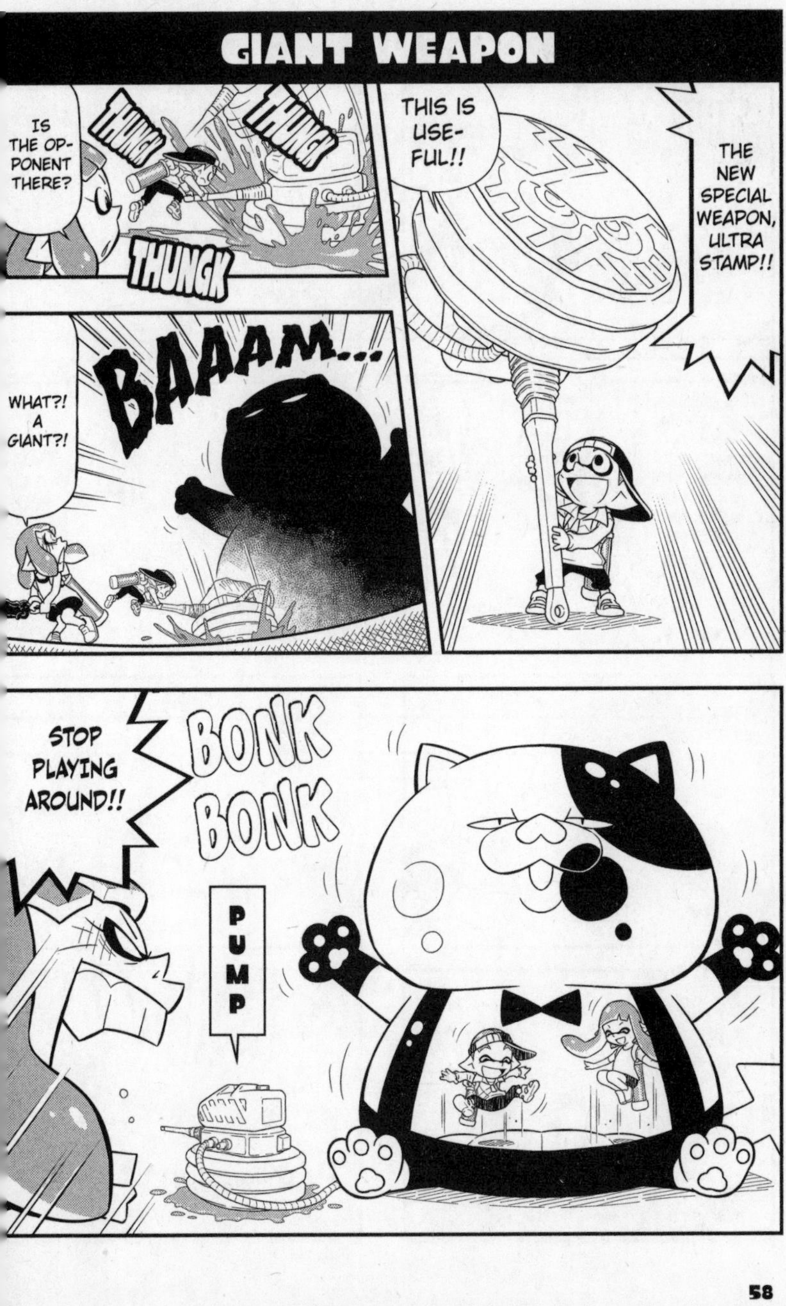
THE NEW SPECIAL WEAPON, ULTRA STAMP!!
THIS IS USE-FUL!!
THUNGK
THUNGK
IS THE OP-PONENT THERE?
THUNGK
BAAAM...
WHAT?! A GIANT?!
BONK BONK
STOP PLAYING AROUND!!
PUMP

EVALUATION

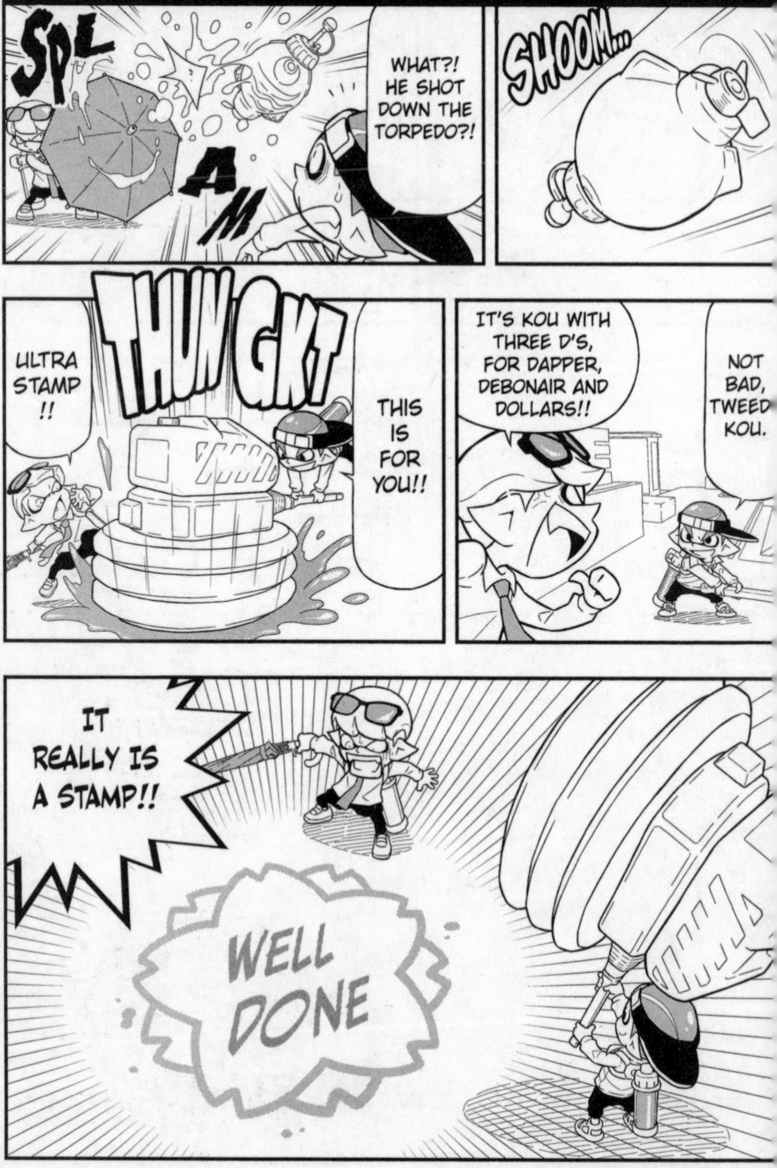

SHOOM...
WHAT?! HE SHOT DOWN THE TORPEDO?!
SPLAM
NOT BAD, TWEED KOU.
IT'S KOU WITH THREE D'S, FOR DAPPER, DEBONAIR AND DOLLARS!!
THIS IS FOR YOU!!
THUNGKT
ULTRA STAMP!!
IT REALLY IS A STAMP!!
WELL DONE

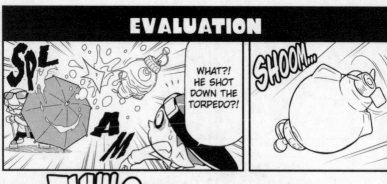

ATTACK ATTACK ATTACK

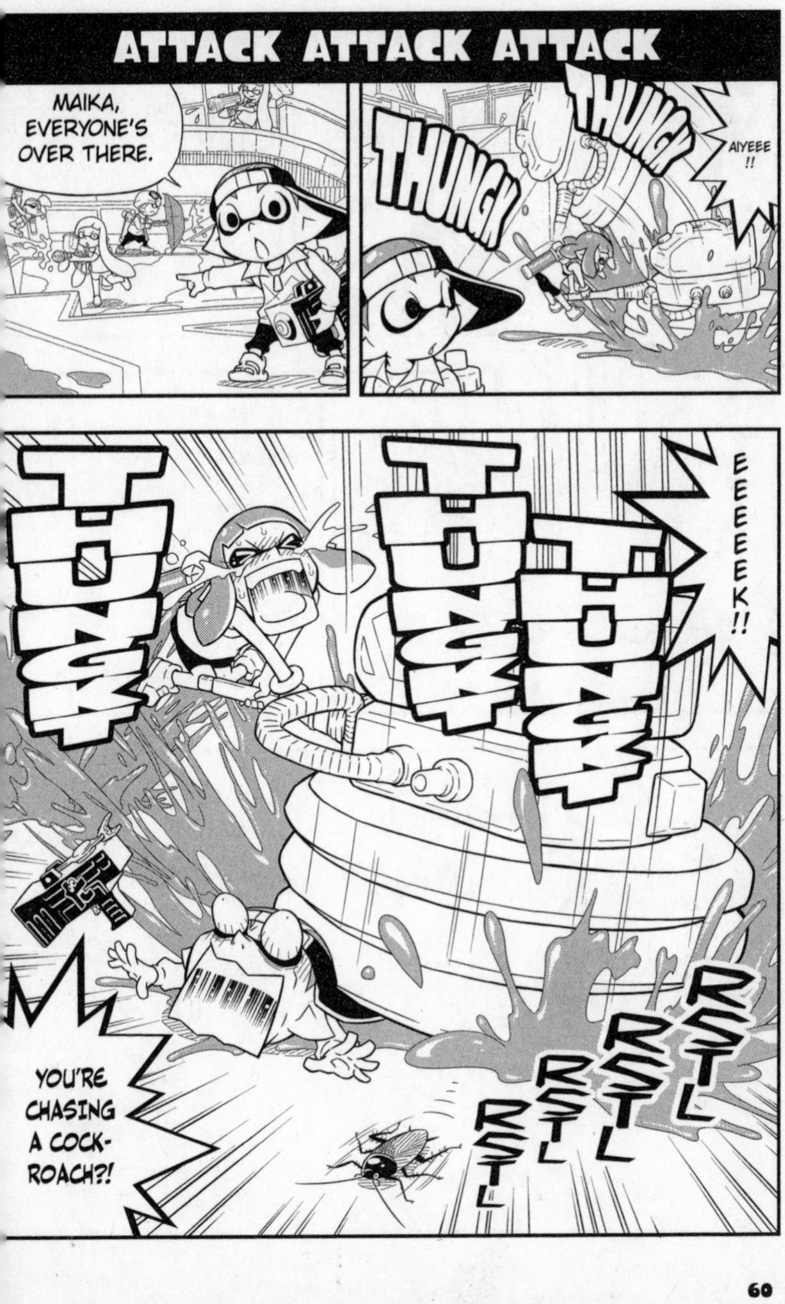
THUNGK
THUNGK
AIYEEE !!
MAIKA, EVERYONE'S OVER THERE.
EEEEEEK!!
THUNGK
THUNGK
THUNGK
RSTL RSTL RSTL RSTL
YOU'RE CHASING A COCK-ROACH?!

BRAWL

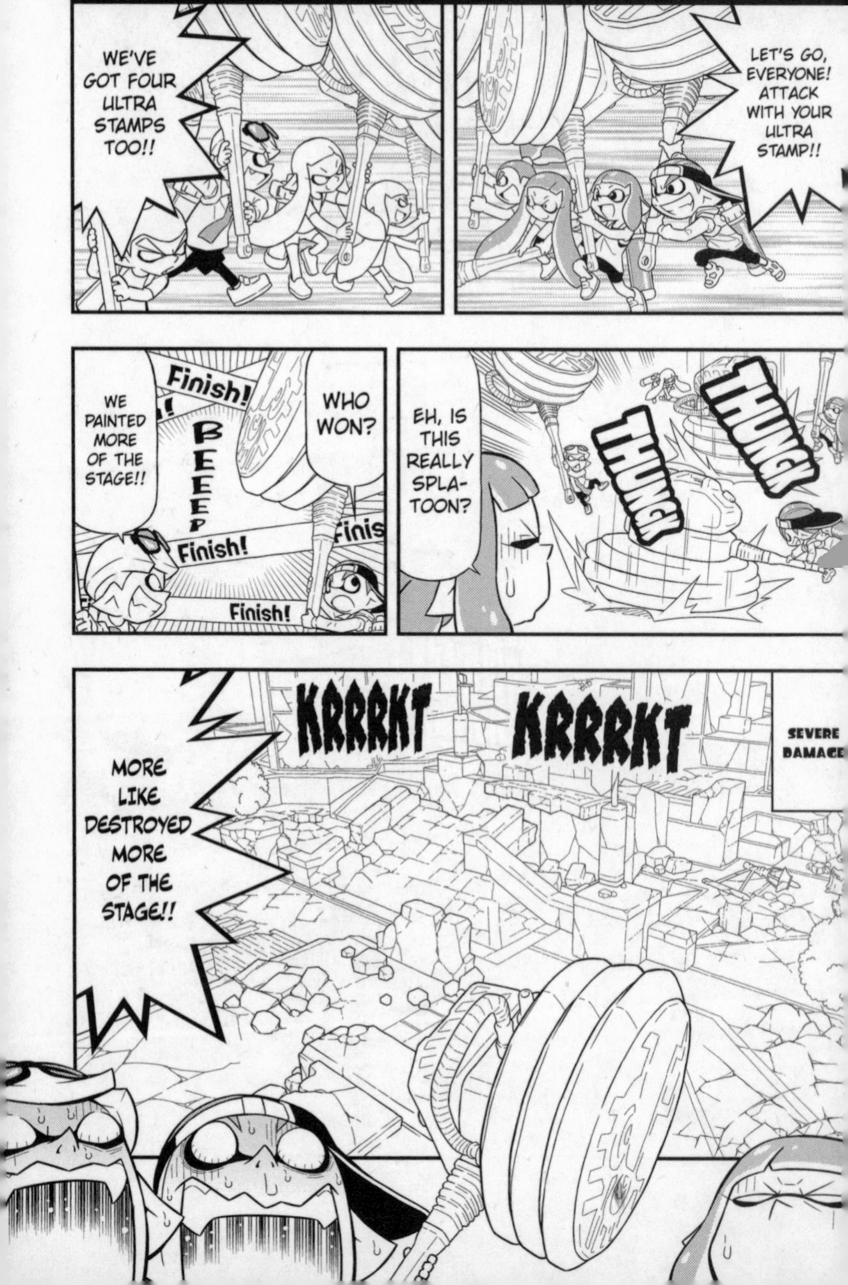
LET'S GO, EVERYONE! ATTACK WITH YOUR ULTRA STAMP!!
WE'VE GOT FOUR ULTRA STAMPS TOO!!
THUNK
THUNK
EH, IS THIS REALLY SPLA-TOON?
WHO WON?
Finish!
BEEEEP
Finish!
Finish!
WE PAINTED MORE OF THE STAGE!!
Finish!
SEVERE DAMAGE
KRRRKT
KRRRKT
MORE LIKE DESTROYED MORE OF THE STAGE!!

Splatoon SQUID KIDS COMEDY SHOW

THUNGKT
You're going to rebuild it with the Ultra Stamp?!

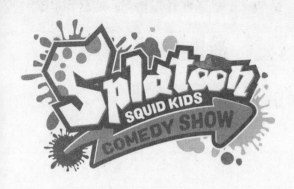

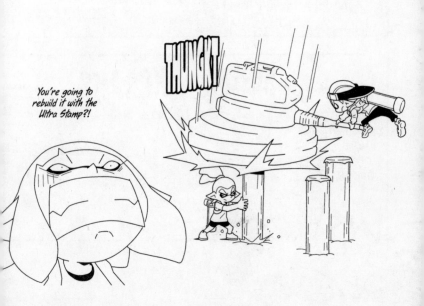

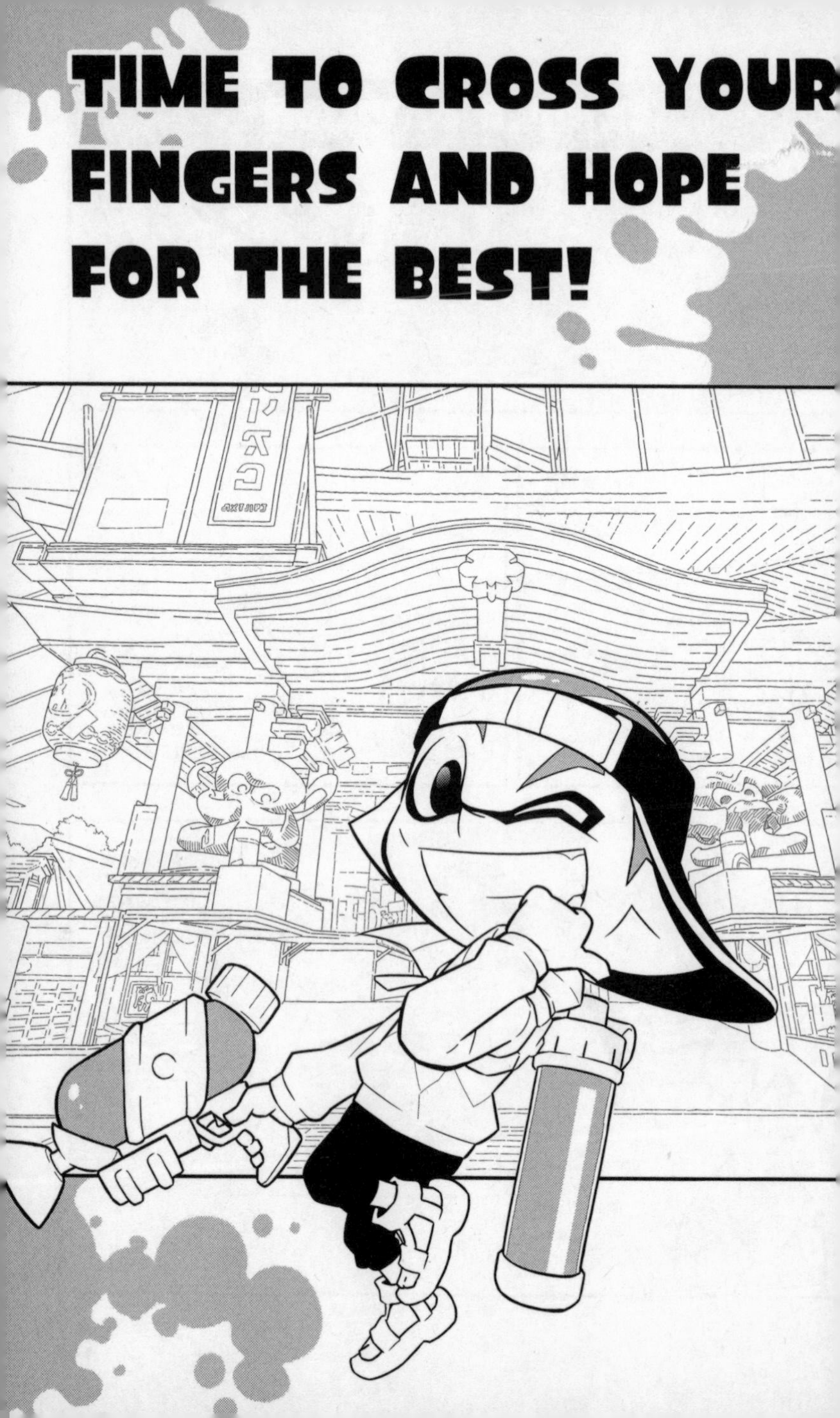
TIME TO CROSS YOUR FINGERS AND HOPE FOR THE BEST!

SKIPPER PAVILION

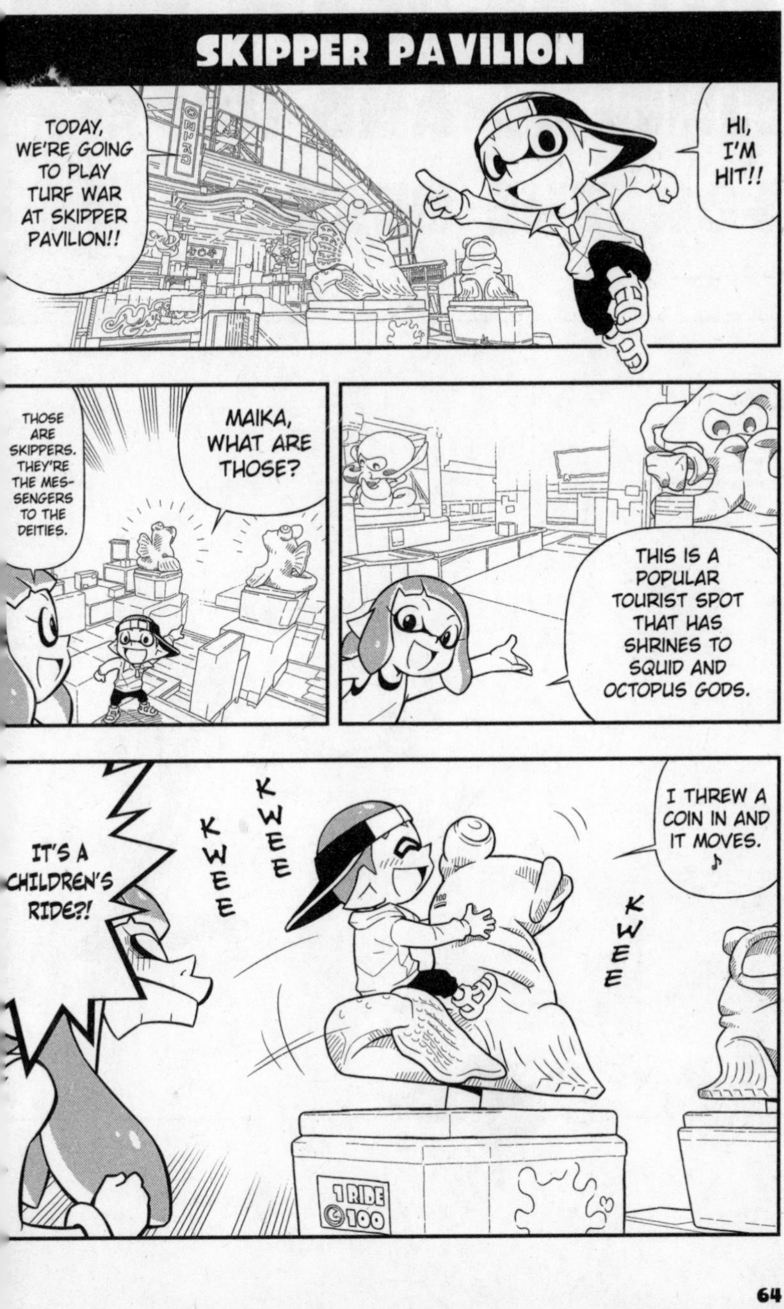
HI, I'M HIT!!
TODAY, WE'RE GOING TO PLAY TURF WAR AT SKIPPER PAVILION!!
THIS IS A POPULAR TOURIST SPOT THAT HAS SHRINES TO SQUID AND OCTOPUS GODS.
MAIKA, WHAT ARE THOSE?
THOSE ARE SKIPPERS. THEY'RE THE MES-SENGERS TO THE DEITIES.
I THREW A COIN IN AND IT MOVES. ♪
KWEE
KWEE
KWEE
IT'S A CHILDREN'S RIDE?!
1 RIDE
100

THE EARLY BIRD GETS THE WORM

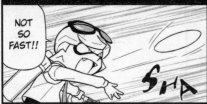

TURF WAR
WE'LL MOVE FASTER THAN THEM!!
NOT SO FAST!!
SHA
I WON'T LOSE TO KOU!! MINE GOES FIRST!!
WHAT ARE YOU THROWING, HIT? THAT'S NOT A BOMB!!
SHA
I WANT TO GO OUT WITH MAIKA.
I WANT TO BE RICH.
WISHING
WE DON'T HAVE TIME FOR WISHES!
CHK

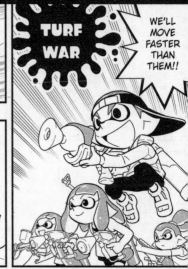

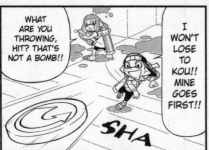

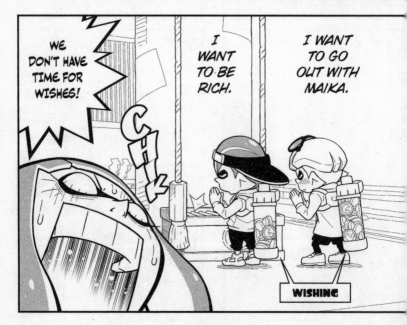

FORTUNES

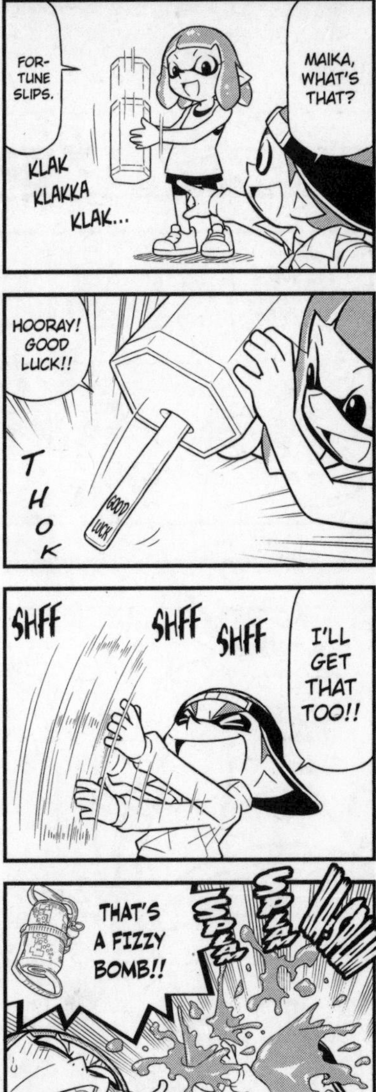
MAIKA, WHAT'S THAT?
FOR-TUNE SLIPS.
KLAK KLAKKA KLAK...
HOORAY! GOOD LUCK!!
THOK
GOOD LUCK
SHFF SHFF SHFF
I'LL GET THAT TOO!!
THAT'S A FIZZY BOMB!!

BELL

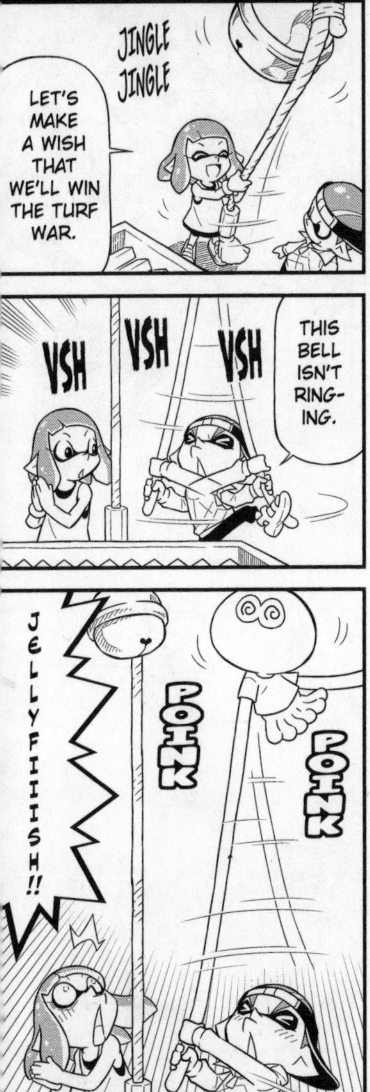
JINGLE JINGLE
LET'S MAKE A WISH THAT WE'LL WIN THE TURF WAR.
THIS BELL ISN'T RING-ING.
VSH VSH VSH
POINK POINK
JELLYFIIIISH!!

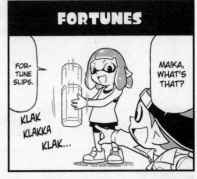

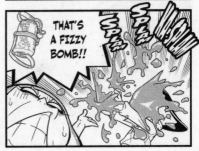

WORKS LIKE A CHARM

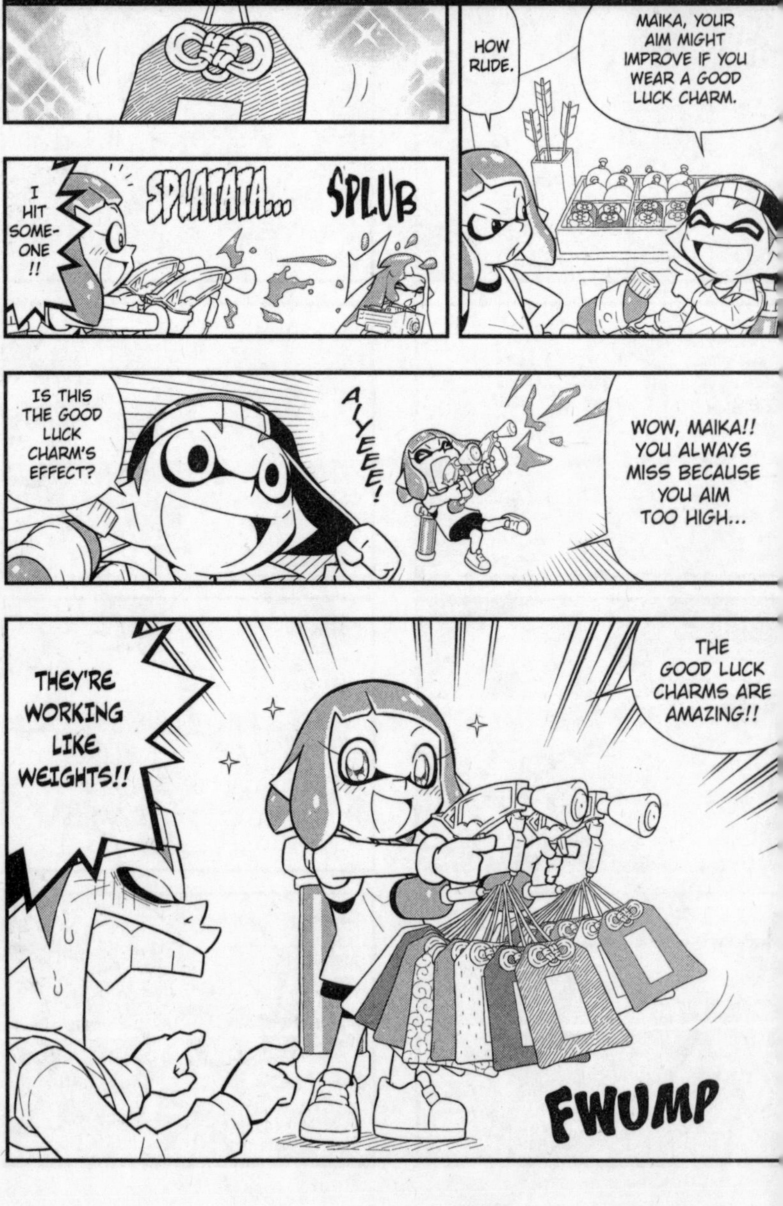
MAIKA, YOUR AIM MIGHT IMPROVE IF YOU WEAR A GOOD LUCK CHARM.
HOW RUDE.
SPLUB
SPLATATA...
I HIT SOME-ONE!!
WOW, MAIKA!! YOU ALWAYS MISS BECAUSE YOU AIM TOO HIGH...
AIYEEE!
IS THIS THE GOOD LUCK CHARM'S EFFECT?
THE GOOD LUCK CHARMS ARE AMAZING!!
THEY'RE WORKING LIKE WEIGHTS!!
FWUMP

WISHING BOARD

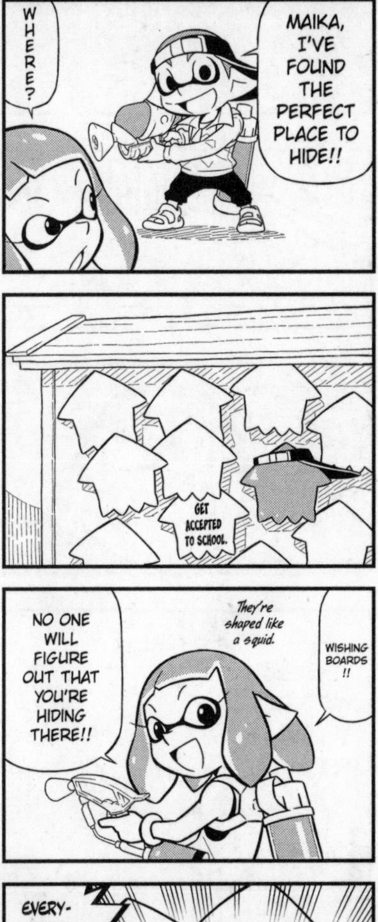
MAIKA, I'VE FOUND THE PERFECT PLACE TO HIDE!!
WHERE?
GET ACCEPTED TO SCHOOL.
WISHING BOARDS!!
They're shaped like a squid.
NO ONE WILL FIGURE OUT THAT YOU'RE HIDING THERE!!
EVERY-ONE'S HIDING THERE?!

WISH

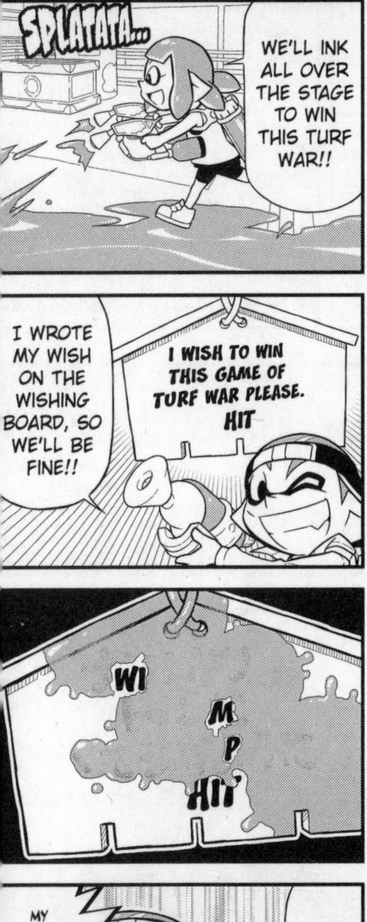
WE'LL INK ALL OVER THE STAGE TO WIN THIS TURF WAR!!
SPLATATA...
I WISH TO WIN THIS GAME OF TURF WAR PLEASE. HIT
I WROTE MY WISH ON THE WISHING BOARD, SO WE'LL BE FINE!!
WI M P HIT
W I M P HIT?
MY WISH HAS DISAP-PEARED BECAUSE OF THE INK!!

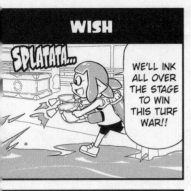

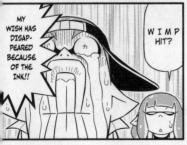

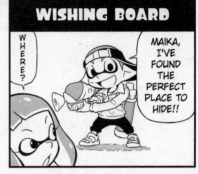

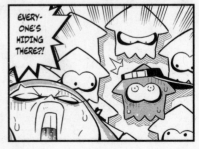

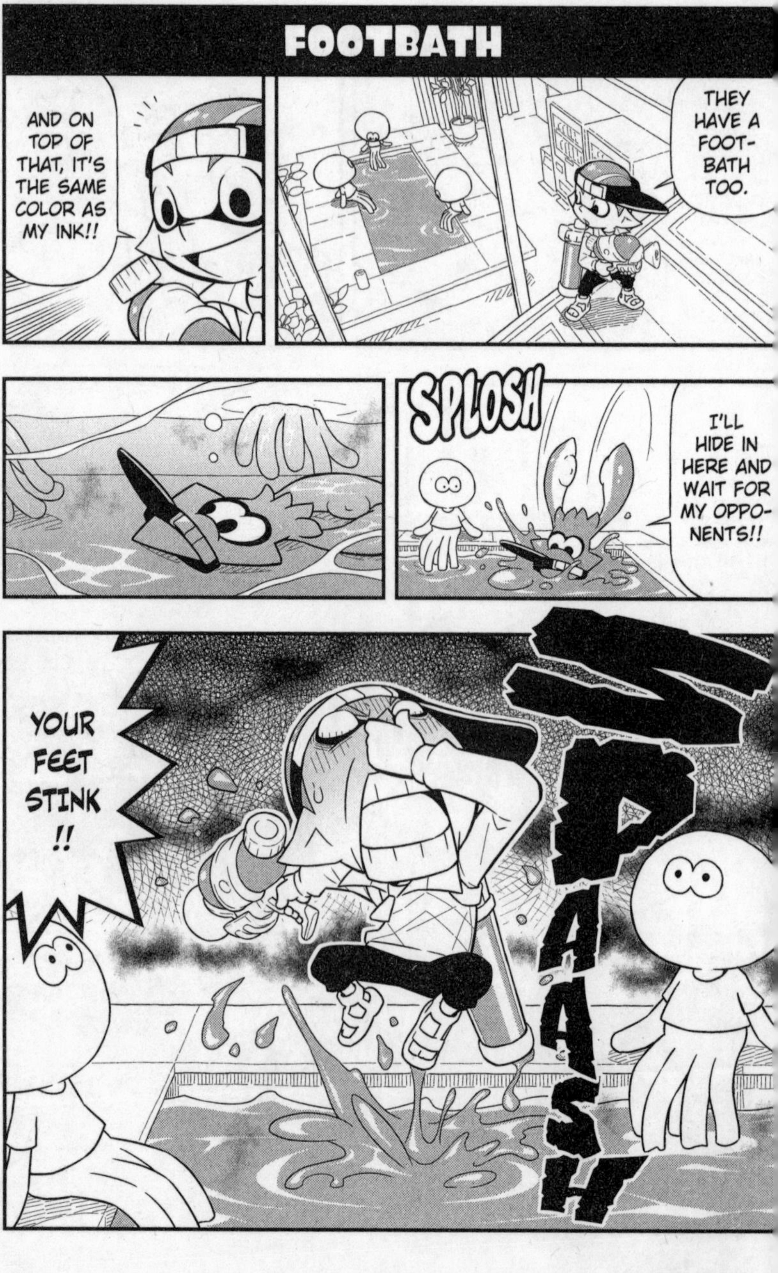
FOOTBATH
THEY HAVE A FOOT-BATH TOO.
AND ON TOP OF THAT, IT'S THE SAME COLOR AS MY INK!!
I'LL HIDE IN HERE AND WAIT FOR MY OPPO-NENTS!!
SPLOSH
SPAAASH
YOUR FEET STINK!!

THE ANGRY RESULT

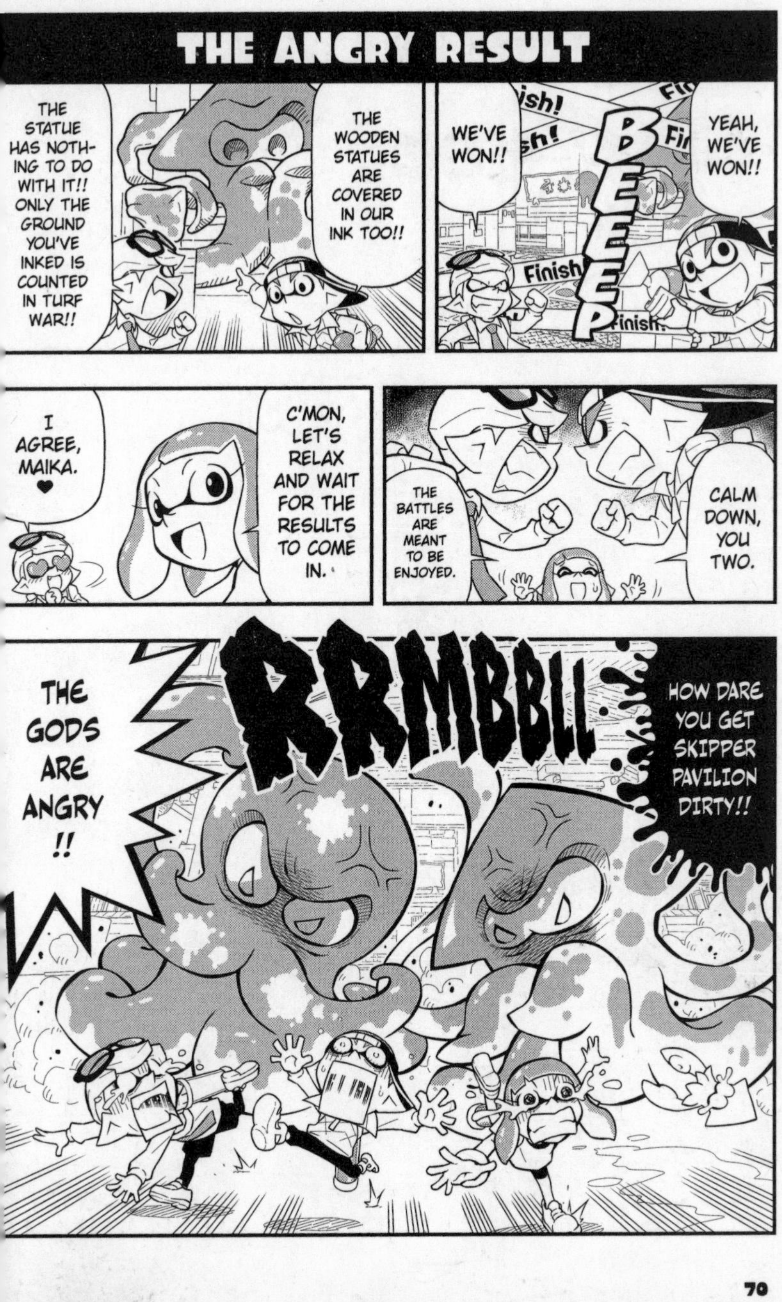

YEAH, WE'VE WON!!
WE'VE WON!!
BEEEEP
Finish!
THE WOODEN STATUES ARE COVERED IN OUR INK TOO!!
THE STATUE HAS NOTHING TO DO WITH IT!! ONLY THE GROUND YOU'VE INKED IS COUNTED IN TURF WAR!!
CALM DOWN, YOU TWO.
THE BATTLES ARE MEANT TO BE ENJOYED.
C'MON, LET'S RELAX AND WAIT FOR THE RESULTS TO COME IN.
I AGREE, MAIKA. ♥
HOW DARE YOU GET SKIPPER PAVILION DIRTY!!
RRMBBLL
THE GODS ARE ANGRY!!

TIME TO PLAY SOME COOL GAMES!

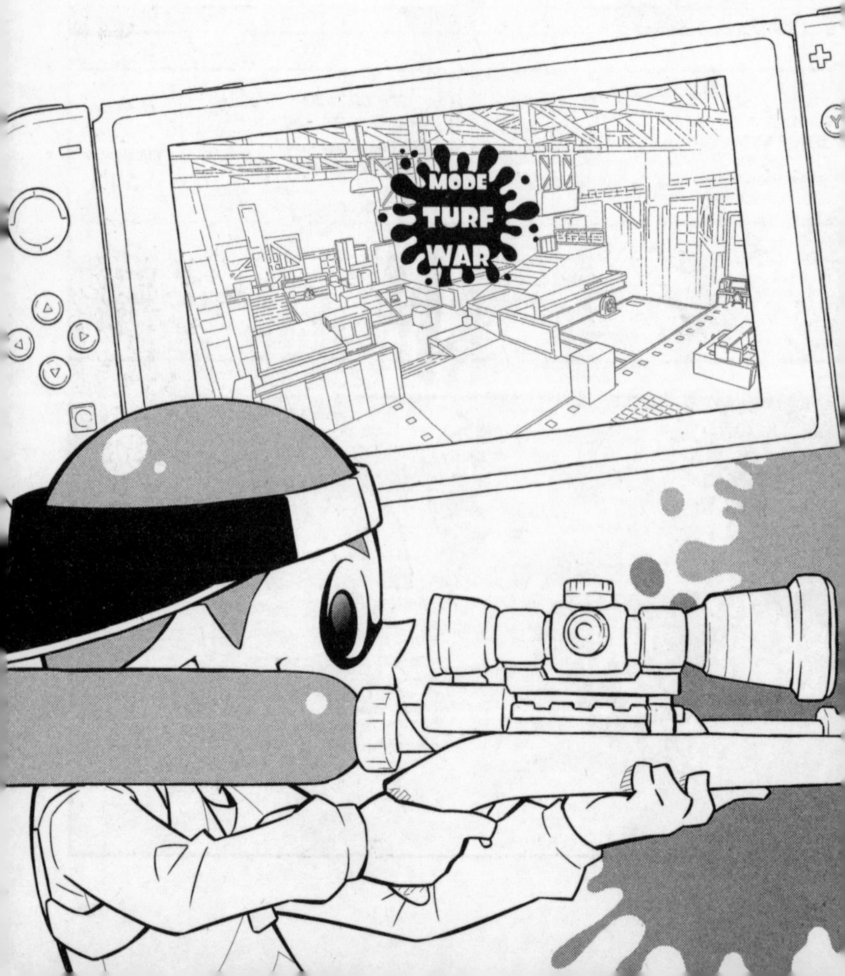
MODE
TURF
WAR

ANCHO-V GAMES

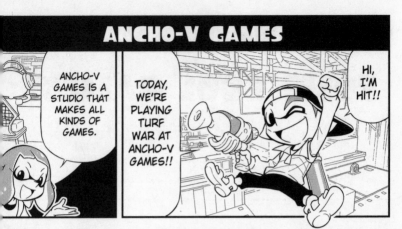

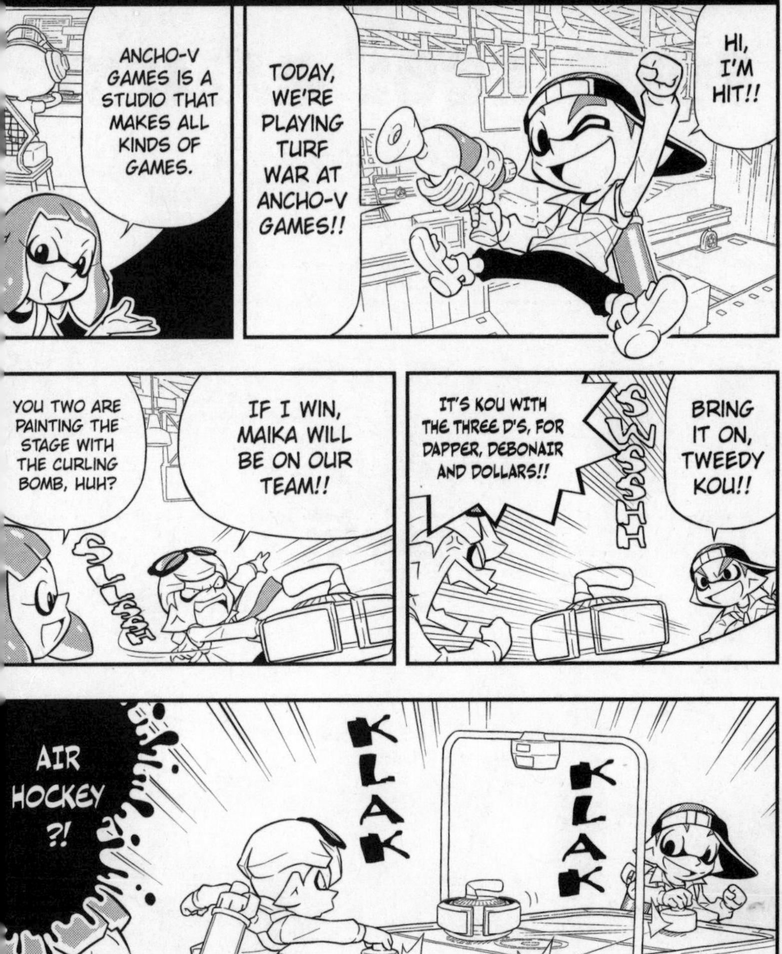
HI, I'M HIT!!
TODAY, WE'RE PLAYING TURF WAR AT ANCHO-V GAMES!!
ANCHO-V GAMES IS A STUDIO THAT MAKES ALL KINDS OF GAMES.
BRING IT ON, TWEEDY KOU!!
IT'S KOU WITH THE THREE D'S, FOR DAPPER, DEBONAIR AND DOLLARS!!
IF I WIN, MAIKA WILL BE ON OUR TEAM!!
YOU TWO ARE PAINTING THE STAGE WITH THE CURLING BOMB, HUH?
KLAK
KLAK
AIR HOCKEY ?!

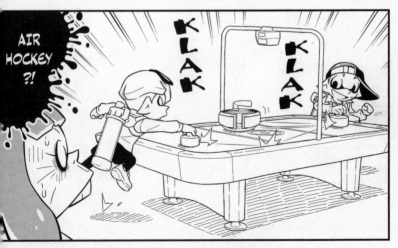

GETTING WEAPONS

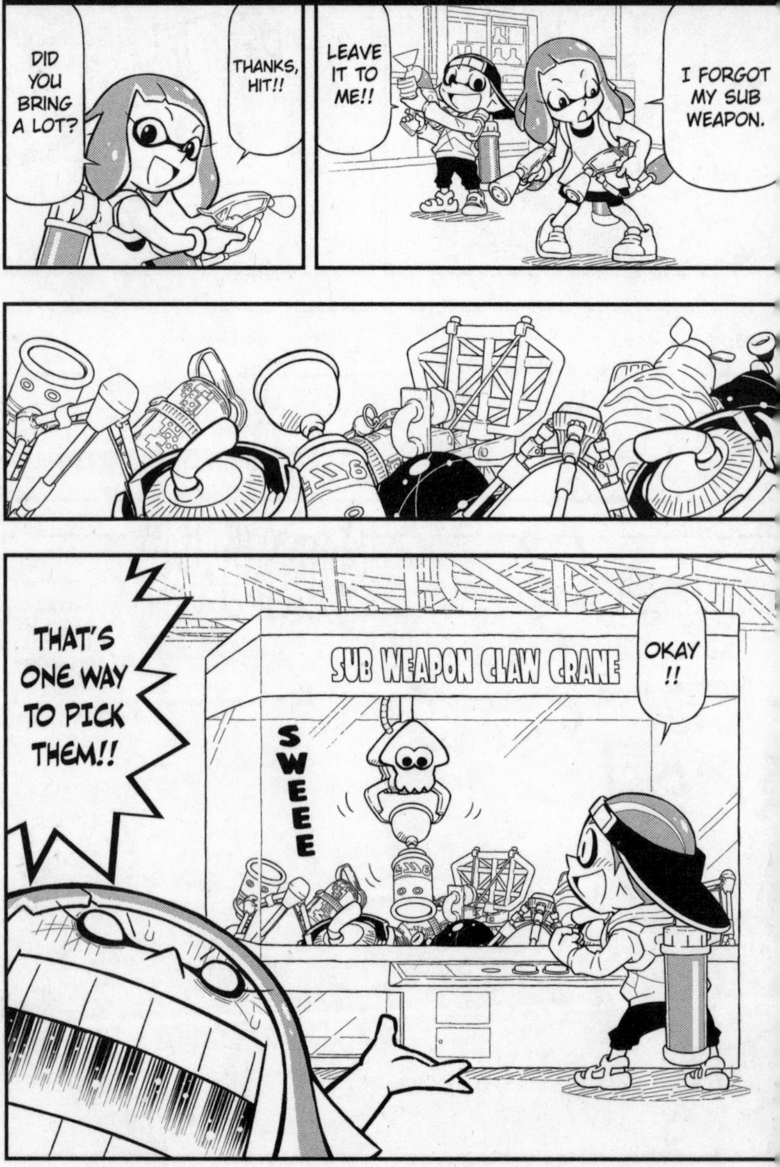
I FORGOT MY SUB WEAPON.
LEAVE IT TO ME!!
THANKS, HIT!!
DID YOU BRING A LOT?
OKAY!!
SUB WEAPON CLAW CRANE
SWEEE
THAT'S ONE WAY TO PICK THEM!!

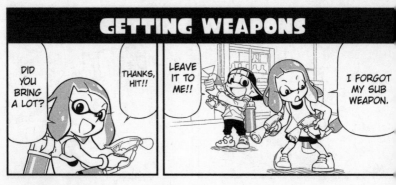

SURROUNDED

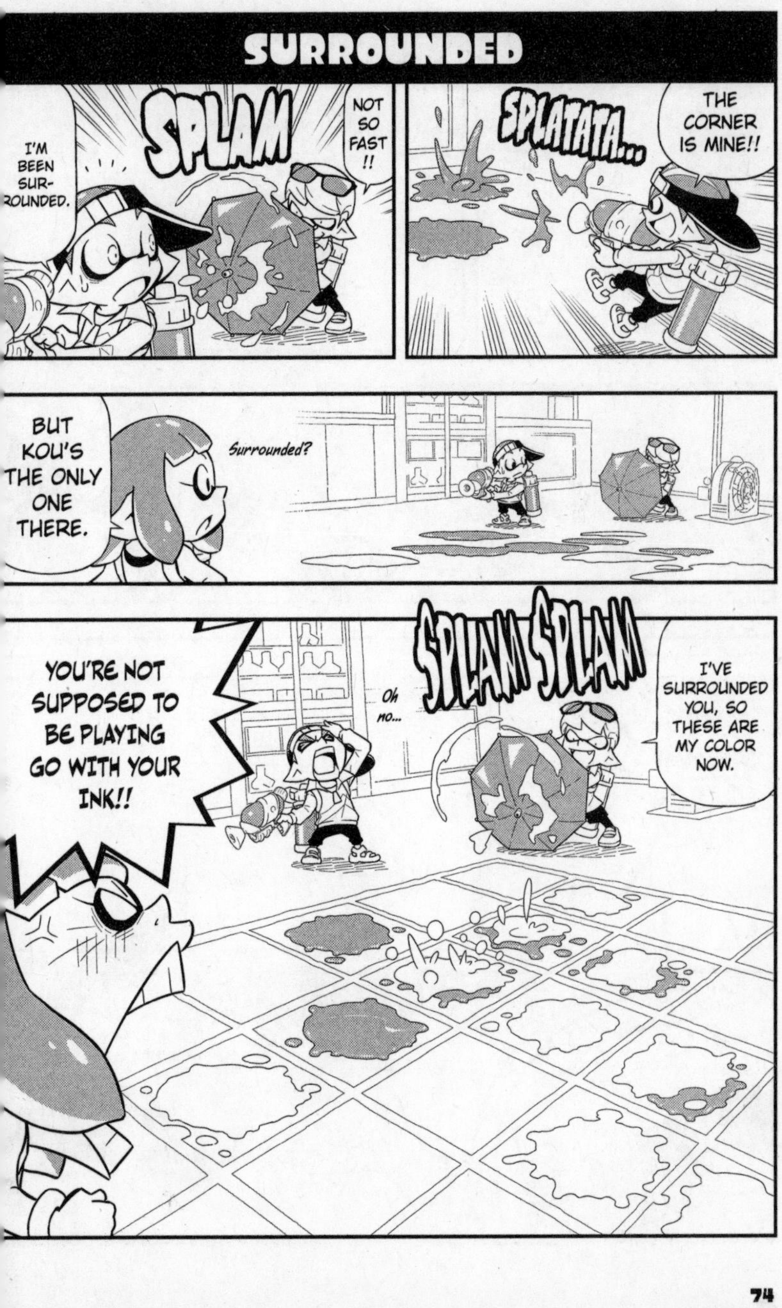
THE CORNER IS MINE!!
SPLATATA...
NOT SO FAST!!
SPLAM
I'M BEEN SUR-ROUNDED.
Surrounded?
BUT KOU'S THE ONLY ONE THERE.
I'VE SURROUNDED YOU, SO THESE ARE MY COLOR NOW.
SPLAM SPLAM
Oh no...
YOU'RE NOT SUPPOSED TO BE PLAYING GO WITH YOUR INK!!

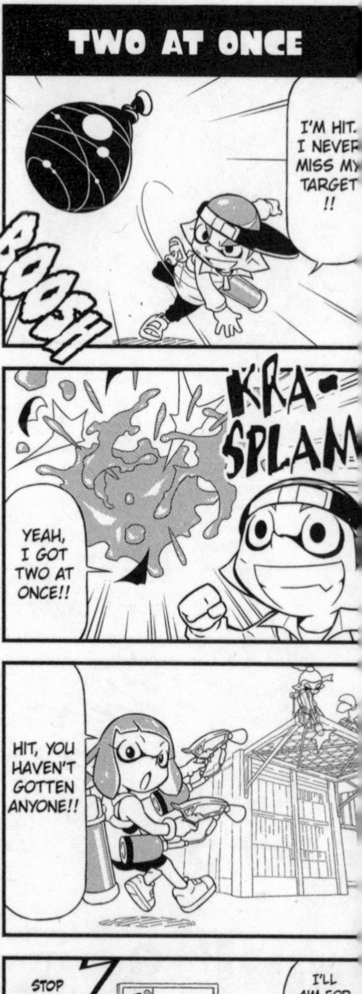
TWO AT ONCE
I'M HIT. I NEVER MISS MY TARGET!!
BOOSH
KRA-SPLAM
YEAH, I GOT TWO AT ONCE!!
HIT, YOU HAVEN'T GOTTEN ANYONE!!
I'LL AIM FOR NUMBER 1 NEXT!!
1 4 5 6 7 8 9
STOP PLAYING AROUND!!

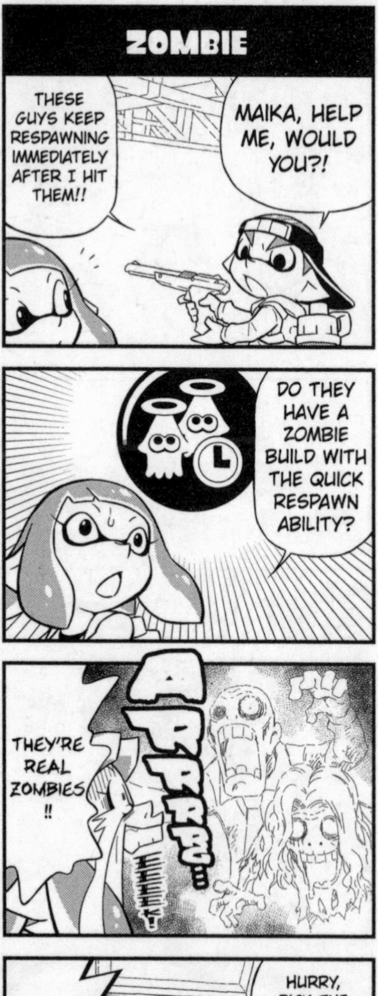
ZOMBIE
MAIKA, HELP ME, WOULD YOU?!
THESE GUYS KEEP RESPAWNING IMMEDIATELY AFTER I HIT THEM!!
DO THEY HAVE A ZOMBIE BUILD WITH THE QUICK RESPAWN ABILITY?
APRRRG...
THEY'RE REAL ZOMBIES!!
HURRY, PICK THE WEAPON UP.
IT'S JUST A SHOOT-ING GAME!!

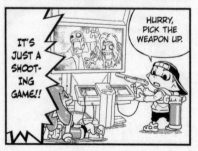

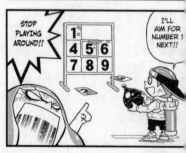

TARGET

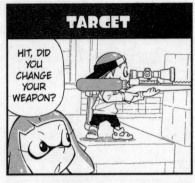

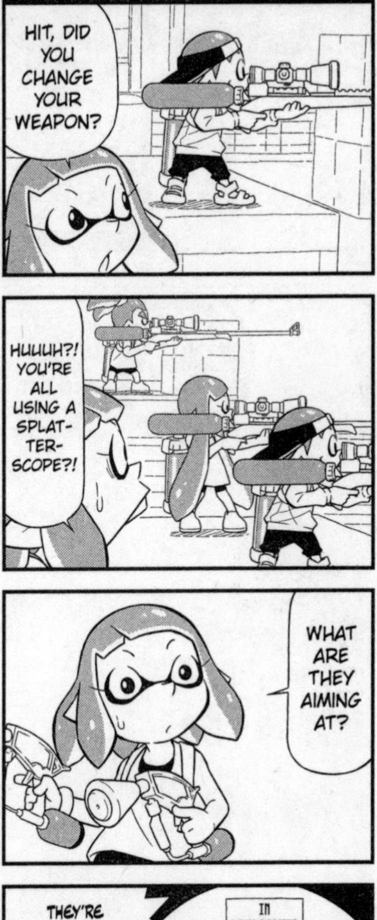
HIT, DID YOU CHANGE YOUR WEAPON?
HUUUH?! YOU'RE ALL USING A SPLAT-TER-SCOPE?!
WHAT ARE THEY AIMING AT?
IN DEVELOPMENT
THEY'RE TAKING A PEEK AT THE LATEST VIDEO GAME!!
KLAK KLAK

PROPELLER FLOOR

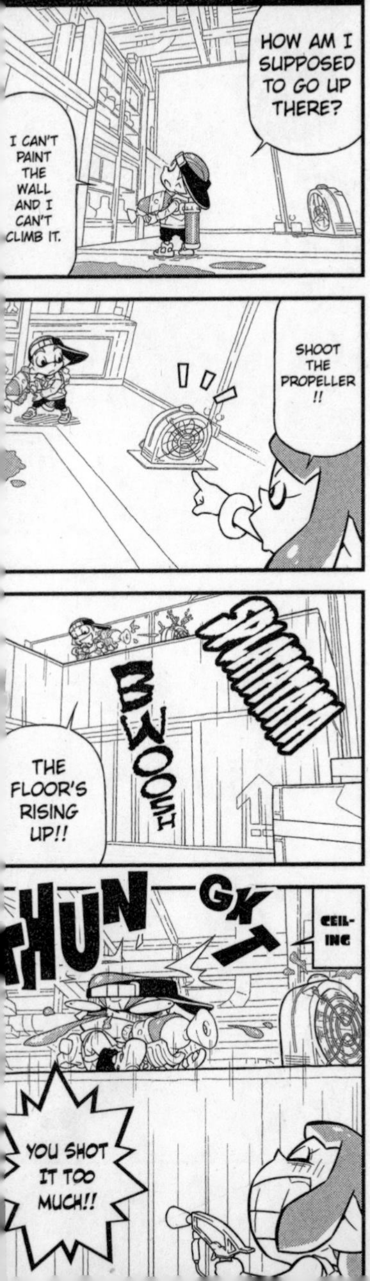
HOW AM I SUPPOSED TO GO UP THERE?
I CAN'T PAINT THE WALL AND I CAN'T CLIMB IT.
SHOOT THE PROPELLER !!
BWOOOSH
THE FLOOR'S RISING UP!!
CEIL-ING
THUNGK
YOU SHOT IT TOO MUCH!!

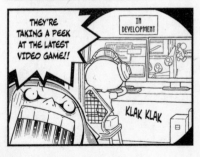

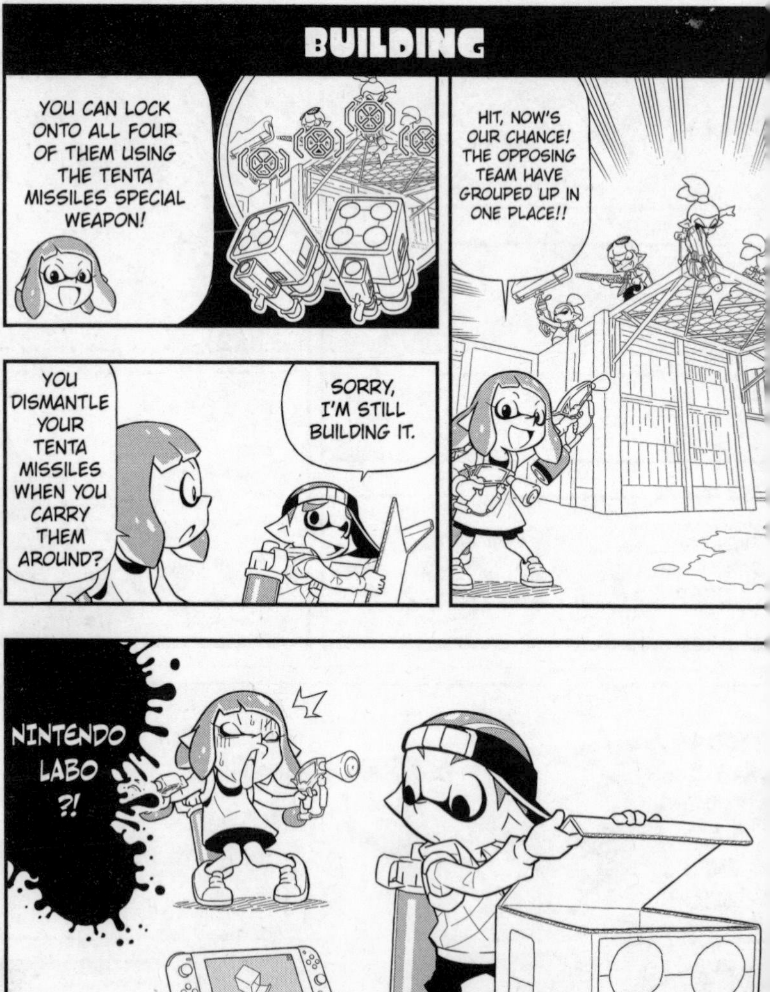
BUILDING
HIT, NOW'S OUR CHANCE! THE OPPOSING TEAM HAVE GROUPED UP IN ONE PLACE!!
YOU CAN LOCK ONTO ALL FOUR OF THEM USING THE TENTA MISSILES SPECIAL WEAPON!
SORRY, I'M STILL BUILDING IT.
YOU DISMANTLE YOUR TENTA MISSILES WHEN YOU CARRY THEM AROUND?
NINTENDO LABO ?!

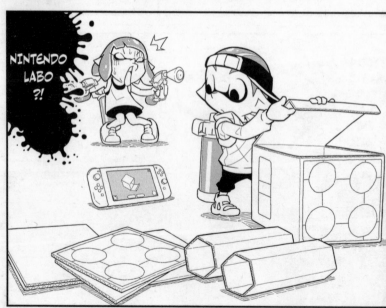

BRUSH VERSUS BRUSH

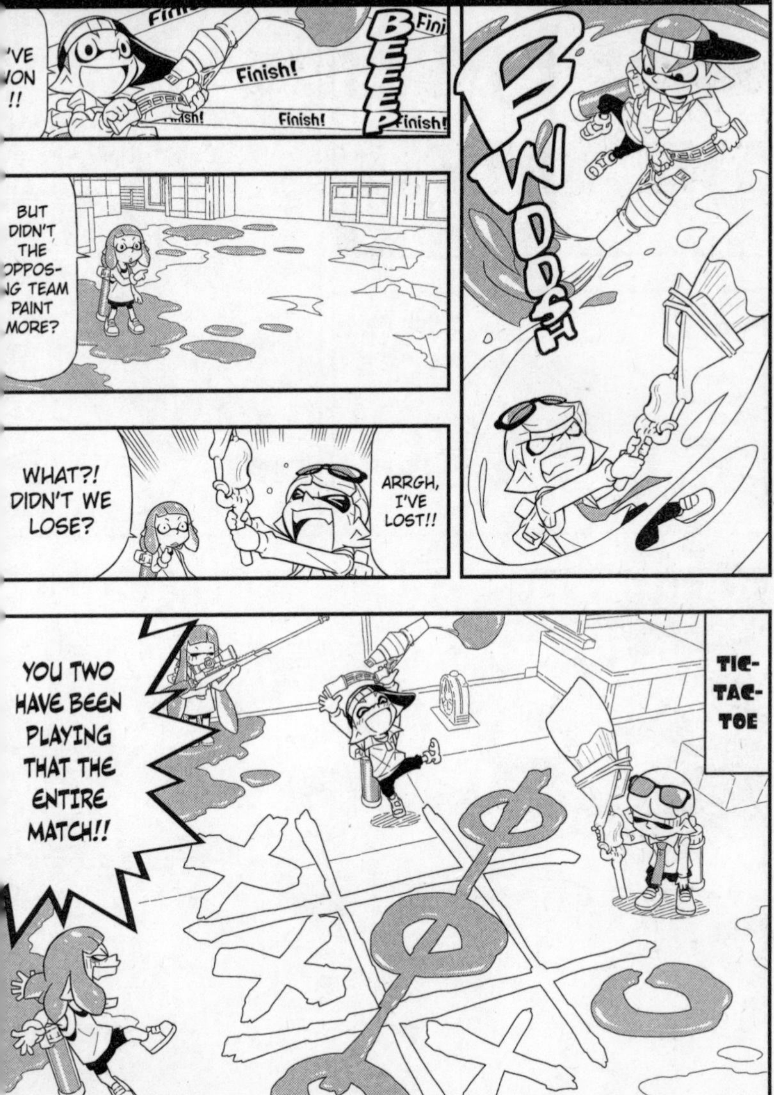
BWOOSH
Finish! Finish! Finish! Finish! Finish! Finish!
BEEEP
'VE ON !!
BUT DIDN'T THE OPPOS- NG TEAM PAINT MORE?
ARRGH, I'VE LOST!!
WHAT?! DIDN'T WE LOSE?
TIC-TAC-TOE
YOU TWO HAVE BEEN PLAYING THAT THE ENTIRE MATCH!!

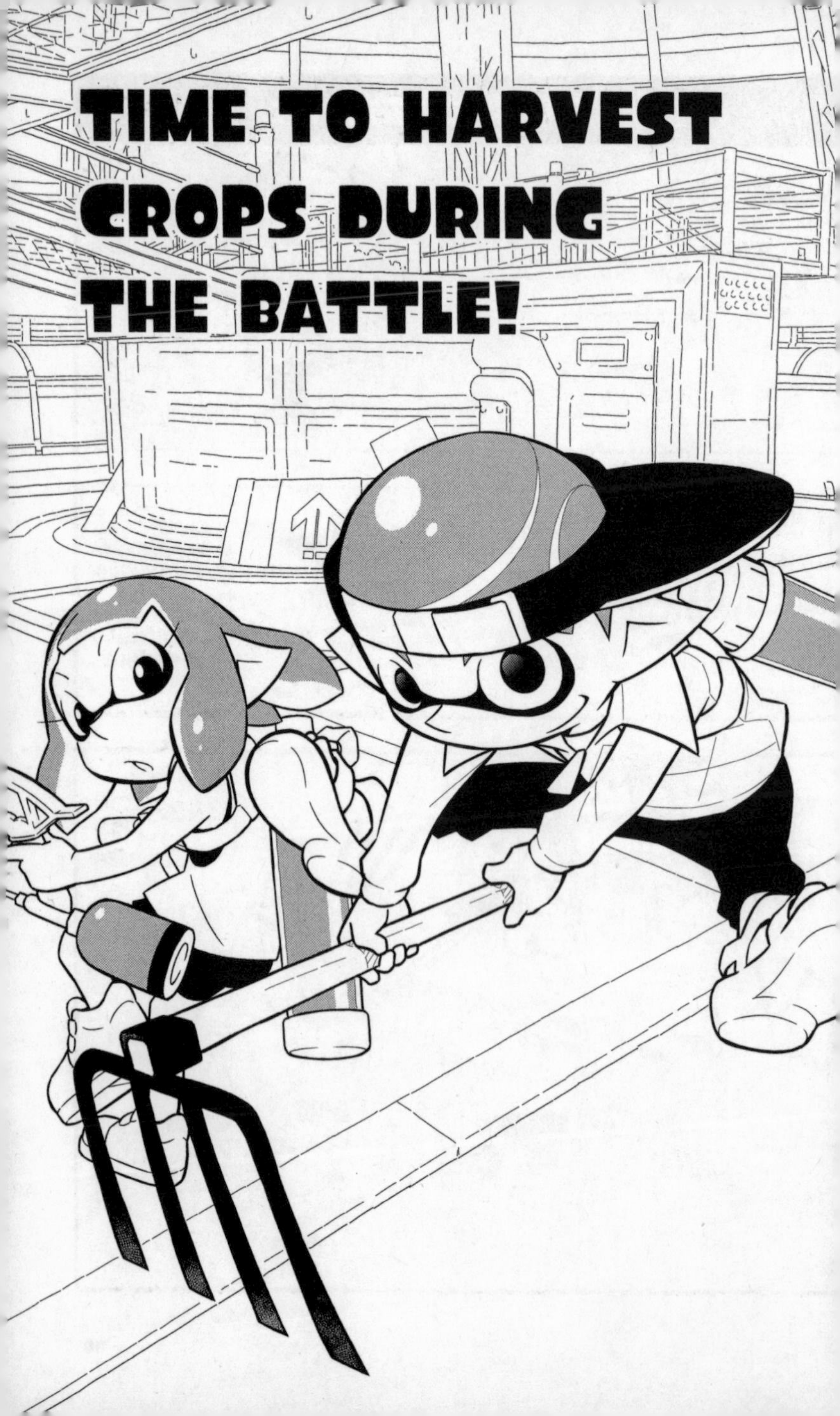
TIME TO HARVEST CROPS DURING THE BATTLE!

KELP DOME

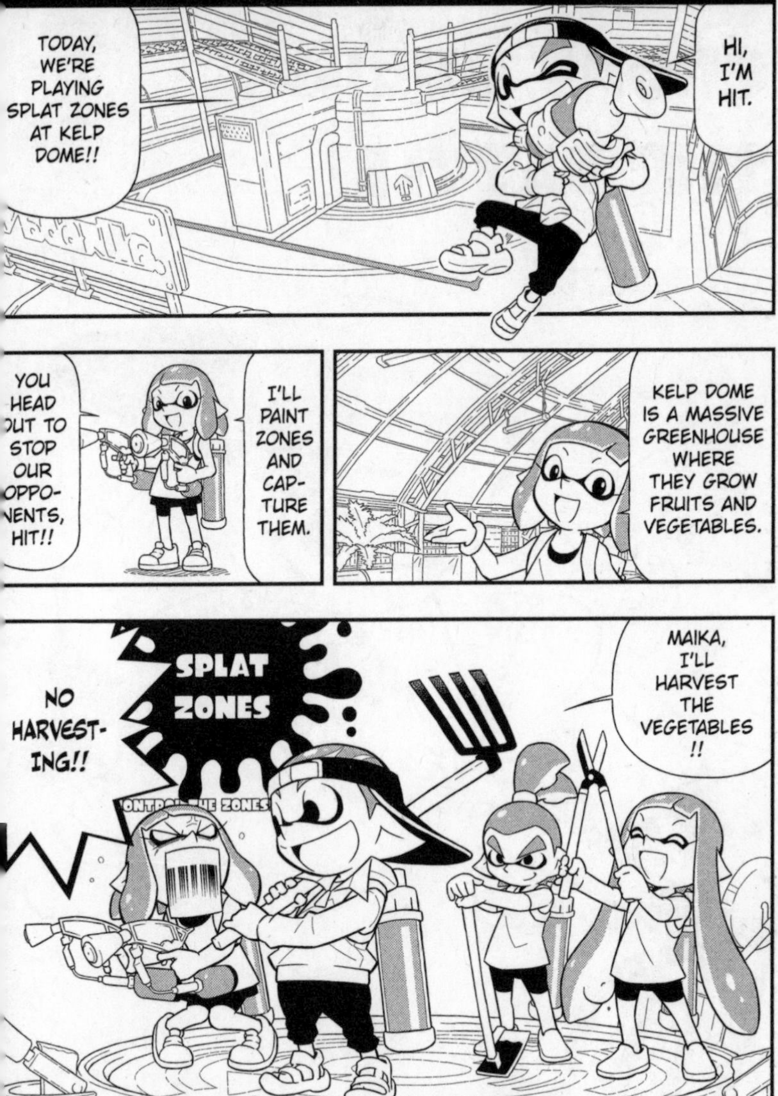

HI, I'M HIT.
TODAY, WE'RE PLAYING SPLAT ZONES AT KELP DOME!!
KELP DOME IS A MASSIVE GREENHOUSE WHERE THEY GROW FRUITS AND VEGETABLES.
I'LL PAINT ZONES AND CAP- TURE THEM.
YOU HEAD OUT TO STOP OUR OPPO- NENTS, HIT!!
MAIKA, I'LL HARVEST THE VEGETABLES !!
SPLAT ZONES
NO HARVEST- ING!!

NO ZONES

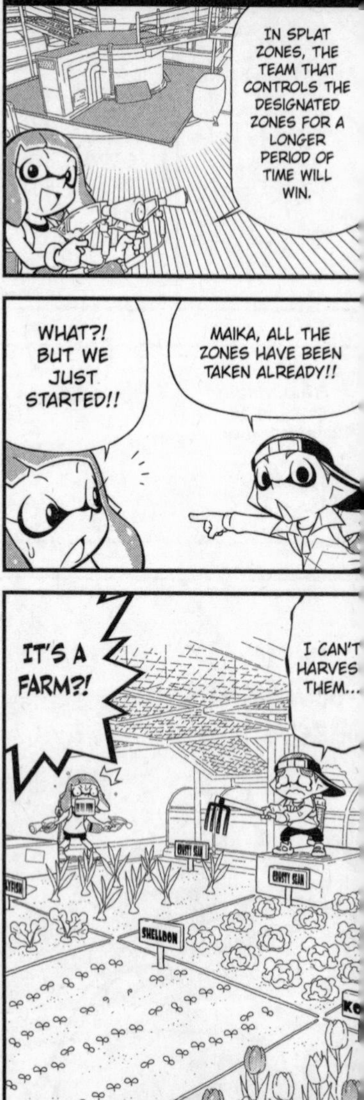

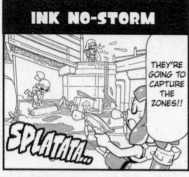

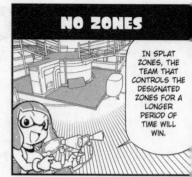

IN SPLAT ZONES, THE TEAM THAT CONTROLS THE DESIGNATED ZONES FOR A LONGER PERIOD OF TIME WILL WIN.
MAIKA, ALL THE ZONES HAVE BEEN TAKEN ALREADY!!
WHAT?! BUT WE JUST STARTED!!
I CAN'T HARVES THEM...
IT'S A FARM?!
CRUSTY SEAN
CRUSTY SEAN
SHELLDON

INK NO-STORM

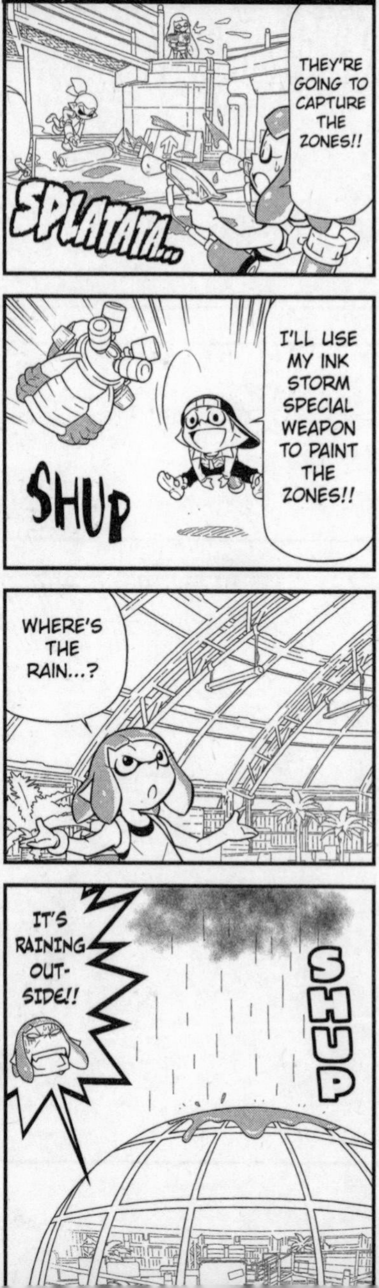

THEY'RE GOING TO CAPTURE THE ZONES!!
SPLATATATA..
I'LL USE MY INK STORM SPECIAL WEAPON TO PAINT THE ZONES!!
SHUP
WHERE'S THE RAIN...?
SHUP
IT'S RAINING OUT-SIDE!!

FOLLOW THE ULTRA STAMP

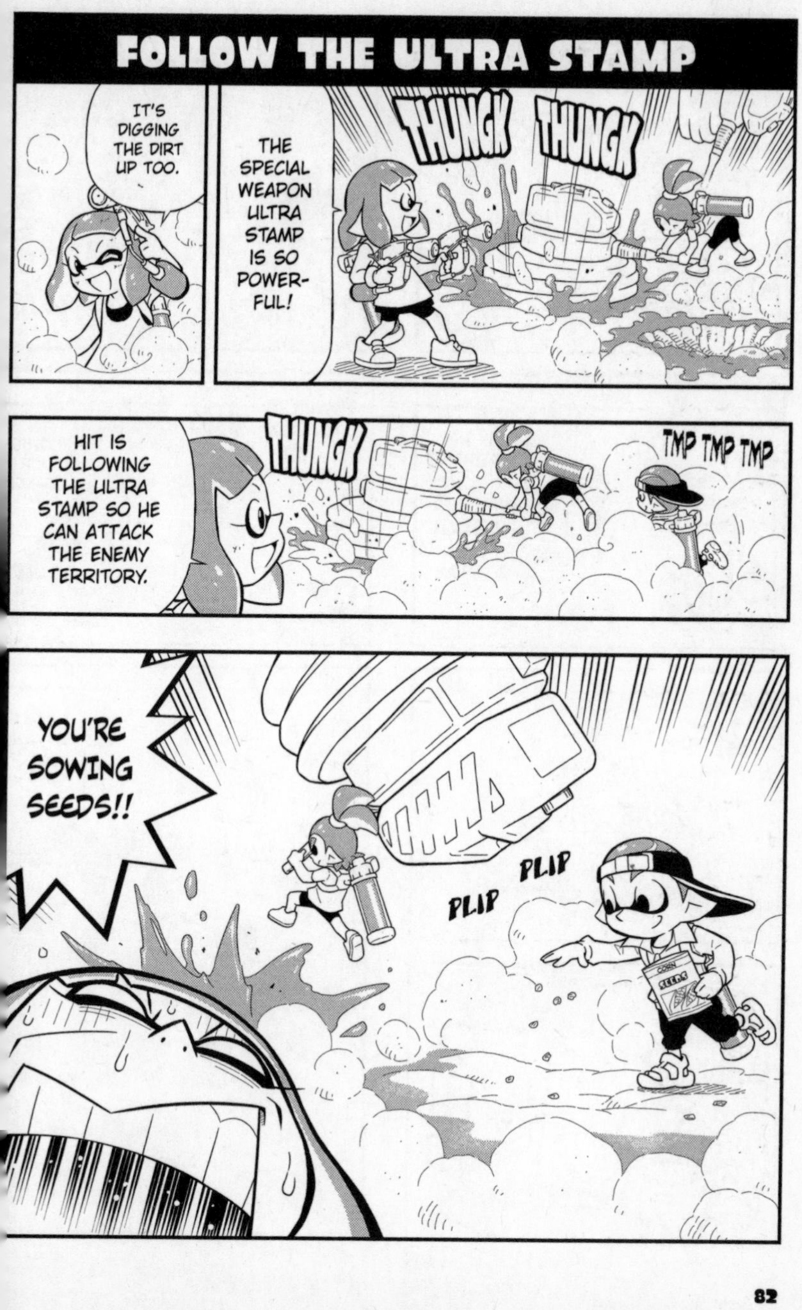
THUNGK THUNGK
THE SPECIAL WEAPON ULTRA STAMP IS SO POWERFUL!
IT'S DIGGING THE DIRT UP TOO.
TMP TMP TMP
THUNGK
HIT IS FOLLOWING THE ULTRA STAMP SO HE CAN ATTACK THE ENEMY TERRITORY.
PLIP
PLIP
CORN SEEDS
YOU'RE SOWING SEEDS!!

INK THE ZONES

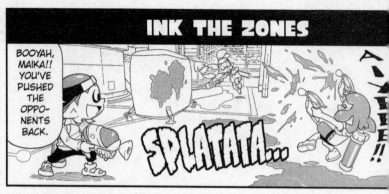

SPLATATA...
BOOYAH, MAIKA!! YOU'VE PUSHED THE OPPONENTS BACK.
NOW'S OUR CHANC !!
YOU'RE GOING TO INK THE ZONES TOGETHER?
I'LL HELP OUT WITH MY DUALIES TOO.
GRO BIG. ♪
SHAAAA
SHWAA
WATERING THE VEGETABLES?!

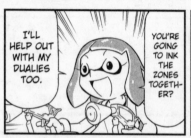

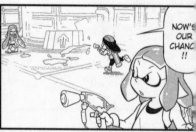

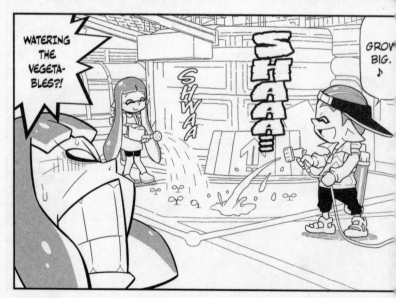

INK STORM WAR

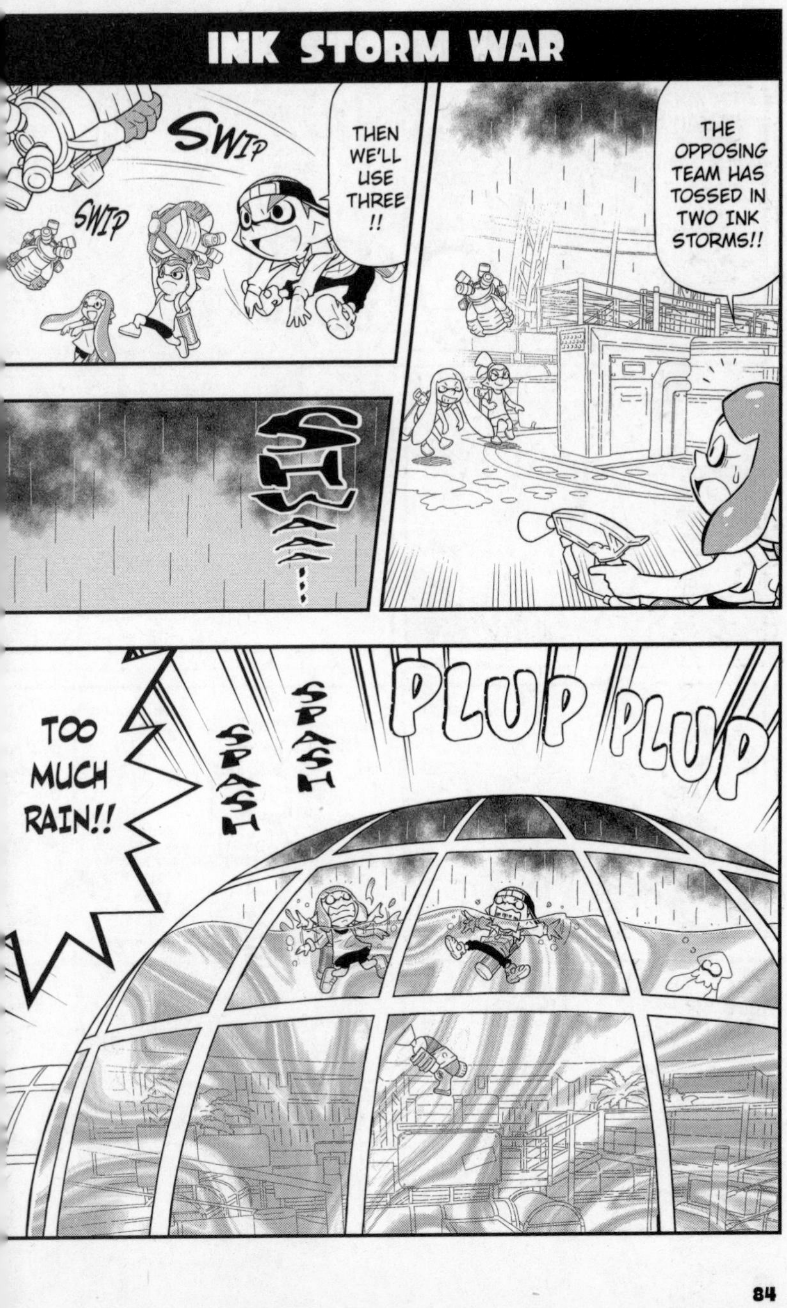
THE OPPOSING TEAM HAS TOSSED IN TWO INK STORMS!!
THEN WE'LL USE THREE!!
SWIP
SWIP
PLUP
PLUP
SPASH
SPASH
TOO MUCH RAIN!!

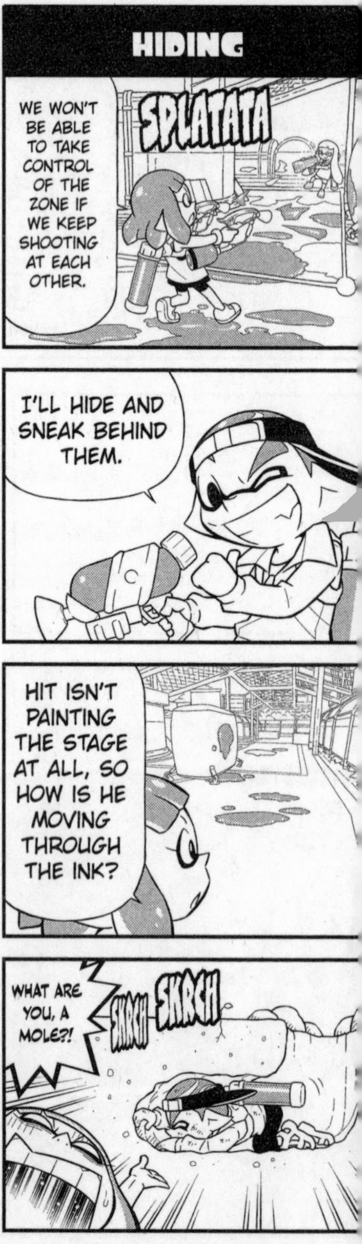
HIDING
SPLATATA
WE WON'T BE ABLE TO TAKE CONTROL OF THE ZONE IF WE KEEP SHOOTING AT EACH OTHER.
I'LL HIDE AND SNEAK BEHIND THEM.
HIT ISN'T PAINTING THE STAGE AT ALL, SO HOW IS HE MOVING THROUGH THE INK?
SKRCH
SKRCH
WHAT ARE YOU, A MOLE?!

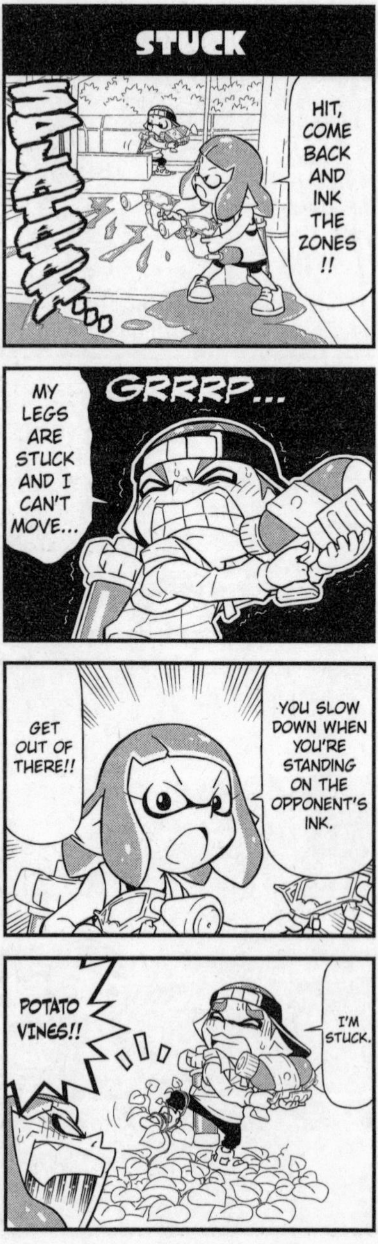
STUCK
HIT, COME BACK AND INK THE ZONES!!
SPLATATA...
GRRRP...
MY LEGS ARE STUCK AND I CAN'T MOVE...
YOU SLOW DOWN WHEN YOU'RE STANDING ON THE OPPONENT'S INK.
GET OUT OF THERE!!
I'M STUCK.
POTATO VINES!!

GROWING IN THE ZONE

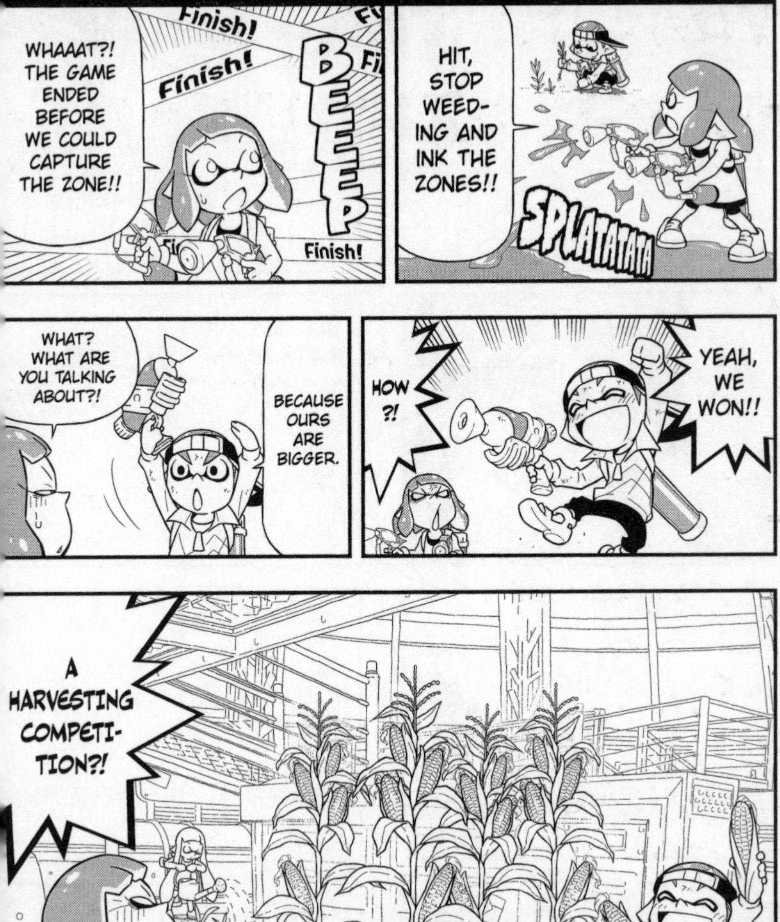
HIT, STOP WEEDING AND INK THE ZONES!!
SPLATATATA
Finish!
Finish!
Finish!
BEEEEP
WHAAAT?! THE GAME ENDED BEFORE WE COULD CAPTURE THE ZONE!!
Finish!
YEAH, WE WON!!
HOW?!
WHAT? WHAT ARE YOU TALKING ABOUT?!
BECAUSE OURS ARE BIGGER.
A HARVESTING COMPETITION?!

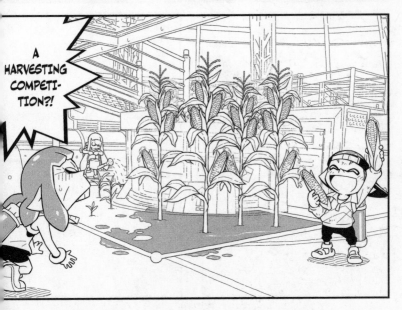

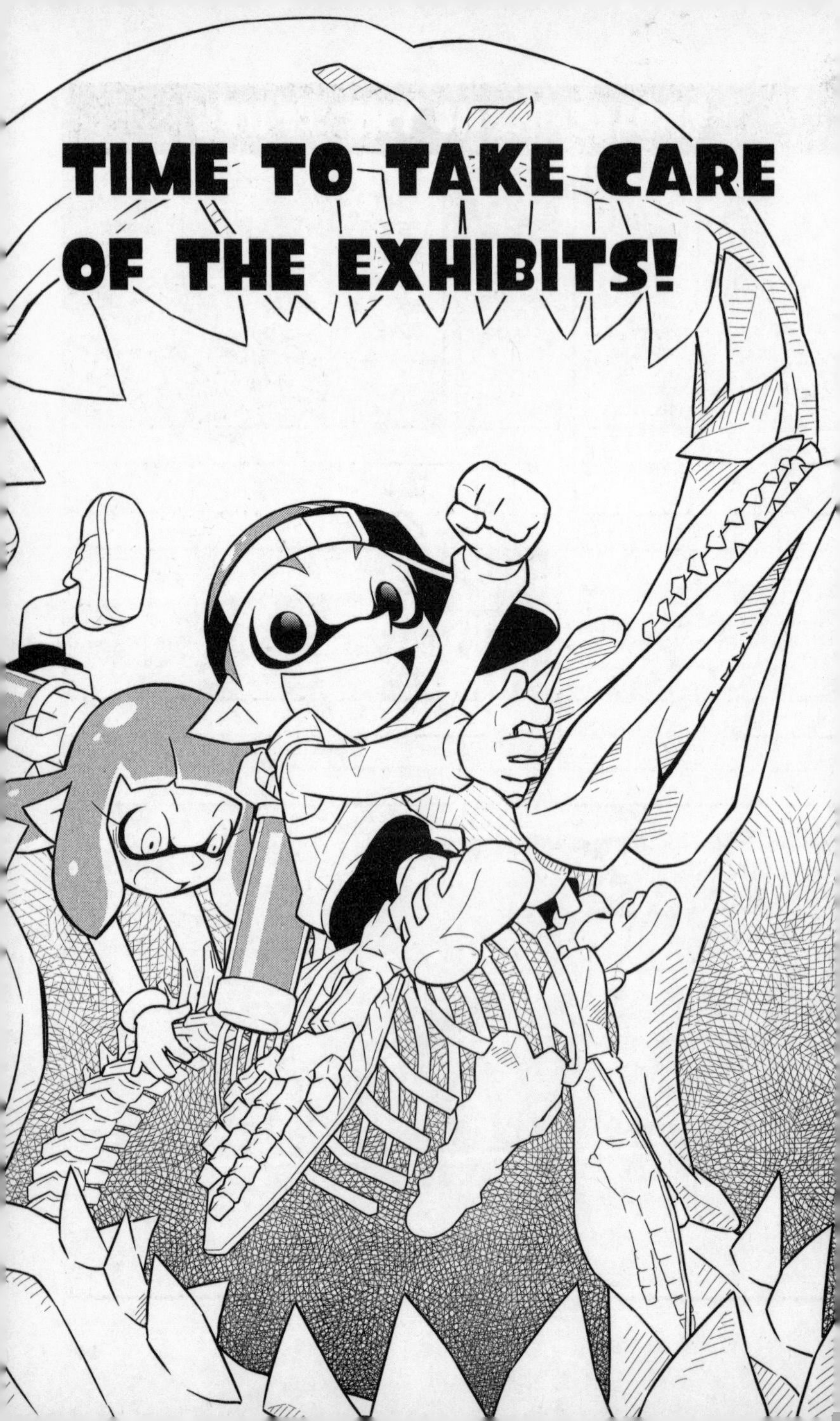
TIME TO TAKE CARE OF THE EXHIBITS!

SHELLENDORF INSTITUTE

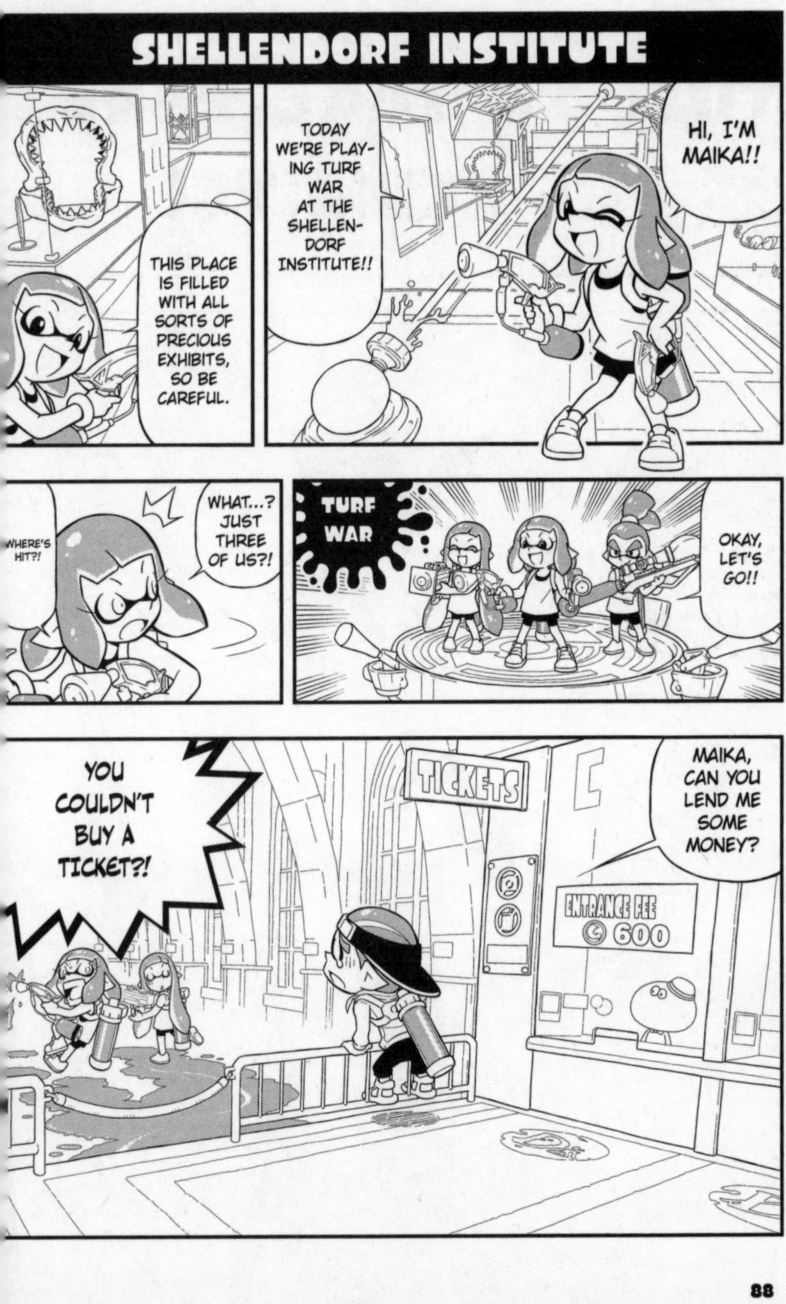
HI, I'M MAIKA!!
TODAY WE'RE PLAYING TURF WAR AT THE SHELLENDORF INSTITUTE!!
THIS PLACE IS FILLED WITH ALL SORTS OF PRECIOUS EXHIBITS, SO BE CAREFUL.
OKAY, LET'S GO!!
TURF WAR
WHAT...? JUST THREE OF US?!
WHERE'S
HIT?!
MAIKA, CAN YOU LEND ME SOME MONEY?
TICKETS
ENTRANCE FEE
600
YOU COULDN'T BUY A TICKET?!

PROTECT THE EXHIBITS!!

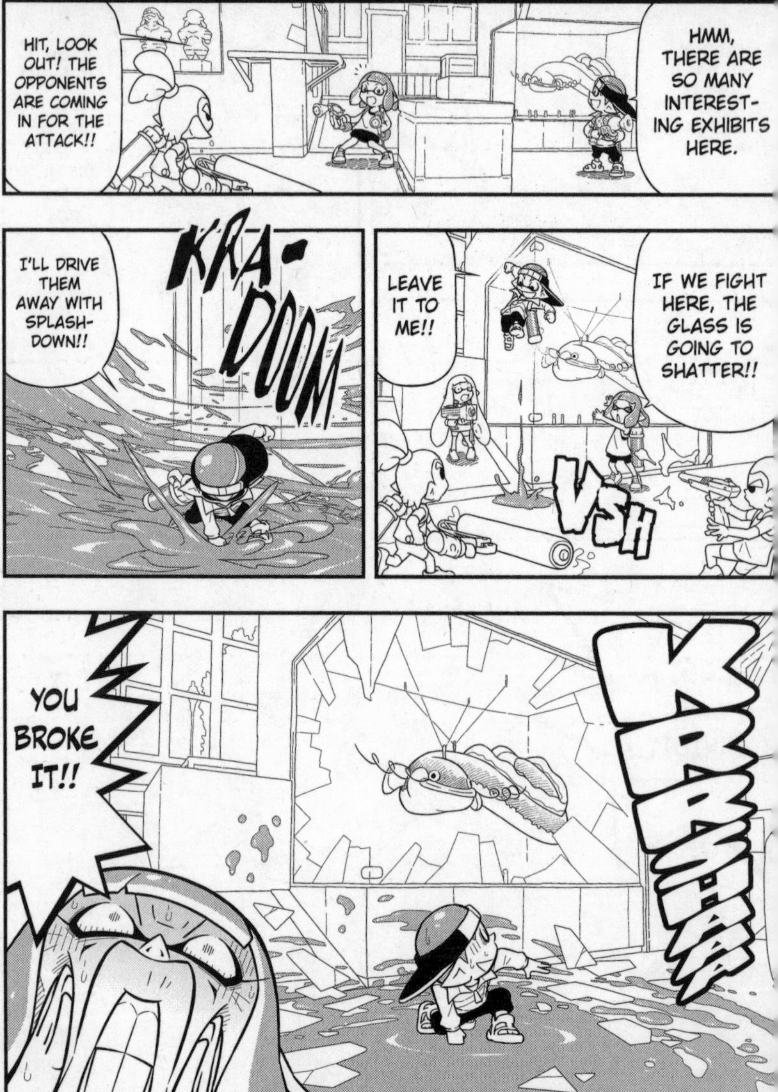
HMM, THERE ARE SO MANY INTEREST-ING EXHIBITS HERE.
HIT, LOOK OUT! THE OPPONENTS ARE COMING IN FOR THE ATTACK!!
IF WE FIGHT HERE, THE GLASS IS GOING TO SHATTER!!
LEAVE IT TO ME!!
VSH
KRA-DOOM
I'LL DRIVE THEM AWAY WITH SPLASH-DOWN!!
KRRSHAAA
YOU BROKE IT!!

INKRAIL

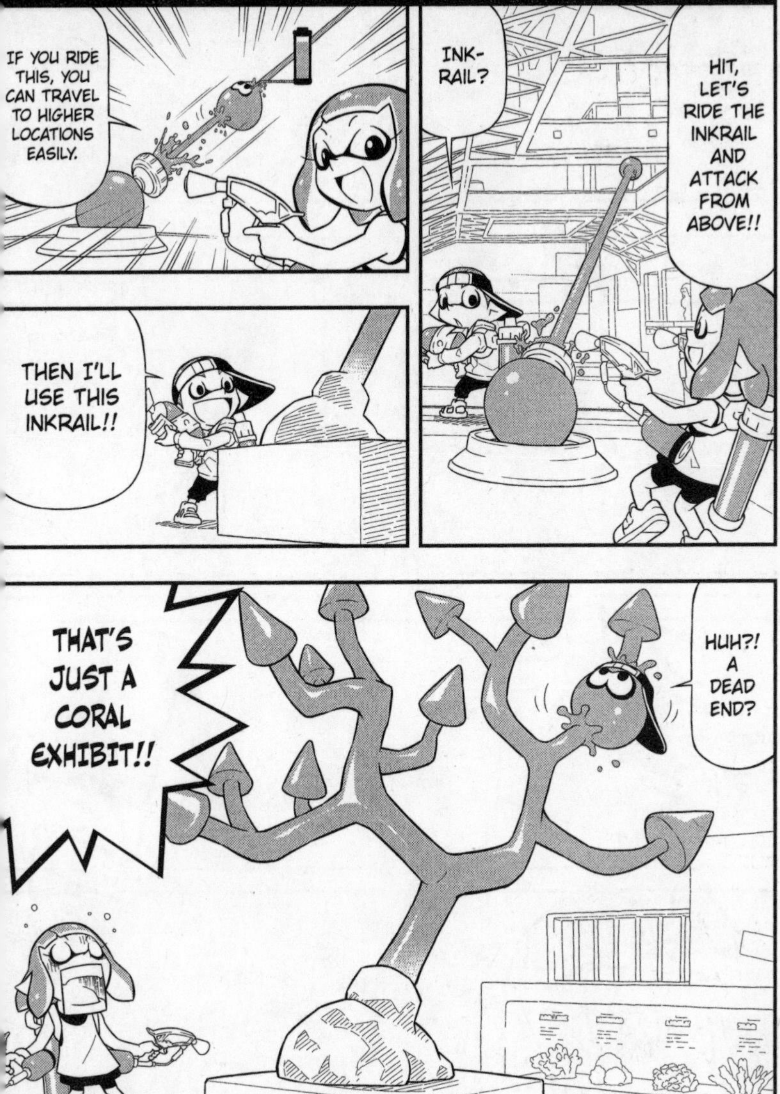

HIT, LET'S RIDE THE INKRAIL AND ATTACK FROM ABOVE!!
INK-RAIL?
IF YOU RIDE THIS, YOU CAN TRAVEL TO HIGHER LOCATIONS EASILY.
THEN I'LL USE THIS INKRAIL!!
HUH?! A DEAD END?
THAT'S JUST A CORAL EXHIBIT!!

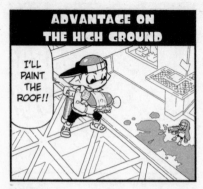

GOING UP

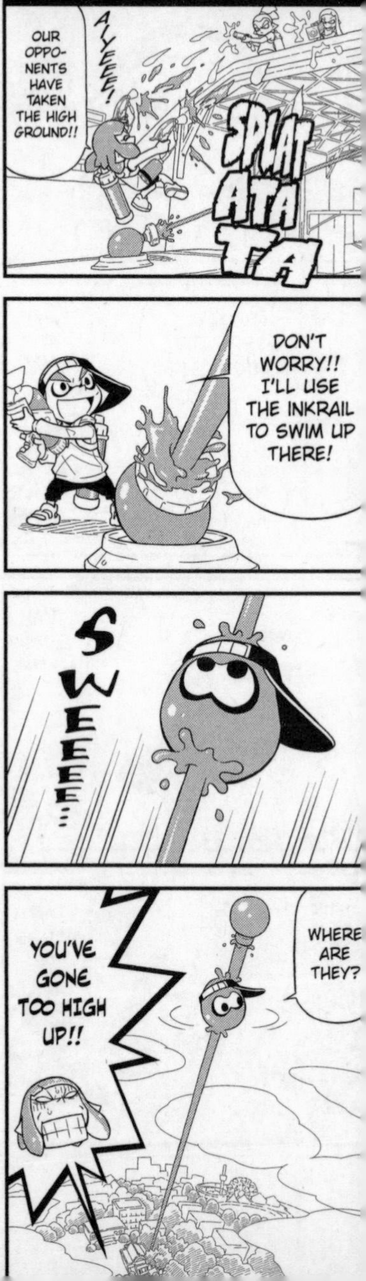
SPLAT ATA TA
AIYEEE!
OUR OPPONENTS HAVE TAKEN THE HIGH GROUND!!
DON'T WORRY!! I'LL USE THE INKRAIL TO SWIM UP THERE!
SWEEEEE...
WHERE ARE THEY?
YOU'VE GONE TOO HIGH UP!!

ADVANTAGE ON THE HIGH GROUND

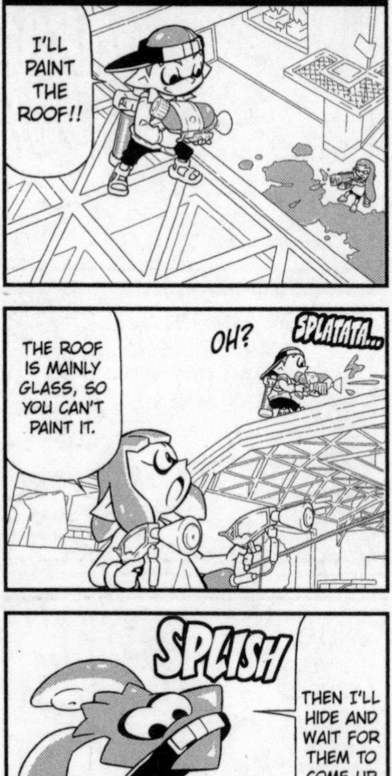
I'LL PAINT THE ROOF!!
SPLATATA...
OH?
THE ROOF IS MAINLY GLASS, SO YOU CAN'T PAINT IT.
THEN I'LL HIDE AND WAIT FOR THEM TO COME UP HERE!!
SPLISH
FWAAASH
I CAN SEE YOU PLAYING ON THE SWITCH!!

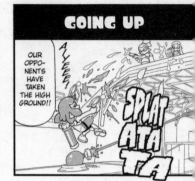

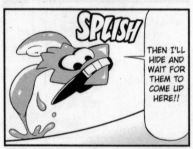

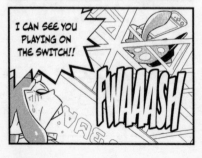

MINES

KRA-SPLAM
ACK!!
SPLATATA
BE CAREFUL, HIT! THE OPPOSING TEAM HAS SET INK MINES!!
KRSHK
WHOA!! I'VE STEPPED ON A MINE TOO!!
OWWW!!
THAT'S AN EXHIBIT!!

IMMOVABLE MAIKA

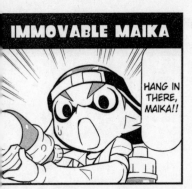

HANG IN THERE, MAIKA!!
CAN'T YOU MOVE?!
DID YOU STEP INTO TOXIC MIST?
I'M OVER HERE.
WHAT?!
TWO MAIKAS?!
I'm not that fat!!
THAT'S A CLAY FIGURINE!!

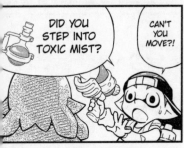

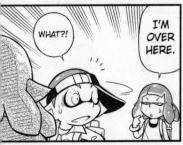

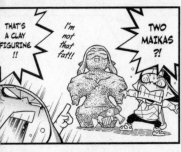

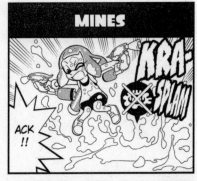

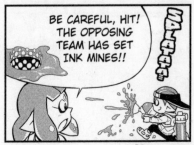

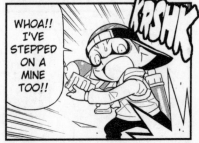

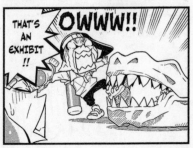

FOSSIL ATTACK

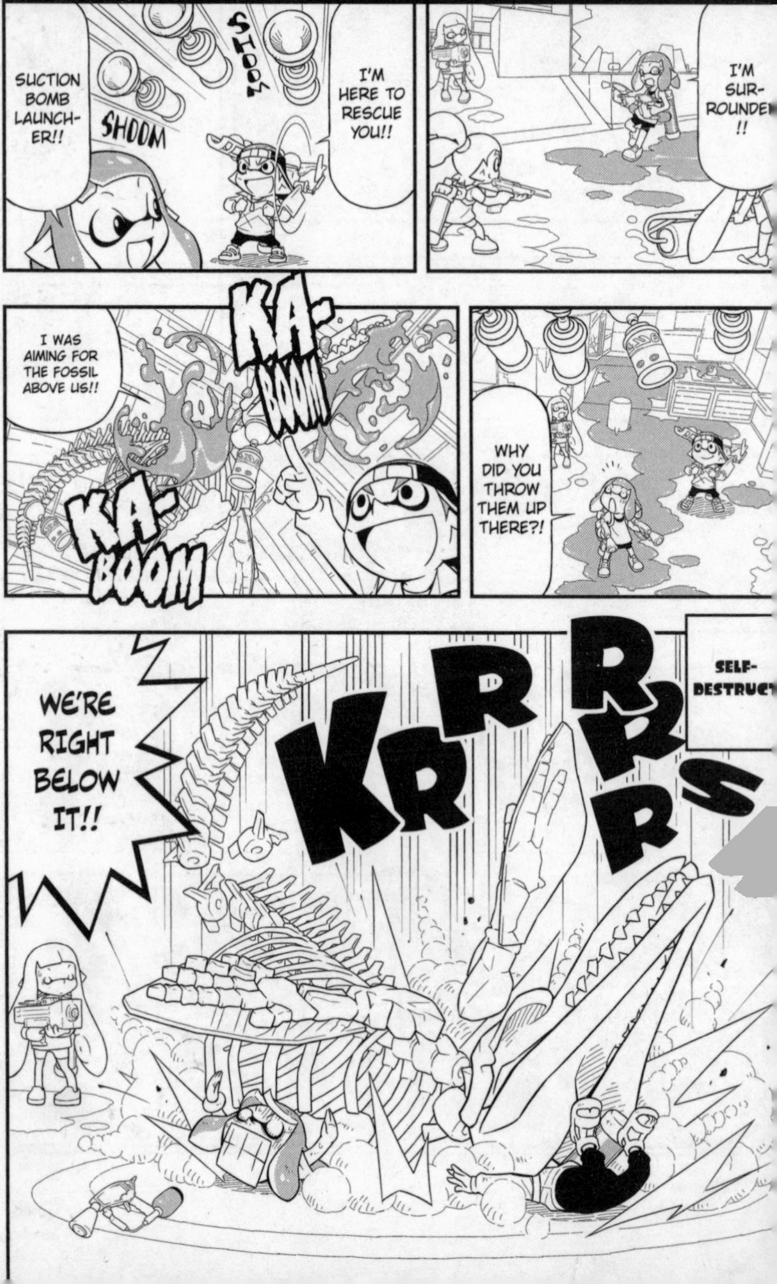
I'M SUR-ROUNDE
!!
I'M HERE TO RESCUE YOU!!
SHOOM
SHOOM
SUCTION BOMB LAUNCH-ER!!
WHY DID YOU THROW THEM UP THERE?!
KA-BOOM
I WAS AIMING FOR THE FOSSIL ABOVE US!!
KA-BOOM
SELF-DESTRUC
KRRRRRS
WE'RE RIGHT BELOW IT!!

GREAT ZAPFISH

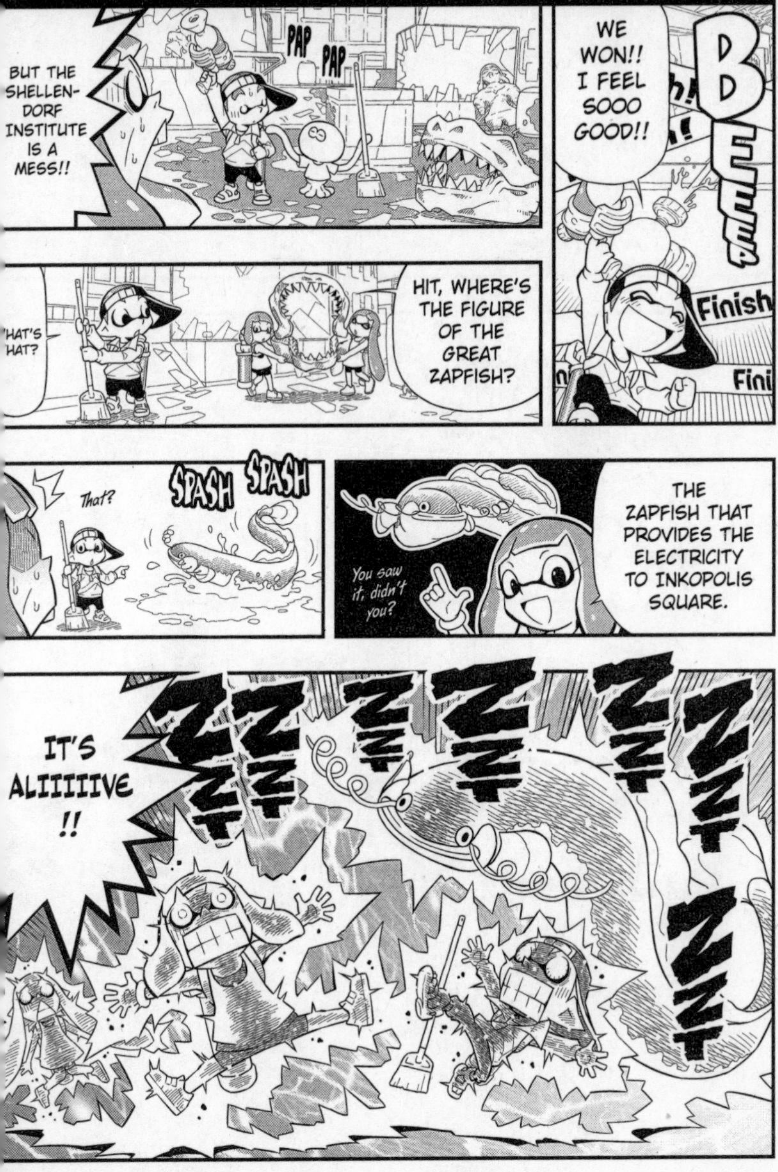

WE WON!! I FEEL SOOO GOOD!!
BEEEEP
Finish
Fini
BUT THE SHELLEN-DORF INSTITUTE IS A MESS!!
PAP PAP
HIT, WHERE'S THE FIGURE OF THE GREAT ZAPFISH?
THE ZAPFISH THAT PROVIDES THE ELECTRICITY TO INKOPOLIS SQUARE.
You saw it, didn't you?
That?
SPASH SPASH
ZZZT ZZZT ZZZT ZZZT ZZZT ZZZT ZZZT
IT'S ALIIIIIVE !!

Splatoon SQUID KIDS COMEDY SHOW

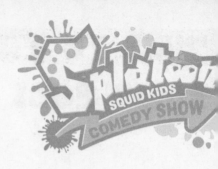

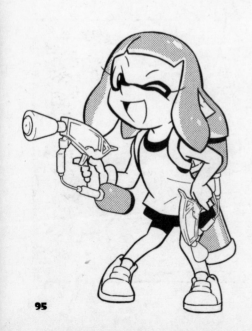

TIME TO CHILL WITH SOME COOL MUSIC!

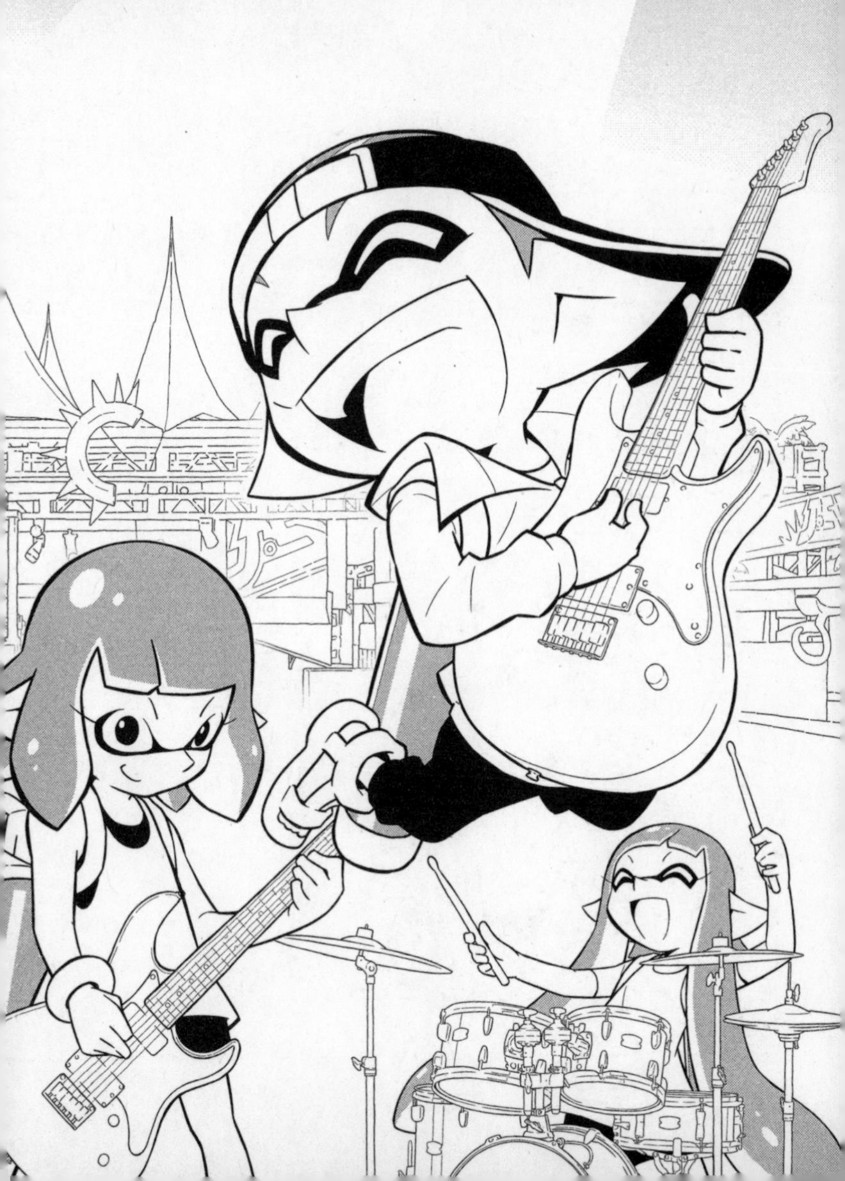

STARFISH MAINSTAGE

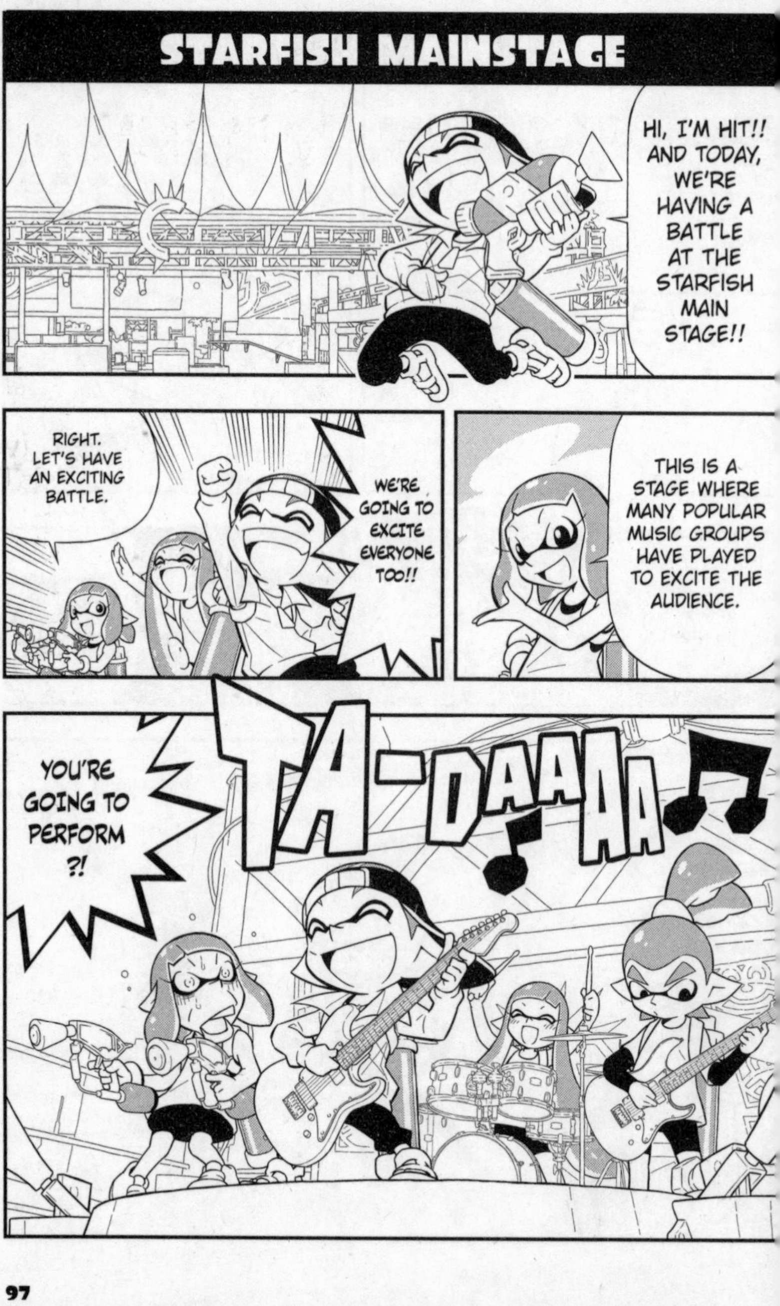
HI, I'M HIT!! AND TODAY, WE'RE HAVING A BATTLE AT THE STARFISH MAIN STAGE!!
THIS IS A STAGE WHERE MANY POPULAR MUSIC GROUPS HAVE PLAYED TO EXCITE THE AUDIENCE.
RIGHT. LET'S HAVE AN EXCITING BATTLE.
WE'RE GOING TO EXCITE EVERYONE TOO!!
TA-DAAAA
YOU'RE GOING TO PERFORM ?!

BATTLE FOR THE CENTER

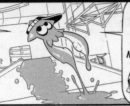

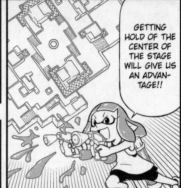

GETTING HOLD OF THE CENTER OF THE STAGE WILL GIVE US AN ADVANTAGE!!
LEAVE IT TO ME, MAIKA!!
I'M THE FIRST ONE AT THE CENTER OF THE STAGE!!
I'M... GETTING THERE FIRST!!
SPLAM
SO MY OPPONENT TODAY IS TWEEDY KOU, HUH?
KRRRSH
IT'S THREE D'S, FOR DAPPER, DEBONAIR AND DOLLARS!!
THIS IS MINE!!
NO, I GOT IT FIRST!!
YOU'RE FIGHTING OVER THE MICROPHONE ON THE CENTER STAGE?!

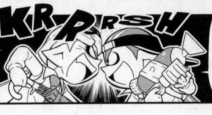

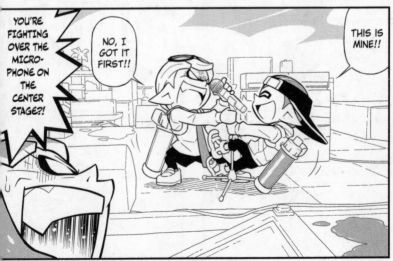

MICROPHONE STAND

I FOUND THE MICRO-PHONE!!
THIS IS A TURF WAR!!
DASH
THIS MICRO-PHONE'S SO LOW...
WHO WAS USING IT BEFORE ME?
SHUUUP
TA-
DA-
DA-
DAA
IT WAS A SUCTION BOMB!!
KRA-

MICROPHONE WITH A CORD

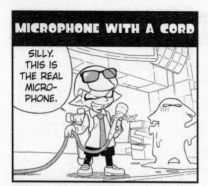

SILLY. THIS IS THE REAL MICRO-PHONE.
OKAY, HERE IT GOES!!
B-BAM
B-BAM
SPLUUB
IT'S A WEAPON!!
H-3 NOZZLENOSE

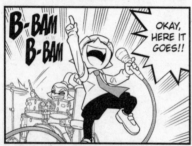

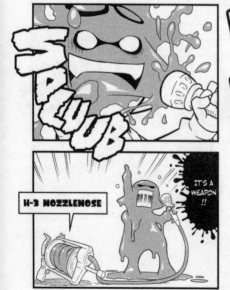

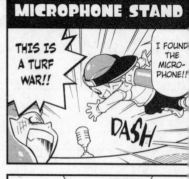

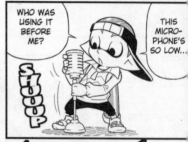

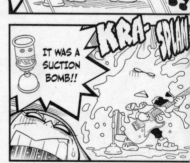

SING FOR BOOYAHS

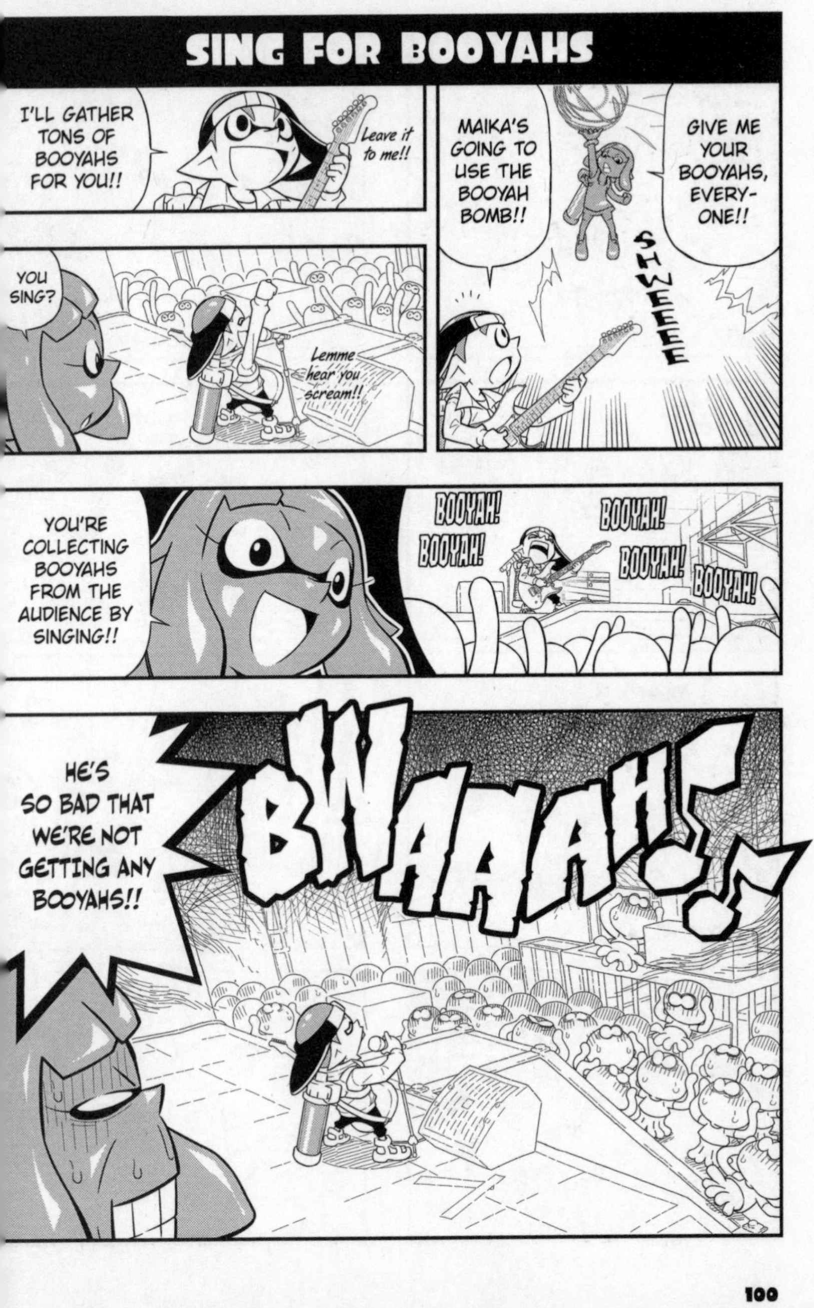
GIVE ME YOUR BOOYAHS, EVERY-ONE!!
MAIKA'S GOING TO USE THE BOOYAH BOMB!!
SHWEEEE
I'LL GATHER TONS OF BOOYAHS FOR YOU!!
Leave it to me!!
YOU SING?
Lemme hear you scream!!
BOOYAH!
BOOYAH!
BOOYAH!
BOOYAH!
BOOYAH!
YOU'RE COLLECTING BOOYAHS FROM THE AUDIENCE BY SINGING!!
BWAAAH!
HE'S SO BAD THAT WE'RE NOT GETTING ANY BOOYAHS!!

UNMOVING TEAMMATES

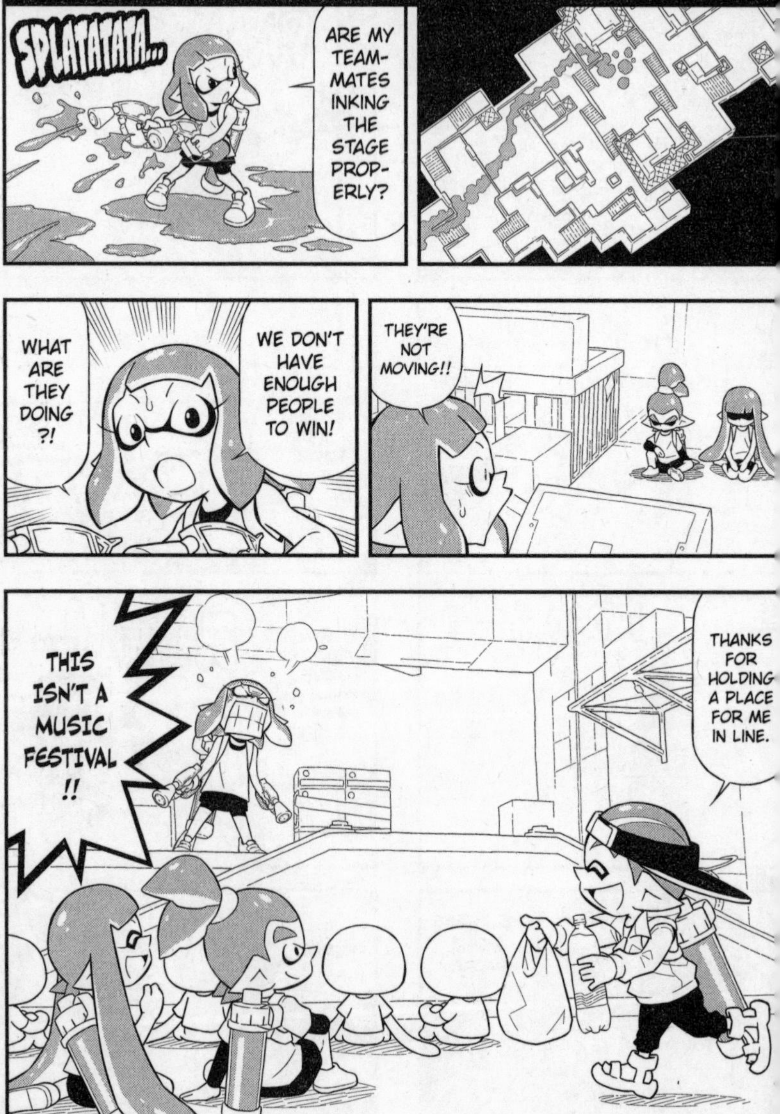
ARE MY TEAM-MATES INKING THE STAGE PROP-ERLY?
SPLATATATA...
THEY'RE NOT MOVING!!
WE DON'T HAVE ENOUGH PEOPLE TO WIN!
WHAT ARE THEY DOING?!
THANKS FOR HOLDING A PLACE FOR ME IN LINE.
THIS ISN'T A MUSIC FESTIVAL!!

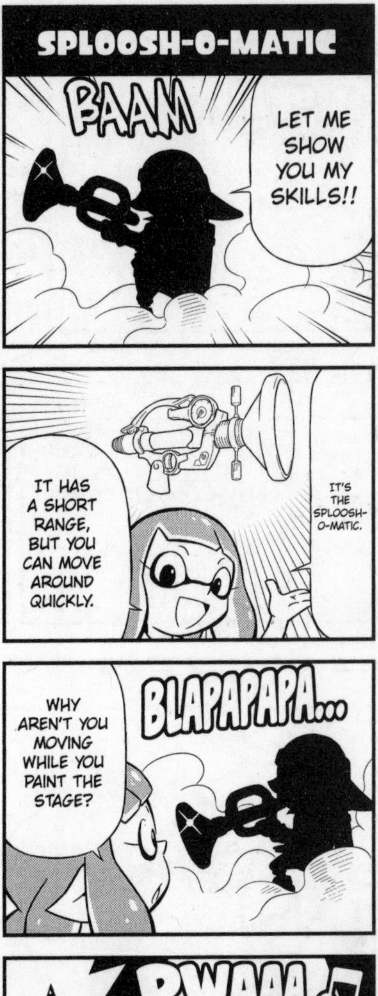
SPLOOSH-O-MATIC
LET ME SHOW YOU MY SKILLS!!
BAAM
IT'S THE SPLOOSH-O-MATIC.
IT HAS A SHORT RANGE, BUT YOU CAN MOVE AROUND QUICKLY.
BLAPAPAPA...
WHY AREN'T YOU MOVING WHILE YOU PAINT THE STAGE?
PWAAA ♪
A TRUMPET!!
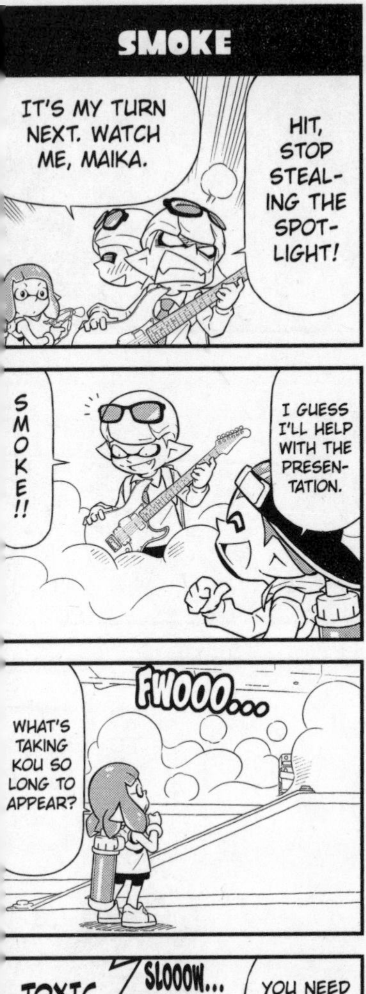
SMOKE
HIT, STOP STEALING THE SPOTLIGHT!
IT'S MY TURN NEXT. WATCH ME, MAIKA.
I GUESS I'LL HELP WITH THE PRESENTATION.
SMOKE!!
FWOOO...
WHAT'S TAKING KOU SO LONG TO APPEAR?
YOU NEED MORE SMOKE?
SLOOOW...
TOXIC MIST!!
A sub weapon that slows you down.

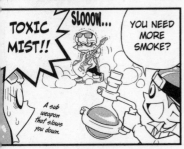

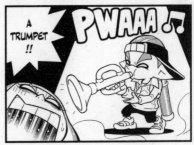

BULLETPROOF BALLER

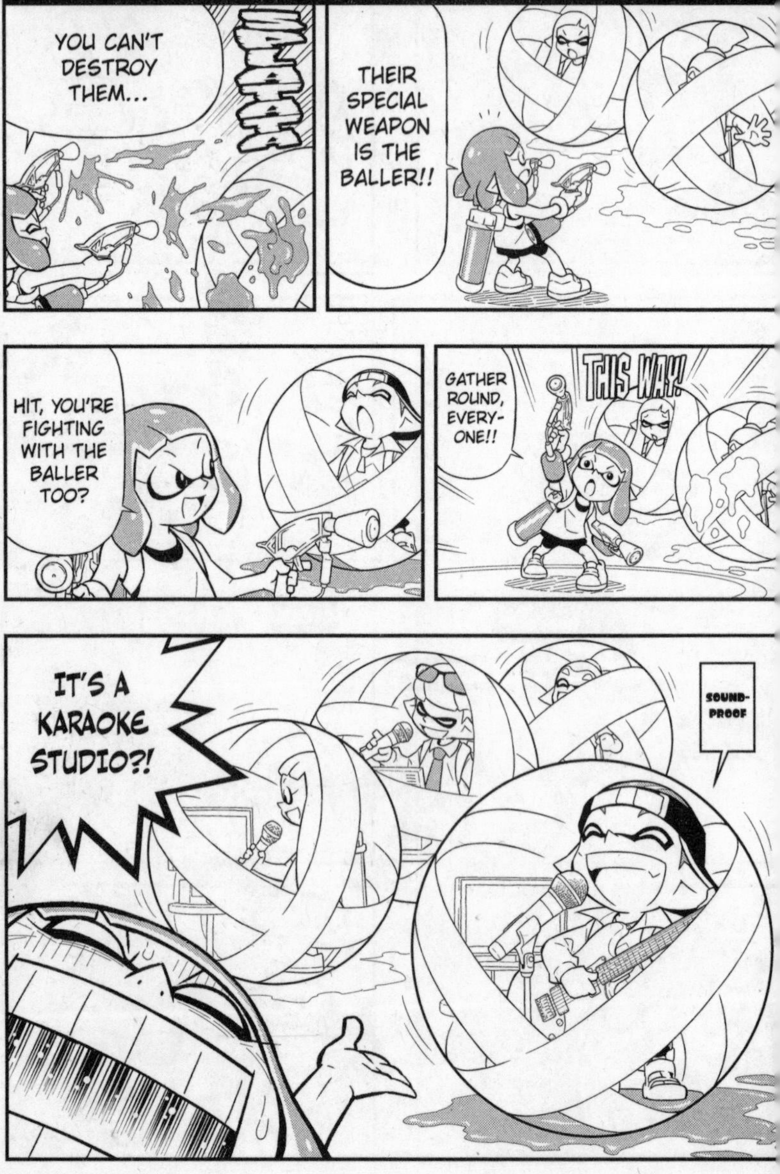

THEIR SPECIAL WEAPON IS THE BALLER!!
YOU CAN'T DESTROY THEM...
THIS WAY!
GATHER ROUND, EVERY-ONE!!
HIT, YOU'RE FIGHTING WITH THE BALLER TOO?
SOUND-PROOF
IT'S A KARAOKE STUDIO?!

JUDGE

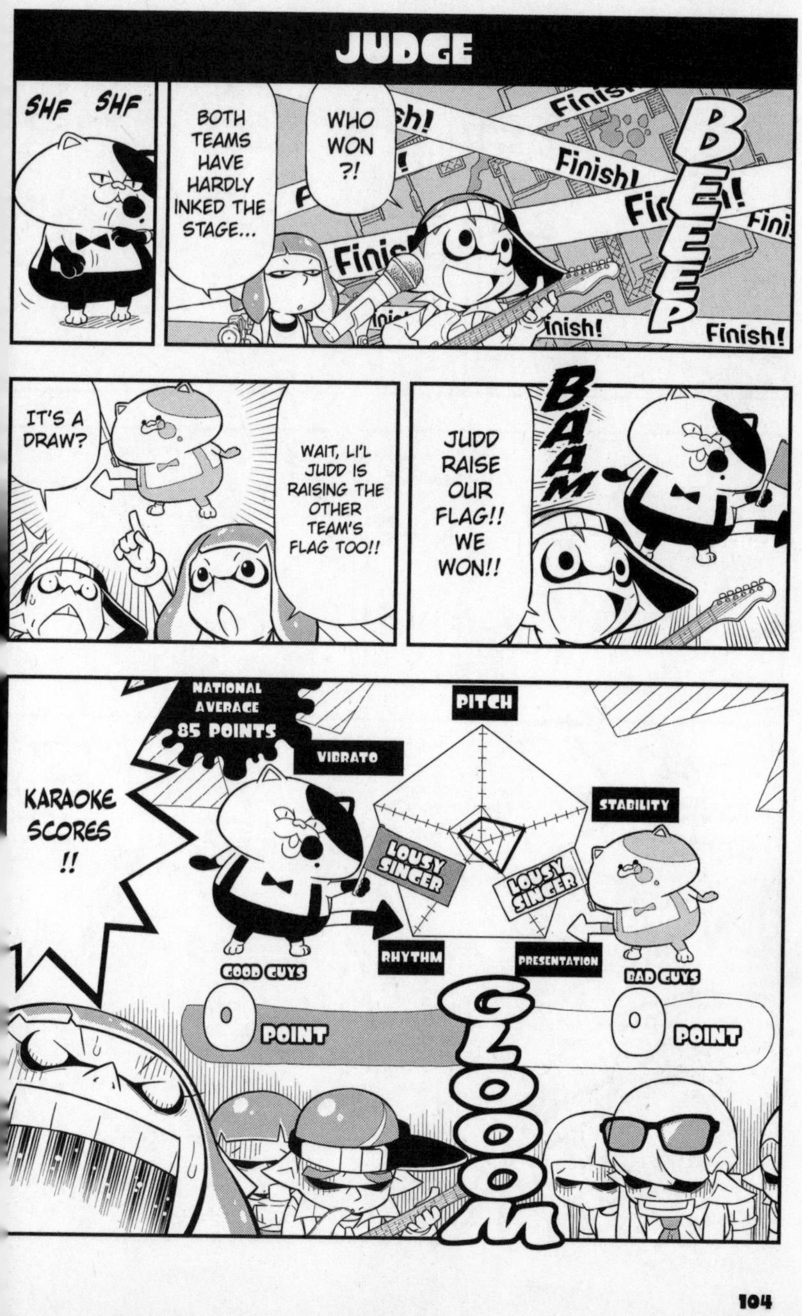

BEEEP
Finish!
Finish!
WHO WON ?!
BOTH TEAMS HAVE HARDLY INKED THE STAGE...
SHF SHF
BAAM
JUDD RAISE OUR FLAG!! WE WON!!
WAIT, LI'L JUDD IS RAISING THE OTHER TEAM'S FLAG TOO!!
IT'S A DRAW?
PITCH
NATIONAL AVERAGE 85 POINTS
VIBRATO
STABILITY
KARAOKE SCORES !!
LOUSY SINGER
LOUSY SINGER
PRESENTATION
RHYTHM
BAD GUYS
0 POINT
GLOOOM
GOOD GUYS
0 POINT

Splatoon
SQUID KIDS
COMEDY SHOW

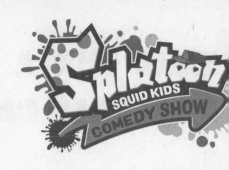

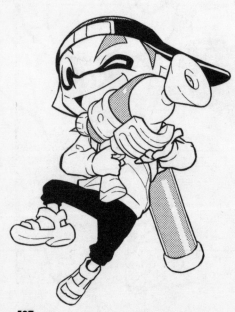

TIME FOR A BASEBALL BATTLE!

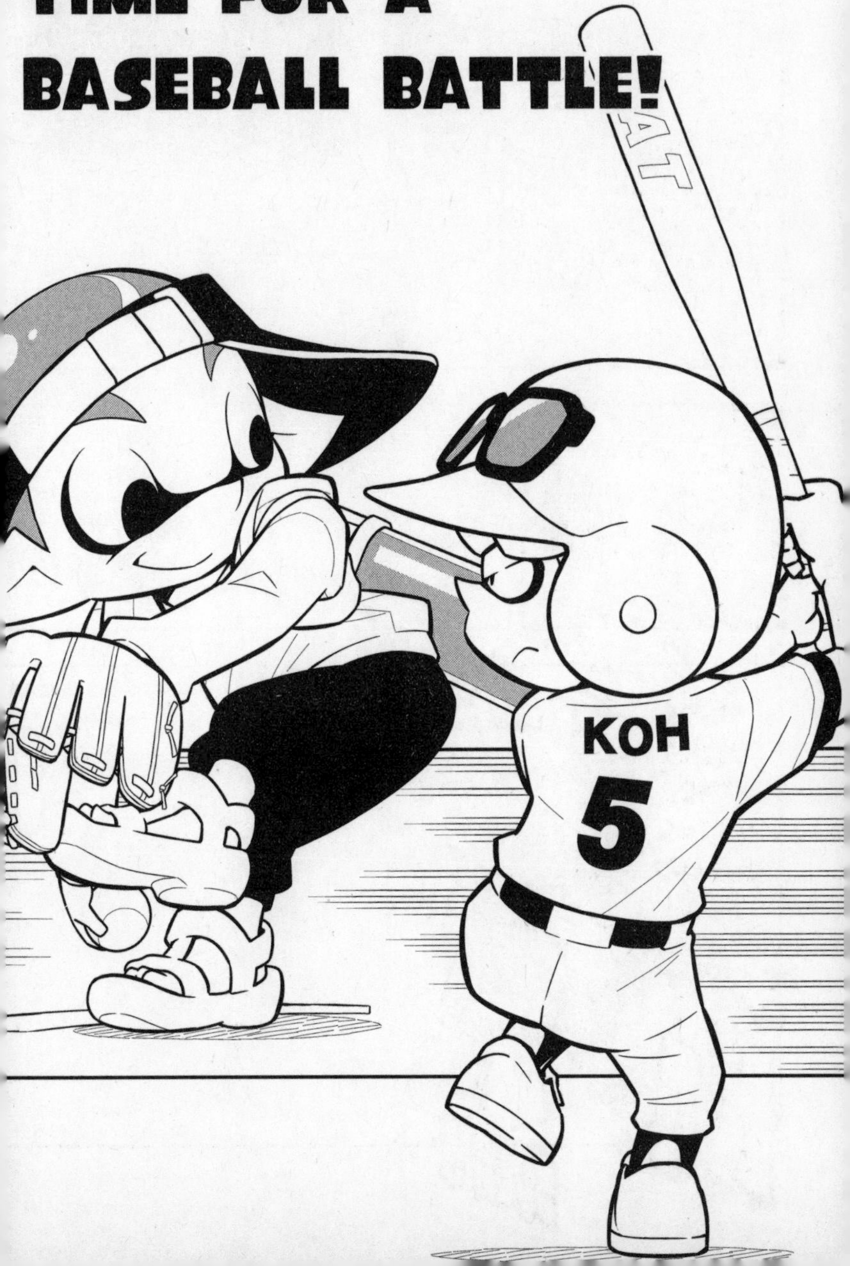
KOH
5

BASEBALL

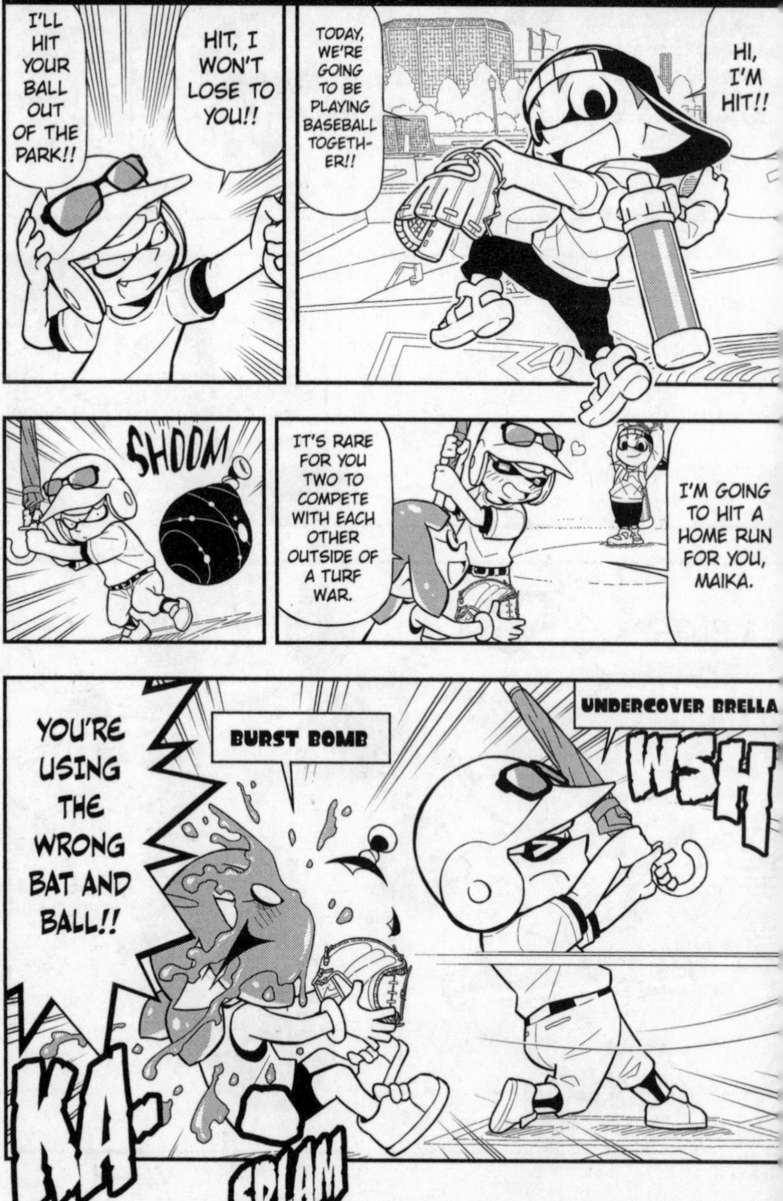
HI, I'M HIT!!
TODAY, WE'RE GOING TO BE PLAYING BASEBALL TOGETH-ER!!
HIT, I WON'T LOSE TO YOU!!
I'LL HIT YOUR BALL OUT OF THE PARK!!
I'M GOING TO HIT A HOME RUN FOR YOU, MAIKA.
IT'S RARE FOR YOU TWO TO COMPETE WITH EACH OTHER OUTSIDE OF A TURF WAR.
SHOOM
UNDERCOVER BRELLA
WSH
BURST BOMB
YOU'RE USING THE WRONG BAT AND BALL!!
KA-
SPLAM

SPECIAL PITCH

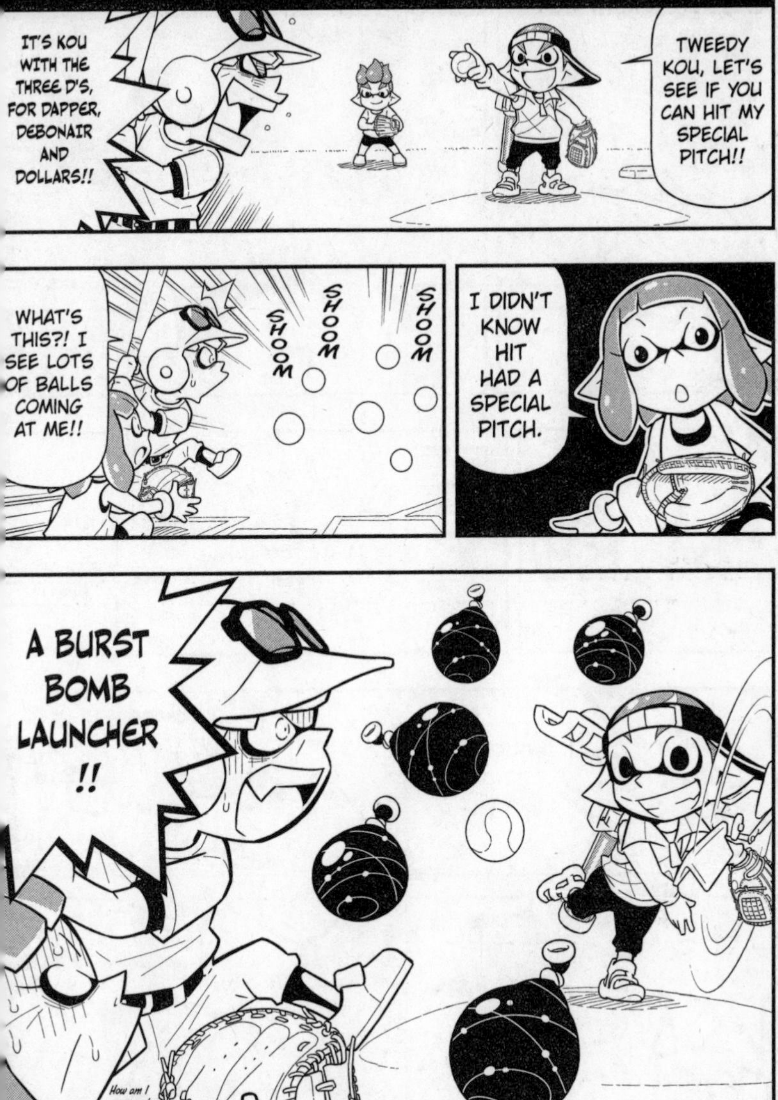

TWEEDY KOU, LET'S SEE IF YOU CAN HIT MY SPECIAL PITCH!!
IT'S KOU WITH THE THREE D'S, FOR DAPPER, DEBONAIR AND DOLLARS!!
I DIDN'T KNOW HIT HAD A SPECIAL PITCH.
SHOOM
SHOOM
SHOOM
WHAT'S THIS?! I SEE LOTS OF BALLS COMING AT ME!!
A BURST BOMB LAUNCHER!!
How am I supposed to catch those?

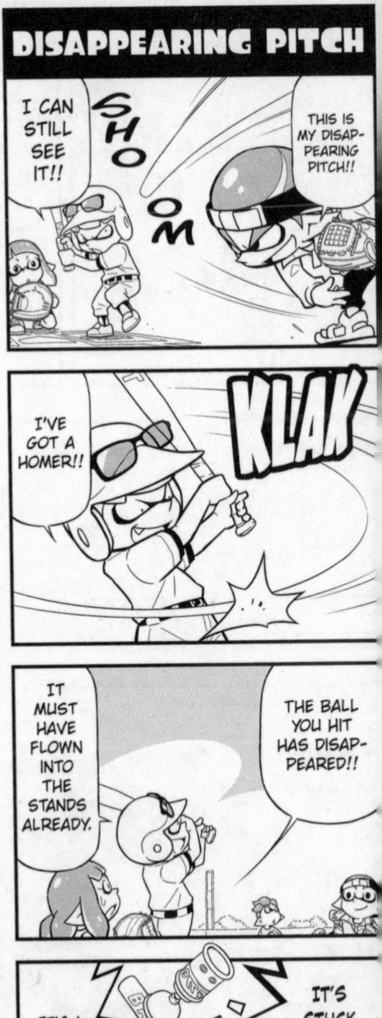
DISAPPEARING PITCH
THIS IS MY DISAP-PEARING PITCH!!
SHOOM
I CAN STILL SEE IT!!
KLAK
I'VE GOT A HOMER!!
THE BALL YOU HIT HAS DISAP-PEARED!!
IT MUST HAVE FLOWN INTO THE STANDS ALREADY.
IT'S STUCK ON YOUR BAT!!
IT'S A SUCTION BOMB!!

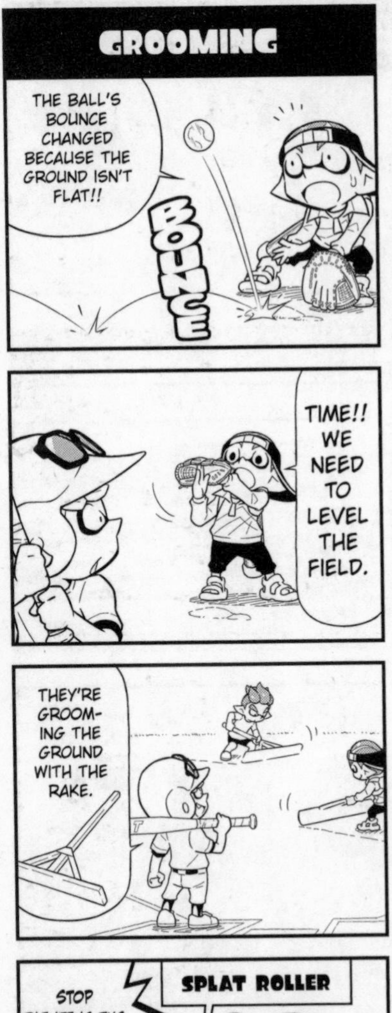
GROOMING
THE BALL'S BOUNCE CHANGED BECAUSE THE GROUND ISN'T FLAT!!
BOUNCE
TIME!! WE NEED TO LEVEL THE FIELD.
THEY'RE GROOM-ING THE GROUND WITH THE RAKE.
SPLAT ROLLER
SLISH
SLISH
STOP PAINTING THE FIELD WITH YOUR INK !!

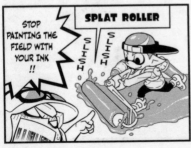

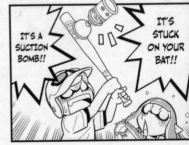

INK GROUND

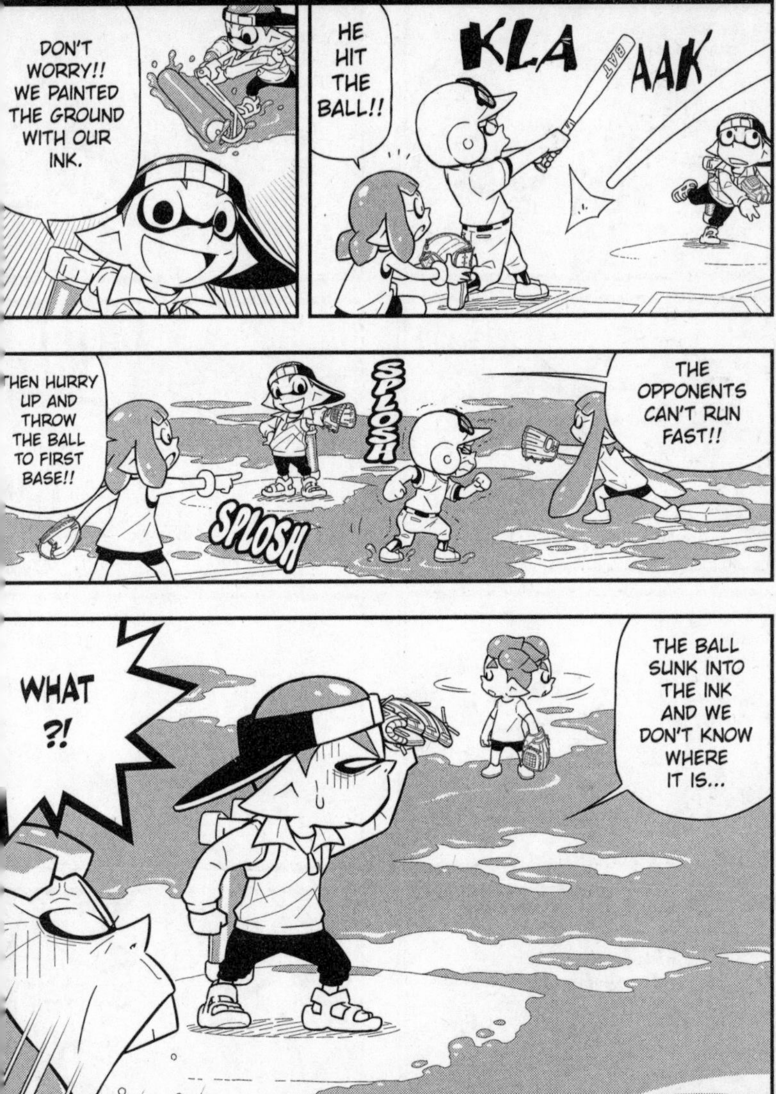
HE HIT THE BALL!!
KLA AAK
BAT
DON'T WORRY!! WE PAINTED THE GROUND WITH OUR INK.
THE OPPONENTS CAN'T RUN FAST!!
SPLOSH
THEN HURRY UP AND THROW THE BALL TO FIRST BASE!!
SPLOSH
THE BALL SUNK INTO THE INK AND WE DON'T KNOW WHERE IT IS...
WHAT ?!

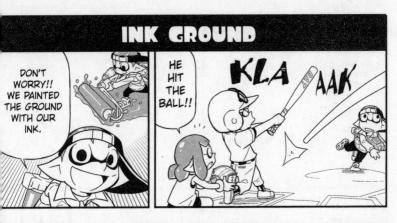

FAST RUNNER

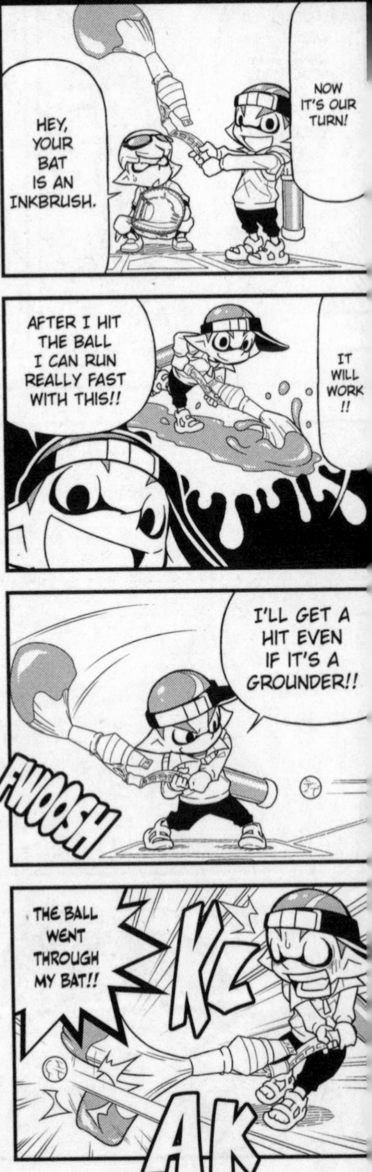
NOW IT'S OUR TURN!
HEY, YOUR BAT IS AN INKBRUSH.
IT WILL WORK!!
AFTER I HIT THE BALL I CAN RUN REALLY FAST WITH THIS!!
I'LL GET A HIT EVEN IF IT'S A GROUNDER!!
FWOOSH
KLAK
THE BALL WENT THROUGH MY BAT!!

SQUID RUNNING

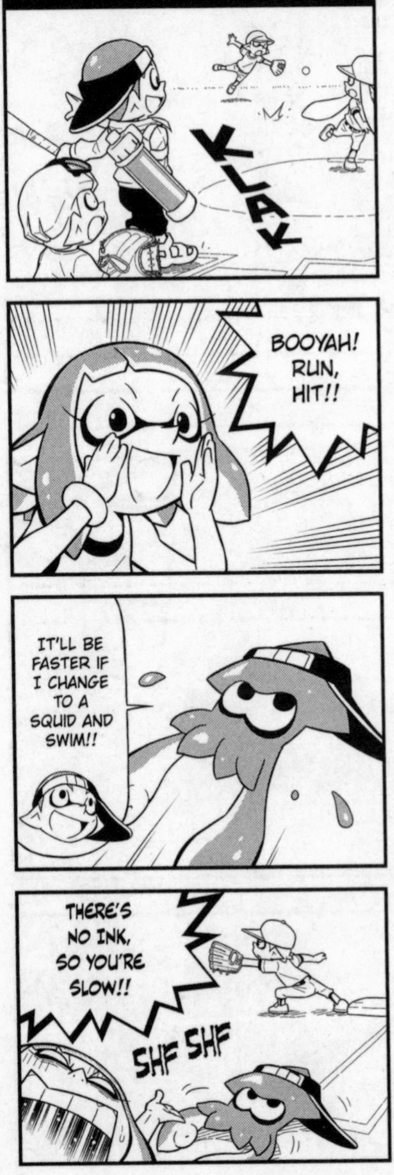
KLAK
BOOYAH! RUN, HIT!!
IT'LL BE FASTER IF I CHANGE TO A SQUID AND SWIM!!
THERE'S NO INK, SO YOU'RE SLOW!!
SHF SHF

BEAKON BACK

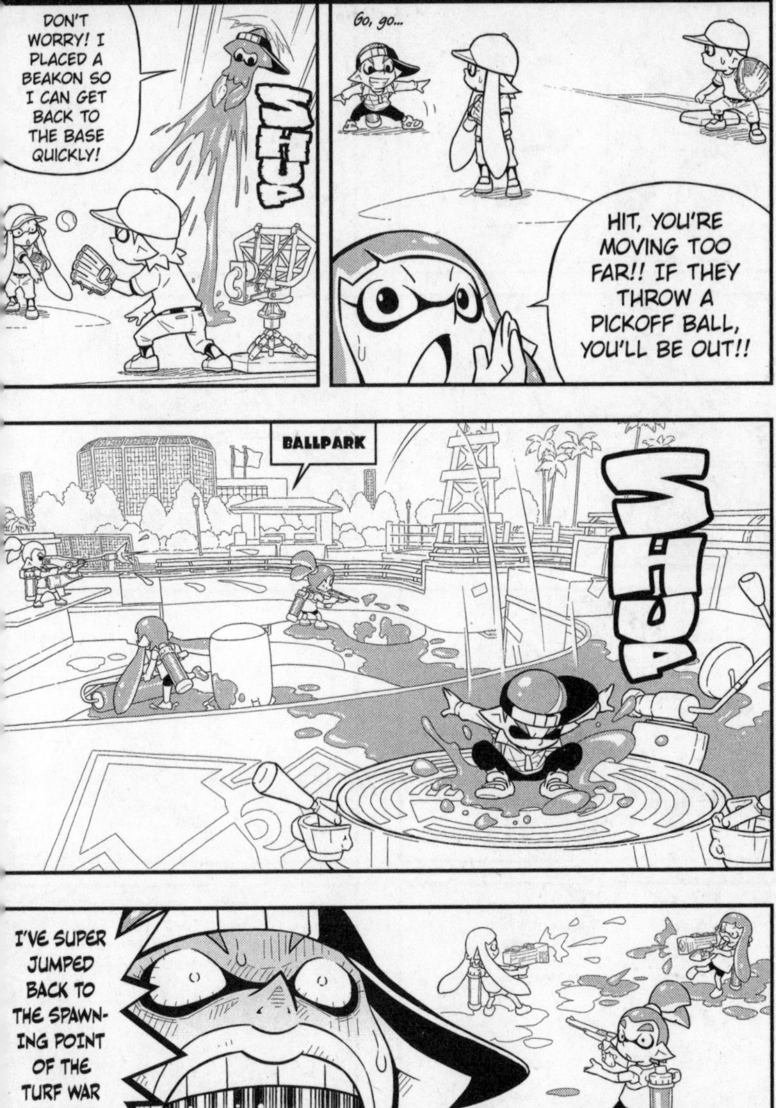

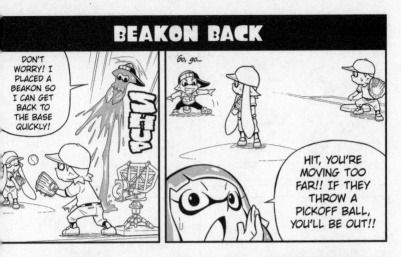

Go, go...
HIT, YOU'RE MOVING TOO FAR!! IF THEY THROW A PICKOFF BALL, YOU'LL BE OUT!!
DON'T WORRY! I PLACED A BEAKON SO I CAN GET BACK TO THE BASE QUICKLY!
BALLPARK
I'VE SUPER JUMPED BACK TO THE SPAWN-ING POINT OF THE TURF WAR STAGE!!

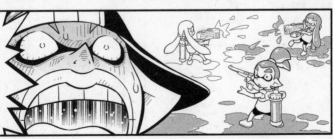

BACK HOME

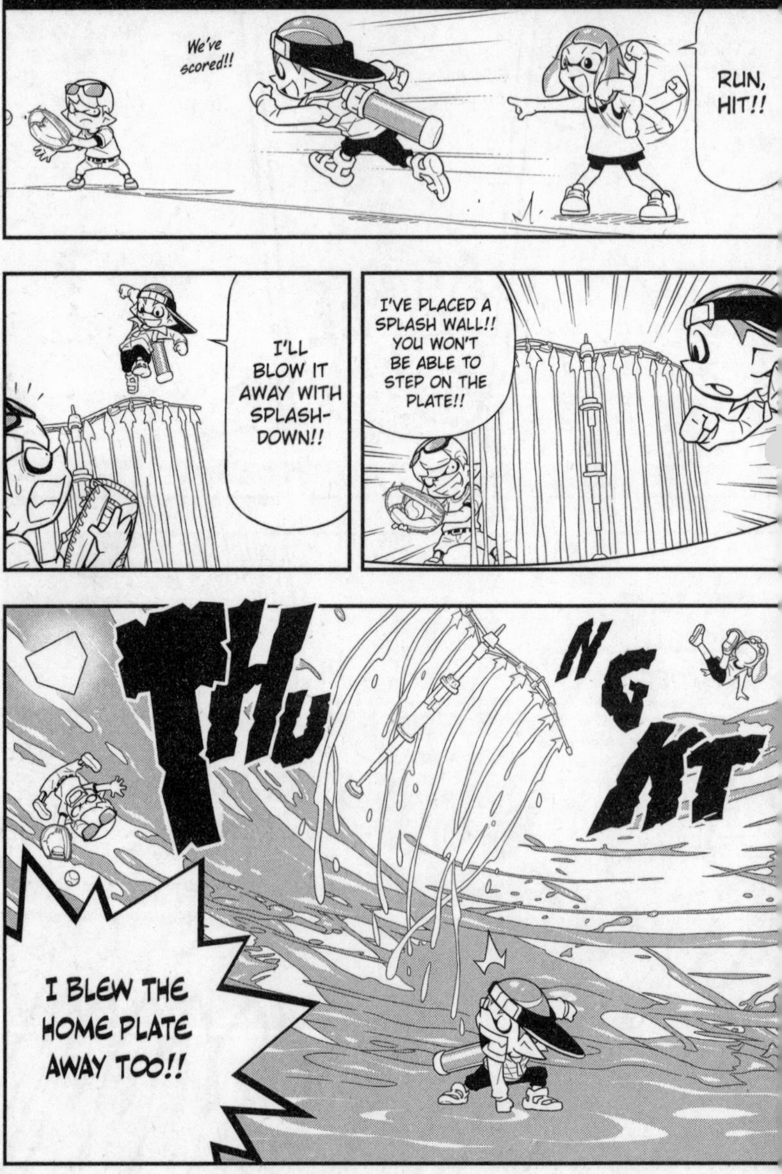
RUN, HIT!!
We've scored!!
I'VE PLACED A SPLASH WALL!! YOU WON'T BE ABLE TO STEP ON THE PLATE!!
I'LL BLOW IT AWAY WITH SPLASH-DOWN!!
THUNGKT
I BLEW THE HOME PLATE AWAY TOO!!

SPECIAL ATTACKS

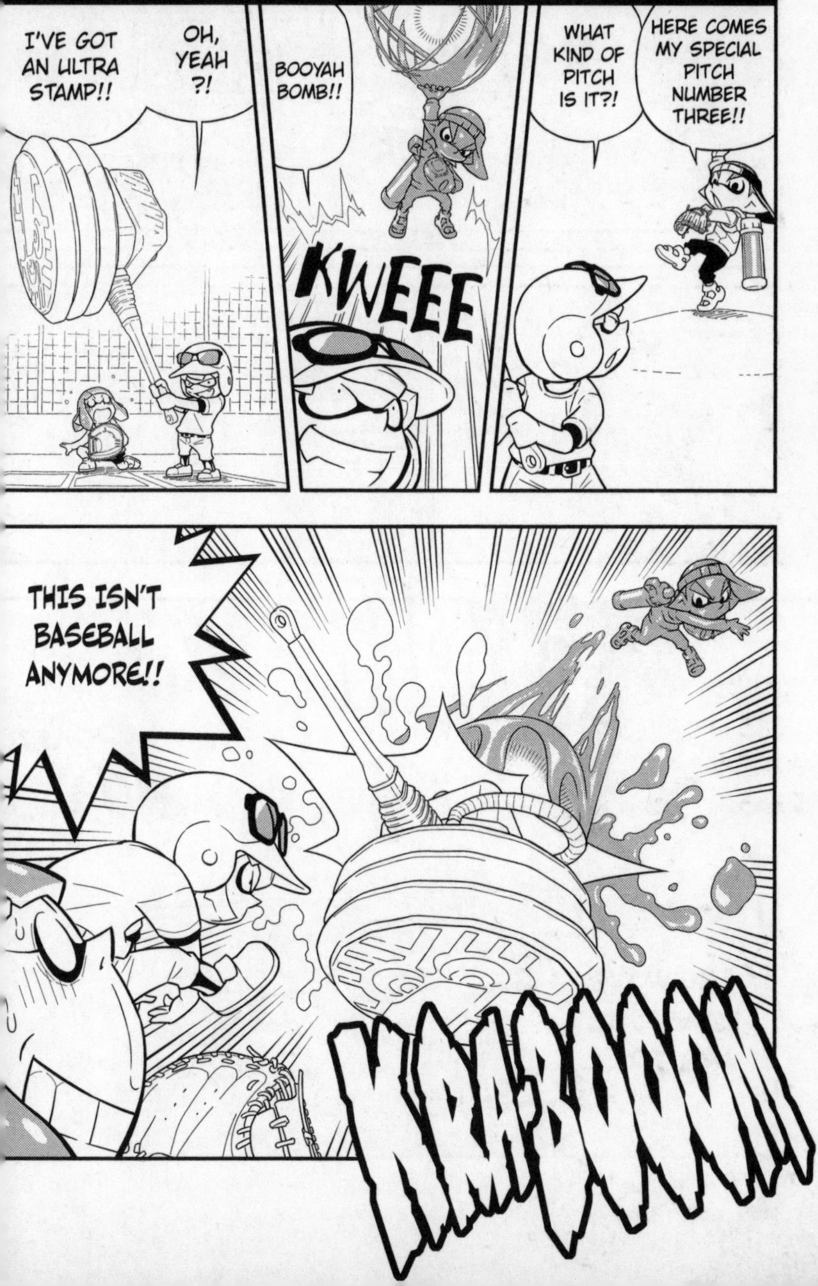

HERE COMES MY SPECIAL PITCH NUMBER THREE!!
WHAT KIND OF PITCH IS IT?!
BOOYAH BOMB!!
KWEEE
OH, YEAH ?!
I'VE GOT AN ULTRA STAMP!!
THIS ISN'T BASEBALL ANYMORE!!
KRA-BOOOM

BALL GATHERING

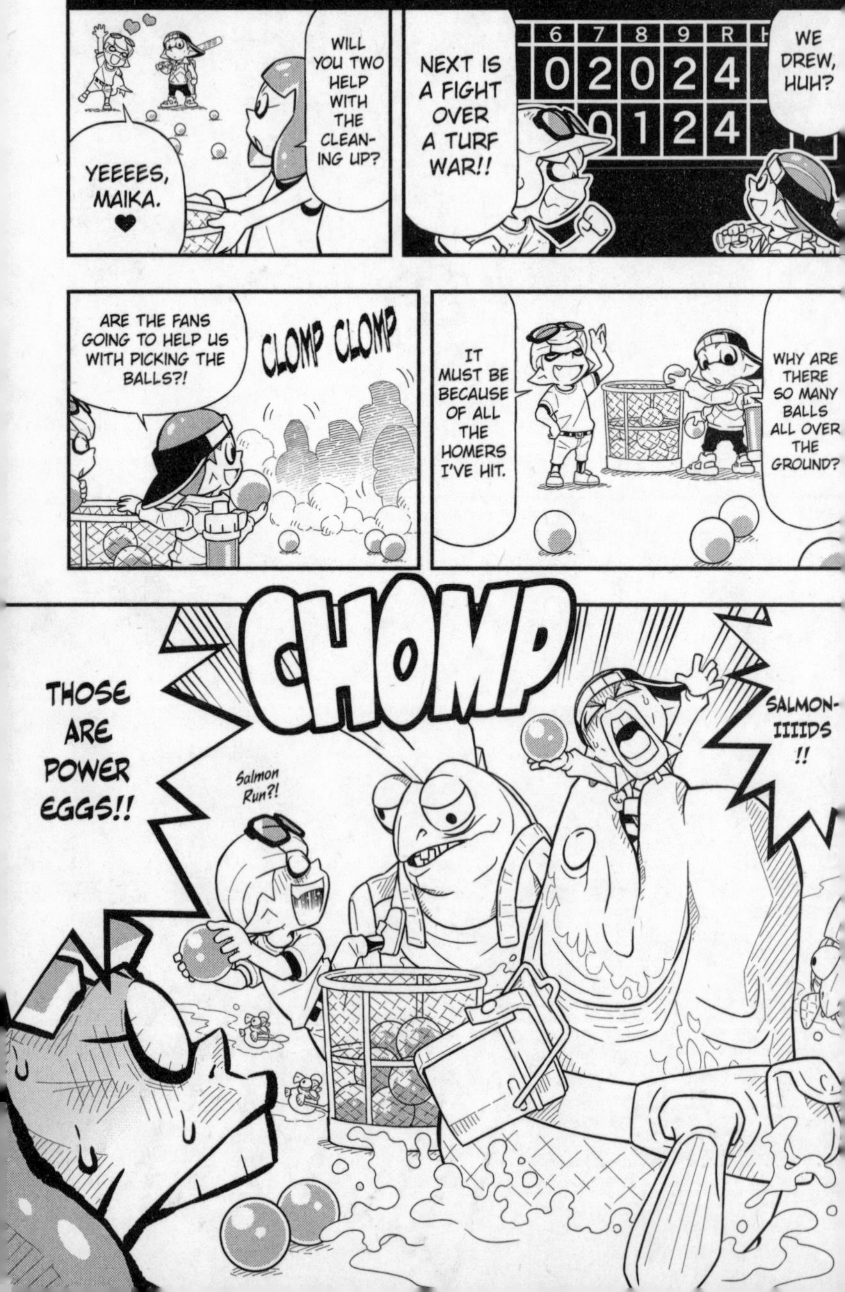
WE DREW, HUH?
6 7 8 9 R H
0 2 0 2 4
0 1 2 4
NEXT IS A FIGHT OVER A TURF WAR!!
WILL YOU TWO HELP WITH THE CLEAN-ING UP?
YEEEES, MAIKA. ♥
WHY ARE THERE SO MANY BALLS ALL OVER THE GROUND?
IT MUST BE BECAUSE OF ALL THE HOMERS I'VE HIT.
ARE THE FANS GOING TO HELP US WITH PICKING THE BALLS?!
CLOMP CLOMP
CHOMP
SALMON-IIIIDS !!
Salmon Run?!
THOSE ARE POWER EGGS!!

Splatoon
SQUID KIDS COMEDY SHOW

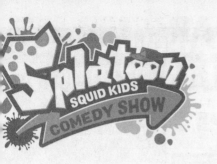

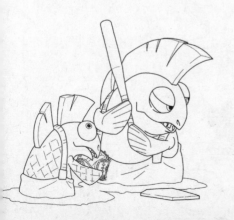

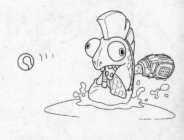

TIME TO PARTICIPATE IN THE FINAL SPLATFEST!

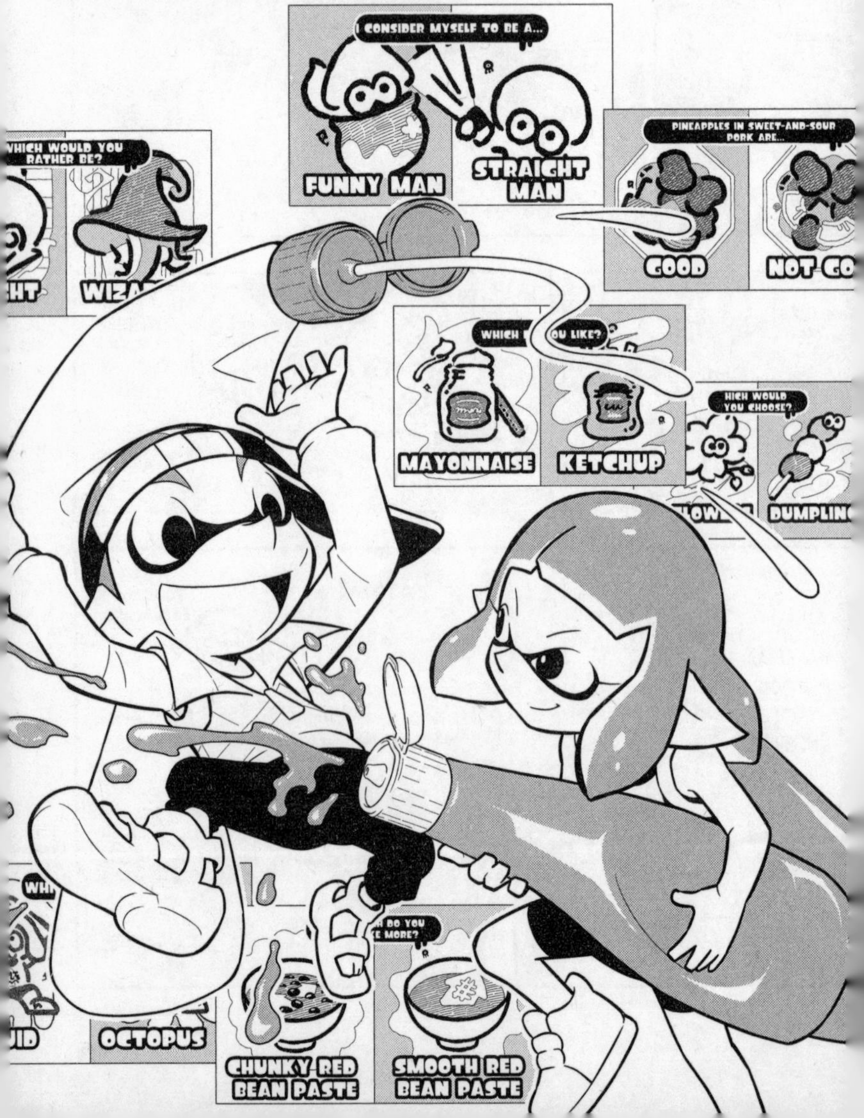
PINEAPPLES IN SWEET-AND-SOUR PORK ARE...
GOOD
CONSIDER MYSELF TO BE A...
STRAIGHT MAN
FUNNY MAN
WHICH WOULD YOU RATHER BE?
WOULD YOU CHOOSE?
KETCHUP
MAYONNAISE
SMOOTH RED BEAN PASTE
CHUNKY RED BEAN PASTE
OCTOPUS

SPLATFEST COMMENCES

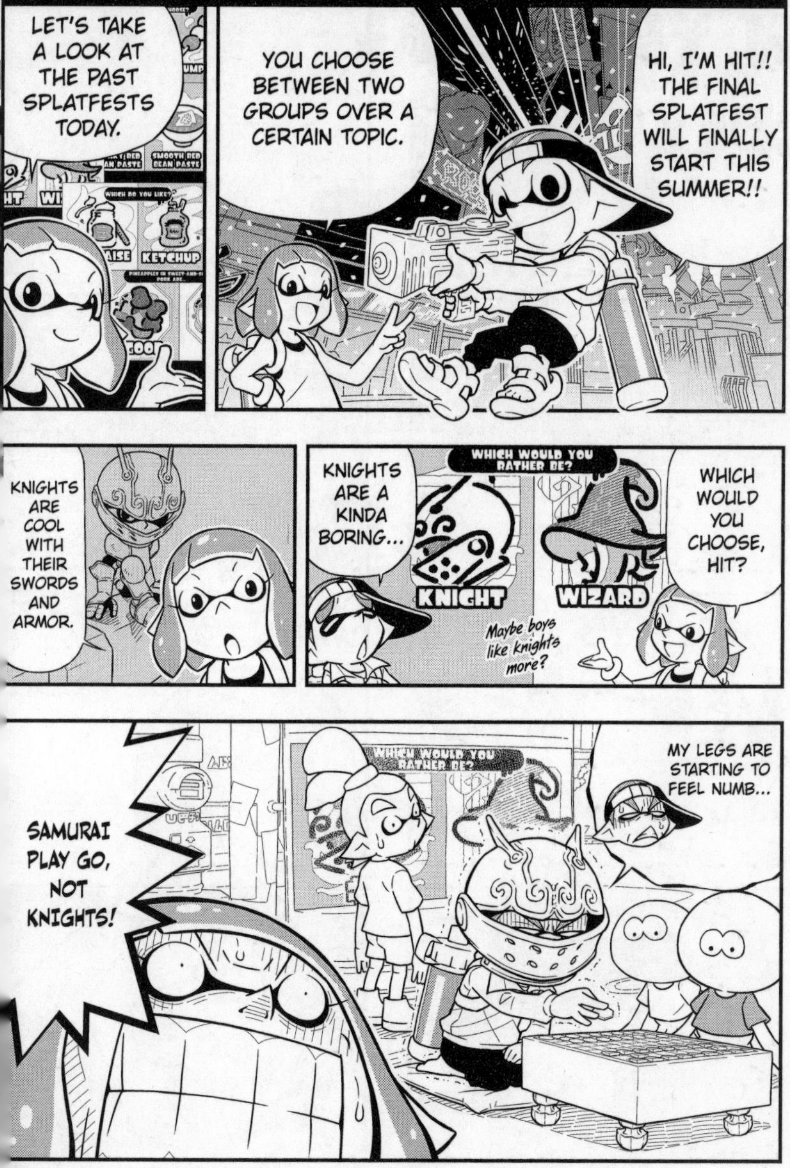
HI, I'M HIT!! THE FINAL SPLATFEST WILL FINALLY START THIS SUMMER!!
YOU CHOOSE BETWEEN TWO GROUPS OVER A CERTAIN TOPIC.
LET'S TAKE A LOOK AT THE PAST SPLATFESTS TODAY.
SMOOTH RED BEAN PASTE
WHICH DO YOU LIKE?
KETCHUP
WHICH WOULD YOU CHOOSE, HIT?
WHICH WOULD YOU RATHER BE?
KNIGHTS ARE A KINDA BORING...
KNIGHT
WIZARD
Maybe boys like knights more?
KNIGHTS ARE COOL WITH THEIR SWORDS AND ARMOR.
MY LEGS ARE STARTING TO FEEL NUMB...
WHICH WOULD YOU RATHER BE?
SAMURAI PLAY GO, NOT KNIGHTS!

FLOWERS VERSUS DUMPLINGS

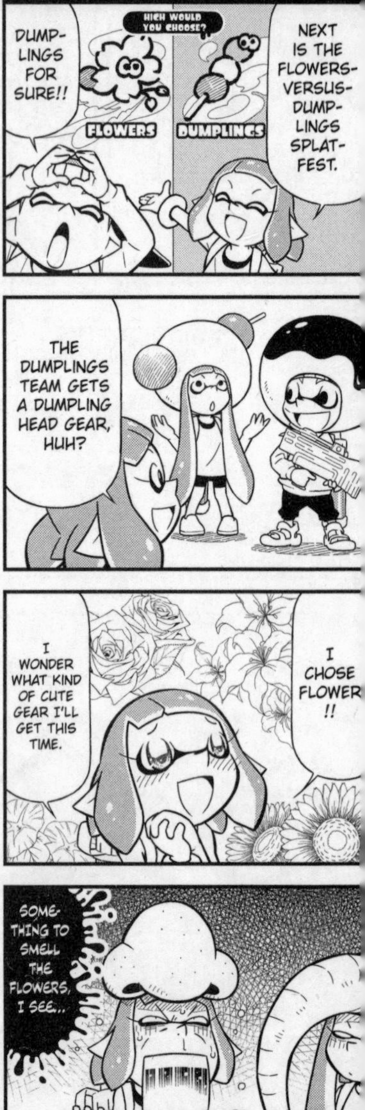
NEXT IS THE FLOWERS-VERSUS-DUMPLINGS SPLATFEST.
HICH WOULD YOU CHOOSE?
DUMPLINGS
FLOWERS
DUMPLINGS FOR SURE!!
THE DUMPLINGS TEAM GETS A DUMPLING HEAD GEAR, HUH?
I CHOSE FLOWER !!
I WONDER WHAT KIND OF CUTE GEAR I'LL GET THIS TIME.
SOMETHING TO SMELL THE FLOWERS, I SEE...

CHUNKY RED BEAN PASTE VERSUS SMOOTH RED BEAN PASTE

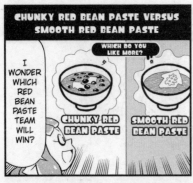

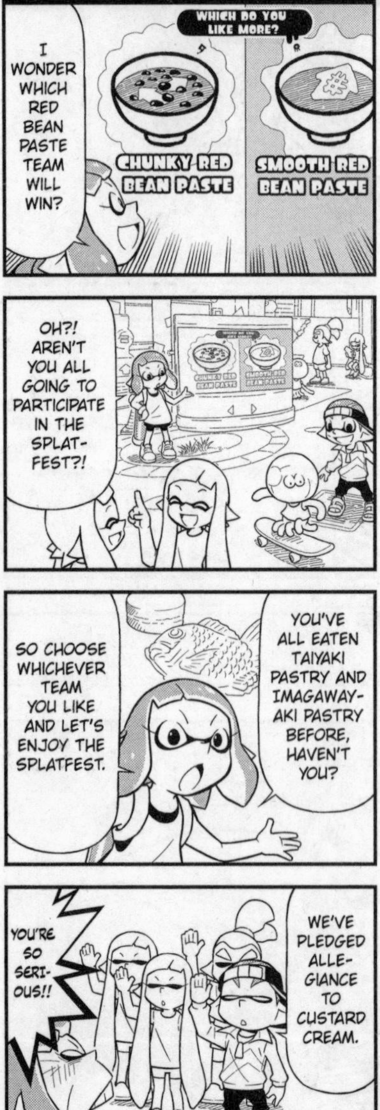
WHICH DO YOU LIKE MORE?
SMOOTH RED BEAN PASTE
CHUNKY RED BEAN PASTE
I WONDER WHICH RED BEAN PASTE TEAM WILL WIN?
OH?! AREN'T YOU ALL GOING TO PARTICIPATE IN THE SPLATFEST?!
YOU'VE ALL EATEN TAIYAKI PASTRY AND IMAGAWAYAKI PASTRY BEFORE, HAVEN'T YOU?
SO CHOOSE WHICHEVER TEAM YOU LIKE AND LET'S ENJOY THE SPLATFEST.
WE'VE PLEDGED ALLEGIANCE TO CUSTARD CREAM.
YOU'RE SO SERIOUS!!

MAYONNAISE VERSUS KETCHUP

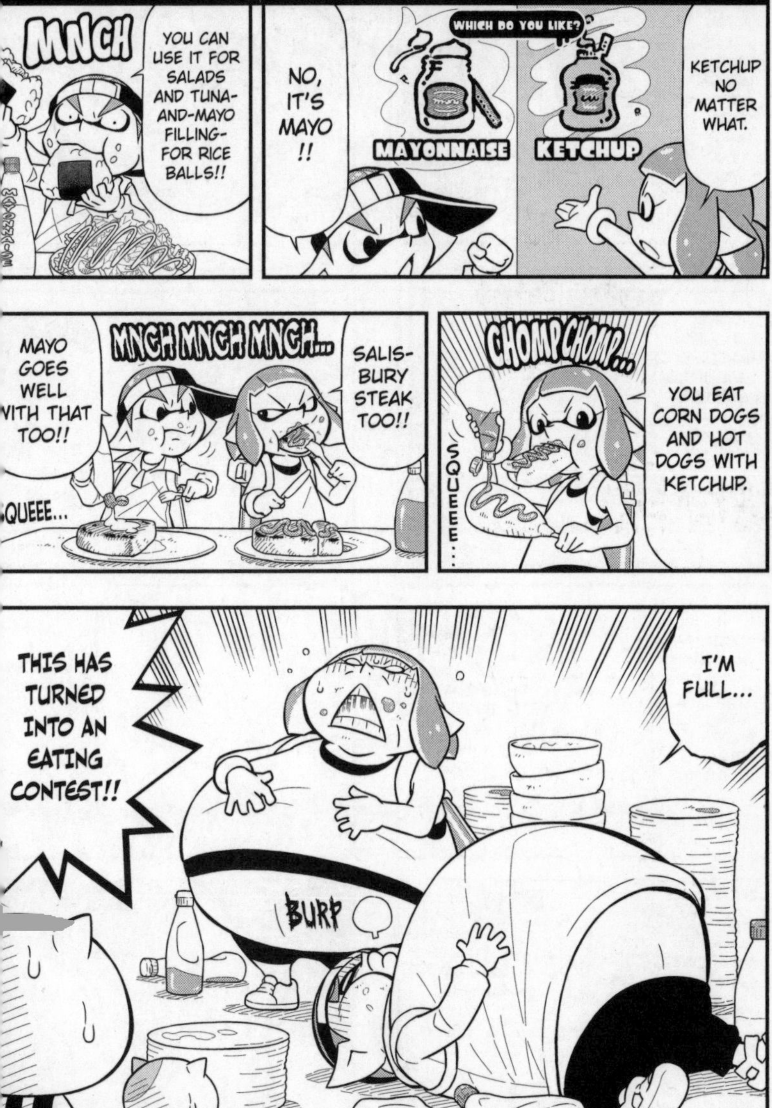
WHICH DO YOU LIKE?
MAYONNAISE
KETCHUP
KETCHUP NO MATTER WHAT.
NO, IT'S MAYO!!
MNCH
YOU CAN USE IT FOR SALADS AND TUNA-AND-MAYO FILLING-FOR RICE BALLS!!
MAYONNAISE
CHOMP CHOMP...
YOU EAT CORN DOGS AND HOT DOGS WITH KETCHUP.
SQUEEEE...
SALIS-BURY STEAK TOO!!
MNCH MNCH MNCH...
MAYO GOES WELL WITH THAT TOO!!
SQUEEE...
I'M FULL...
THIS HAS TURNED INTO AN EATING CONTEST!!
BURP

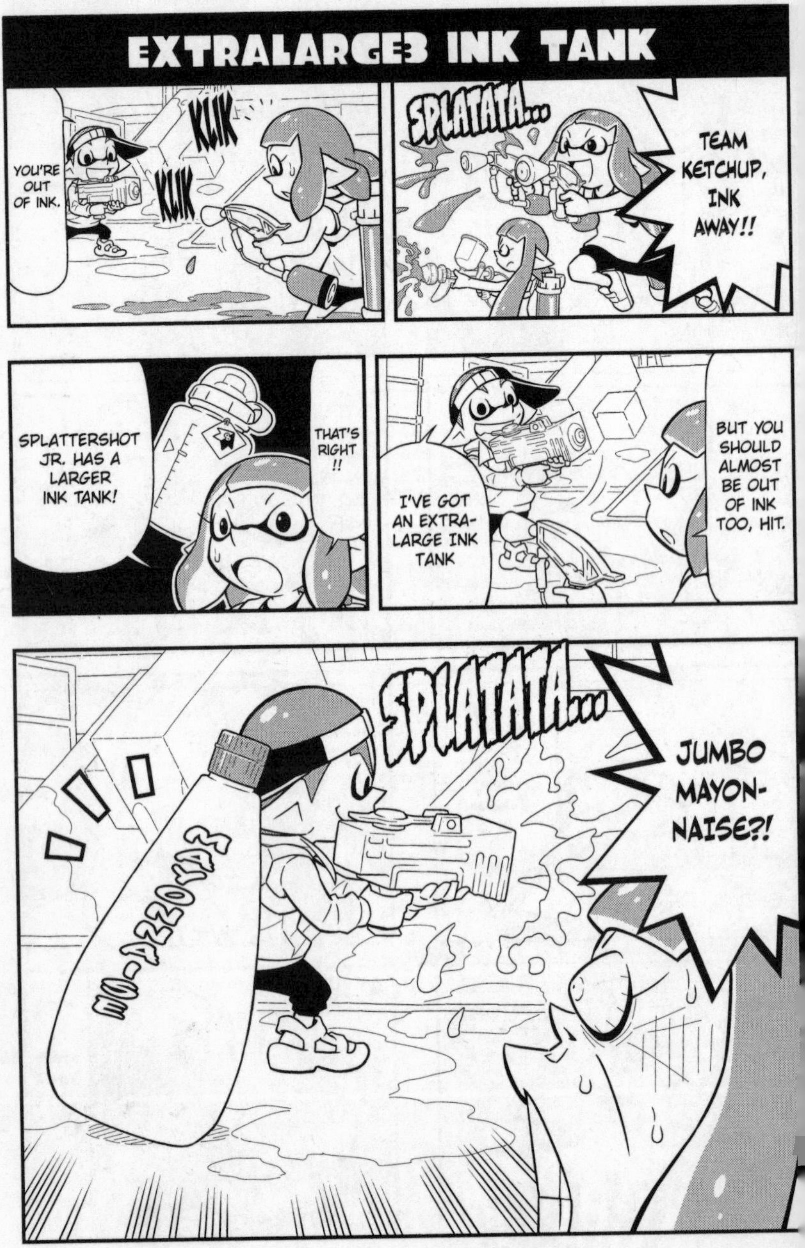
EXTRALARGE INK TANK
KLIK
KLIK
YOU'RE OUT OF INK.
SPLATATA...
TEAM KETCHUP, INK AWAY!!
SPLATTERSHOT JR. HAS A LARGER INK TANK!
THAT'S RIGHT!!
BUT YOU SHOULD ALMOST BE OUT OF INK TOO, HIT.
I'VE GOT AN EXTRA-LARGE INK TANK
SPLATATA...
JUMBO MAYON-NAISE?!
MO-A-ZZOYA?

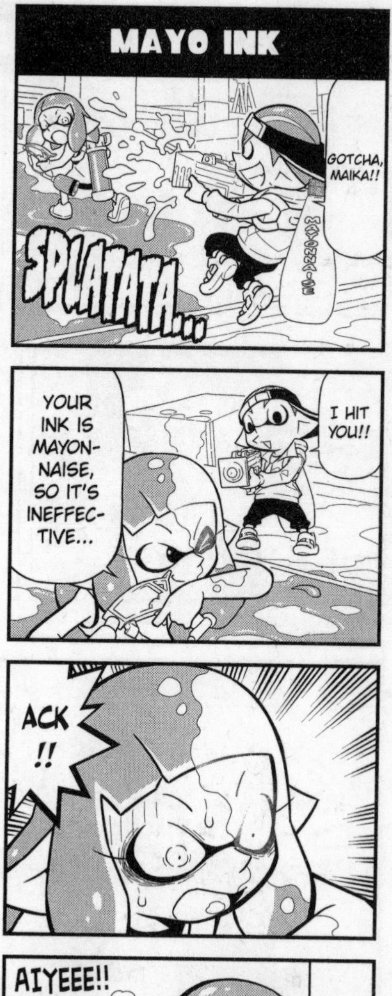
MAYO INK
GOTCHA, MAIKA!!
MAYONNAISE
SPLATATA...
I HIT YOU!!
YOUR INK IS MAYONNAISE, SO IT'S INEFFECTIVE...
ACK!!
MUSTARD MAYO
AIYEEE!!

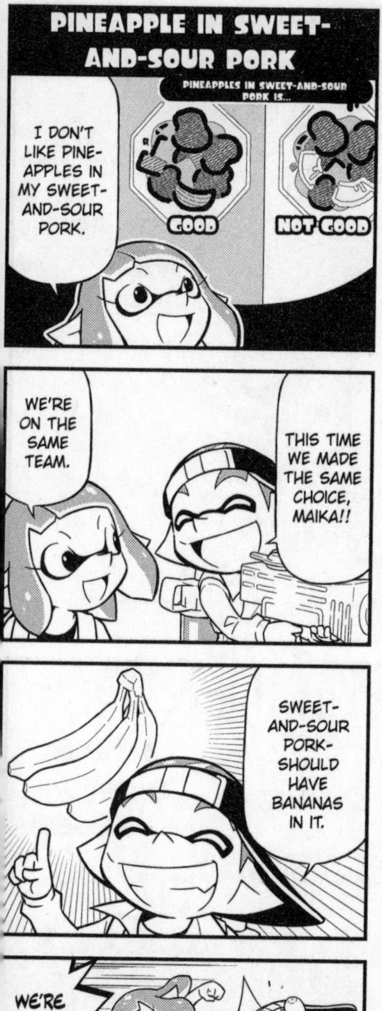
PINEAPPLE IN SWEET-AND-SOUR PORK
PINEAPPLES IN SWEET-AND-SOUR PORK IS...
NOT GOOD
GOOD
I DON'T LIKE PINEAPPLES IN MY SWEET-AND-SOUR PORK.
THIS TIME WE MADE THE SAME CHOICE, MAIKA!!
WE'RE ON THE SAME TEAM.
SWEET-AND-SOUR PORK-SHOULD HAVE BANANAS IN IT.
Go away!!
WE'RE NOT THE SAME!!
THUNGK

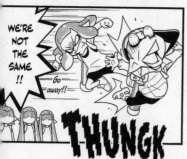

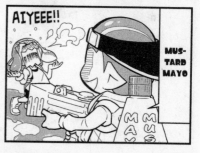

SQUID VERSUS OCTOPUS

WHICH WOULD YOU CHOOSE?
OCTOPUS
SQUID
LET'S GO, TEAM SQUID!!
SWSH
SPLATATATA...
GOOD, WE'VE WON!!
BEEEEP
Finish!
THE PERCENTAGE OF THE VOTES WILL ALSO AFFECT THE RESULT OF THE SPLATFEST!!
JELLYFISH
OCTOPUS
SQUID
90.00%
5.96%
4.04% POPULARITY
JELLY-FIIIIISH?!
BAAAM

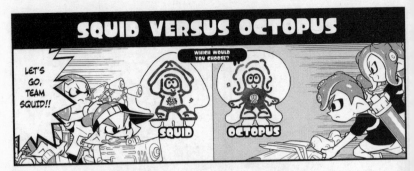

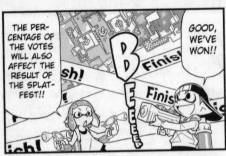

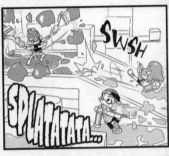

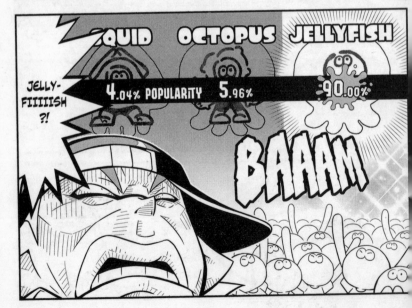

FUNNY MAN VERSUS STRAIGHT MAN

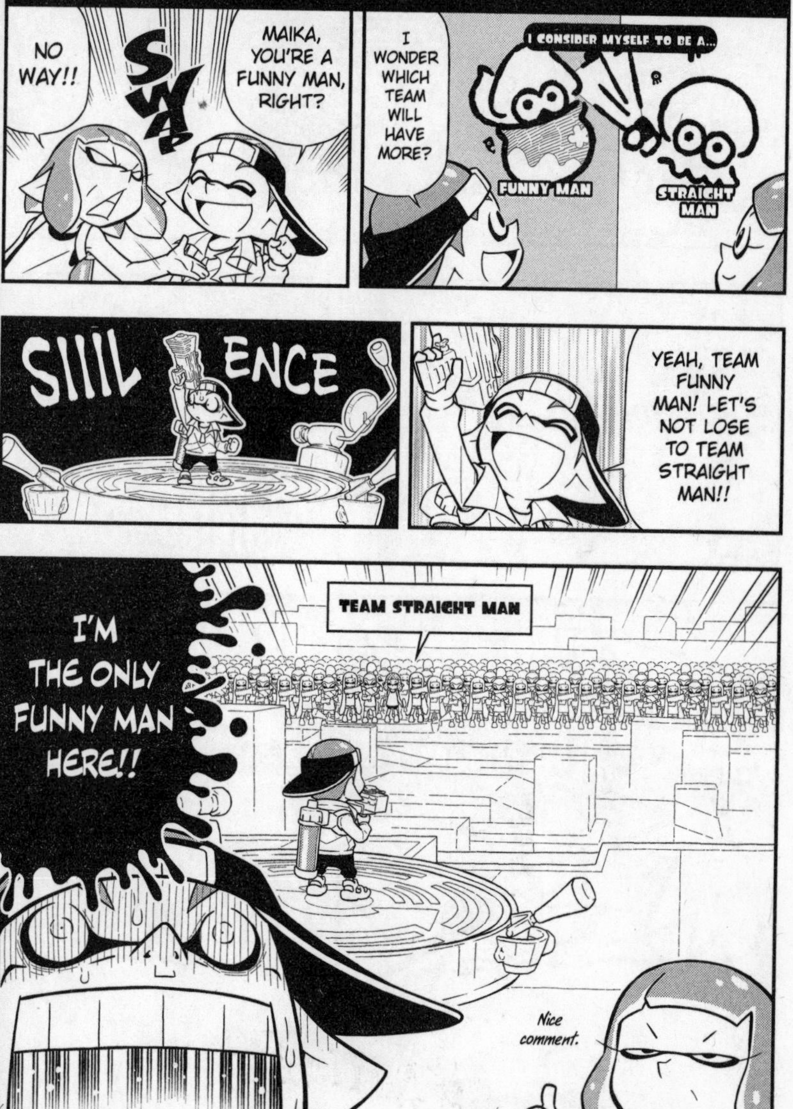
I WONDER WHICH TEAM WILL HAVE MORE?
I CONSIDER MYSELF TO BE A...
FUNNY MAN
STRAIGHT MAN
MAIKA, YOU'RE A FUNNY MAN, RIGHT?
SWAP
NO WAY!!
YEAH, TEAM FUNNY MAN! LET'S NOT LOSE TO TEAM STRAIGHT MAN!!
SIIIL ENCE
TEAM STRAIGHT MAN
I'M THE ONLY FUNNY MAN HERE!!
Nice comment.

Splatoon
SQUID KIDS
COMEDY SHOW

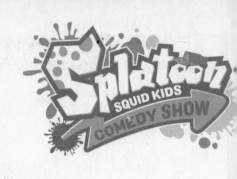

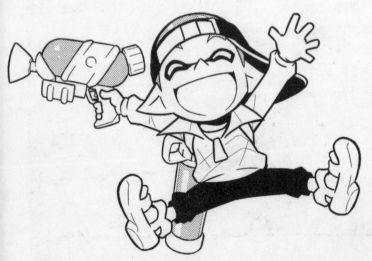

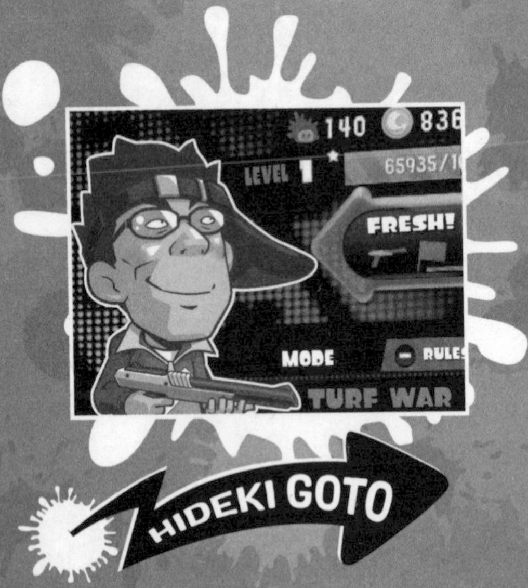
140
836
LEVEL 1
65935/1
FRESH!
MODE
RULES
TURF WAR
HIDEKI GOTO

I have reached the level cap of level 99 and have become level 1★. My rank hasn't risen at all, though.

Hideki Goto was born in Gifu Prefecture, Japan. He received an honorable mention in the 38th Shogakukan Newcomers' Comic Awards, Kids' Manga Division in 1996 for his one-shot *Zenryoku Dadada*. His first serialization was *Manga de Hakken Tamagotchi: Bakusho 4-koma Gekijo*, which began in *Monthly Coro Coro Comics* in 1997. *Splatoon: Squid Kids Comedy Show* began its serialization in *Bessatsu Coro Coro Comics* in 2017 and is Goto's first work to be published in English.

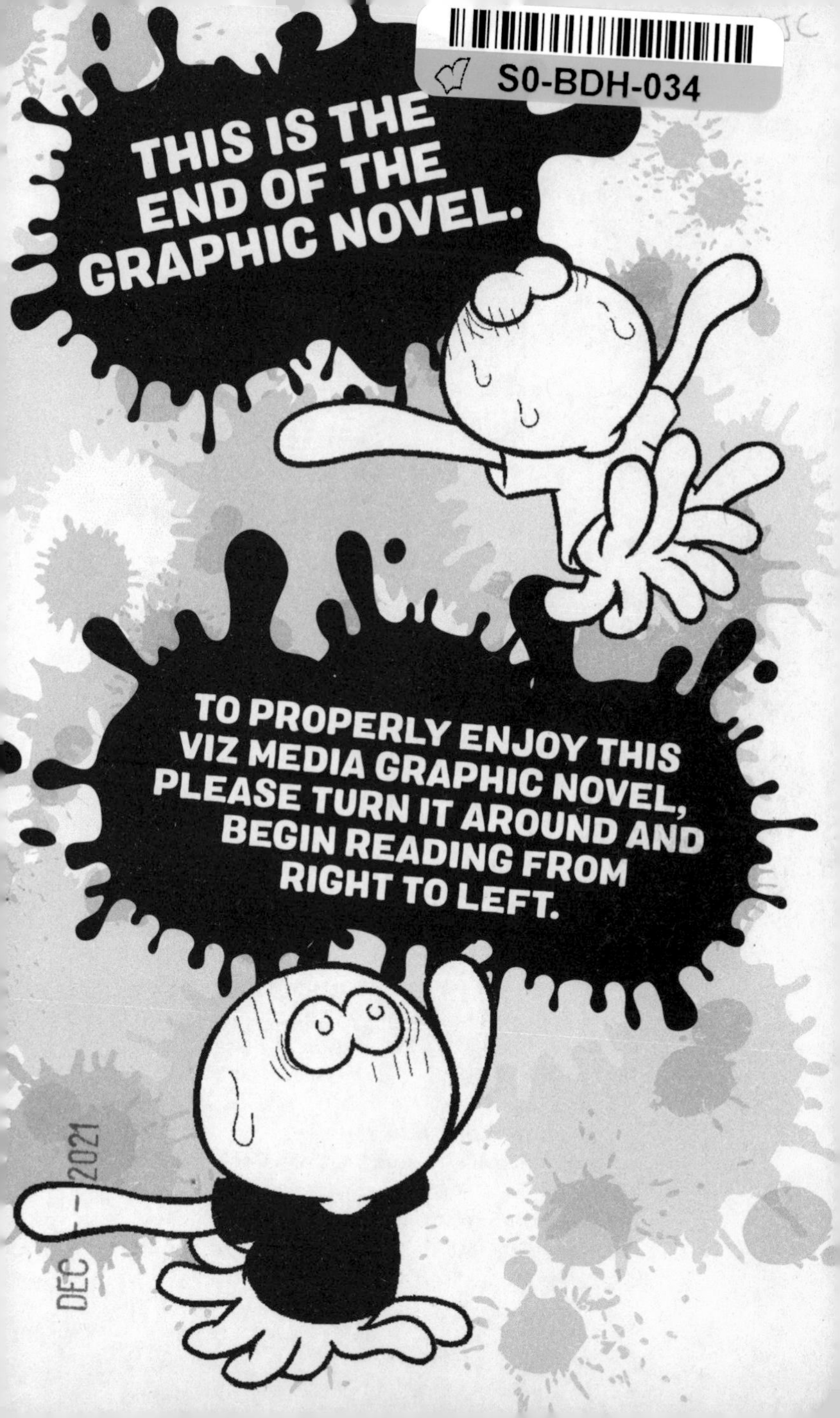
THIS IS THE END OF THE GRAPHIC NOVEL.
TO PROPERLY ENJOY THIS VIZ MEDIA GRAPHIC NOVEL, PLEASE TURN IT AROUND AND BEGIN READING FROM RIGHT TO LEFT.